# ANTONIO MACHADO

*Selected Poems*

# ANTONIO MACHADO

*Selected Poems*

Translated and with an Introduction by

*Alan S. Trueblood*

Harvard University Press

Cambridge, Massachusetts, and London, England

1982

*Library of Congress Cataloging in Publication Data*

Machado, Antonio, 1875–1939.
   Selected poems.

   Text in English and Spanish.
   Includes index.
I. Trueblood, Alan S.    II. Title.
PQ6623.A3A282   1982    861'.62    81-13481
ISBN 0-674-04065-1       AACR2

*To the memory of my mother*

# Preface

The translations in this volume had their start some fifteen
years ago under unusual circumstances. While staying in Madrid in the winter of 1966 I was surprised, agreeably, to read
in the press that a homage to Antonio Machado was to take
place on the twentieth of February in the southeastern city of
Baeza, where the poet had spent seven years as a high school
teacher of French and Spanish. The news was heartening to
Spanish liberals and lovers of poetry everywhere in the pen-
insula. They read it as a sign that the Franco regime had realized it could no longer ignore an artist whose reputation had
withstood more than twenty-five years of officially imposed
silence. This pall had settled on Machado in 1939 after the
defeat of the Republican cause, for which he had been an
eloquent spokesman. He himself had died in exile shortly before.

Machado's devotees proved overoptimistic. When Republi-
cans from all over Spain began converging on Baeza in unexpected numbers, the government had second thoughts. The
most implacable voices within the regime prevailed: the homage was forcibly canceled and crowds of expectant partici-
pants were turned away at the last moment. A bronze head
of Machado created for dedication on this occasion by the
eminent Spanish sculptor Pablo Serrano was spirited away by
its creator, as were posters designed by Joan Miró, the well
known painter. One of the latter, which subsequently
reached me from under the counter of a Madrid bookshop, is
reproduced on the jacket of this book. More notably, Brown
University was presented by the sculptor with his powerful
bust of the poet, one of four in existence. A single

proviso was attached: that the University sponsor a homage
to the poet who could not be publicly acclaimed in his own
country. The homage took place in Providence, Rhode Island,
in October 1967. For the audience gathered on that occasion I
first translated a handful of poems by Machado.

Translation, as disciplined re-creation, cannot but sharpen
one's perceptions of the many-faceted creative activity that
has preceded it. The experience of 1967 substantiated the admiration I had long felt for Machado's art, while the response
of the audience to the poetic voice that came through, however shakily, that day convinced me that a fuller selection of
Machado's verse should be made available to English-lan-
guage readers. Though the poet was not untranslated, he was
still scarcely known. I hoped that lending him my voice
might help make his own carry further into the English-
speaking world. I have sought to give this voice an English
embodiment without surrendering too much of its Spanish
timbre. My aim, like that of most literary translators, has
been to enlarge the experience of poetry open to the English-
speaking reader by unblocking one more current of expression originating outside his traditional domain. To achieve
this end most effectively Machado's voice needs to be heard
in the fullness of its range. Short of translating the entire
opus, the best hope for such a hearing lies in selecting gen-
erously among poems covering all stages and directions of
the poet's development. This is particularly indicated in the
case of an artist like Machado, whose growth never ceased.

This anthology aspires to be representative, although I
must add that views regarding what constitutes representa-
tiveness are bound to be relative, since every poem is ultimately a unique creation. Knowledgeable readers of Machado will not concur in all of my choices, perhaps noting
the absence of this or that familiar piece. Questions of judgment aside, I must acknowledge that in a few cases the reason for an absence is simply the resistance a particular poem
offered to "Englishing" at my hands.

"Englishing"—the term was a favorite during the great
burgeoning of translation in the Elizabethan age. It rests on
an uncomplicated assumption that naturalization in a new
milieu is easily achieved. Such thorough transplantation no
longer seems so possible or so desirable in an age to which

the shrinkage of the globe has brought awareness of irreducible diversity. One cannot hold today that a poet's voice in translation should sound as if he had been writing in English all along. While the translator's voice will ease accommodation into a new literary medium that has its own impositions to make, he becomes a usurper once his voice overpowers or supplants the voice originally heard in the text. Some aura of foreignness, individually and culturally marked, should survive re-creation; it surely will if not dissipated in the process.

In Machado's case the reader quickly notes the central position the "heart" and the "soul" occupy in this poetic world. The Latin "rhetoric of emotion," so unforced and unselfconscious in a poet of Machado's stature, has no equivalent in English poetic expression today, in which traditional reticence and contemporary bluntness so often contend unceremoniously. Although Machado has a reticence of his own, it derives less from reservation of feeling than from restraint in conveying the circumstances surrounding it.

That translation is a form of criticism does not need restating. Continually imposing options that entail some sacrifice for every gain, translation must unavoidably call on critical judgment if it is to proceed nonimpressionistically. The translator has not only to choose among the suggestions that particular contexts insinuate; he must arrive at a sense of order which reconciles local suggestions with the shape of the larger artistic entity and which ultimately obeys the lines of force governing a total opus. Like all critics, the translator does not count only on his own developed awareness of the way texts function, and on the insights of others; he draws also on reflections made by the author on his art and on art itself. While the pertinence of such reflections varies, it is surely clear when the artist evinces keen critical powers of his own, as does Machado.

The positions Machado holds in the realm of poetics will become evident in the pages that follow. Only one needs underscoring here: his insistence on the temporal nature of poetry. To write poetry is to place "the word in time." This means reliance on the temporal resources of language—prosodic, metrical, grammatical, syntactic. These in turn subserve the poet's ultimate aim: the impregnation of language by "the poet's vital time with its own pulsation." Machado

wrote no nonmetrical lines nor indeed any lines without at
least vowel rhyme. For all the differences between the
English and the Spanish metrical systems, it is essential that
the English translator employ the temporal resources of his
language to re-create the sense of a temporal continuum and
of rhythmic pulsatings within it, without which Machado's
poetic utterance ceases to be recognizable. To achieve this
goal without overemphasizing it is no easy matter. Machado's
consistent rhyming cannot be carried over into English, simply because the relative paucity of rhyme-words in our language, in contrast to their abundance in Spanish—and the
differing relief which rhyme consequently assumes in the two
languages—could lead to serious distortions. Ill-supplied with
rhyme, Machado's English translator must marshal other
temporal resources—some, such as vowel quantity, more
subtle than in Spanish—by way of compensation. He must
beware at the same time of manipulating stress, so much
more pronounced in English metrics than in Spanish, as a re-
placement for rhyme. Rhyme should be reserved for those
occasions when its contribution to the total pattern of meaning is crucial. I have dealt with problems of this kind more
pragmatically than systematically and, needless to say, lay no
claim to their full resolution.

   The first intention of this anthology is to assimilate into the
corpus of English poetry a voice carrying intonations not native to it and thus capable of enriching it. The English texts,
one hopes, will stand sufficiently on their own to allow a
reader so inclined to pass over the Spanish entirely. Nevertheless, the work is designed to be read at other levels. The
presence of the Spanish texts is an invitation to the reader to
explore them, along with the English, whatever the extent of
his knowledge of Spanish. The Introduction is intended as a
guide both to Machado and to this selection of his work, in
the hope that the reader's appreciation of the poet may be
deepened. Many of the notes offer leads and establish con-
nections which a more critical reader may wish to pursue. I
nourish a hope that the Hispanist already familiar with Machado may find in this book some contribution to an increased understanding of his work. The Introduction devel-
ops views of Machado and his poetry that I have touched on
elsewhere; the annotation to the Introduction provides some

substantiation of these views; the notes to the poems offer particular readings growing out of the intimacy with the texts which an unhurried translator acquires.

In my view, translators cannot be divided, as they often are, into two bands: the academic and the creative. This book is, among other things, an attempt to close a supposed gap. I have at all stages of its composition greatly benefited from the help of friends and colleagues. Their learning, their advice, and their specific suggestions have improved the quality of the work. For the shortcomings that remain, I am responsible, not they. My thanks go to all of them, but I should like to recall in particular the late Don Tomás Navarro, Machado's close associate in his last years, who shared with me personal reminiscences of the poet. I am indebted to Machado's literary heir, Dr. José Rollán Riesco, of Madrid, for his generous permission to make whatever selection I wished from Machado's work, and for numerous other favors. The Ossabaw Island Foundation of Savannah, Georgia, and Merton College, Oxford University, provided hospitality and stimulation which helped greatly to bring this book to fruition. The Hispanic Society of America kindly placed its Machado collection at my disposal. Alexander A. Parker's encouragement and the valued critiques of Arthur Terry were particularly beneficial at an early stage. Geoffrey W. Ribbans, Andrew P. Debicki, and Claudio Guillén read the entire manuscript; their comments removed numerous imperfections. Edwin Honig's careful reading of the English versions produced invaluable suggestions. Nelson R. Orringer made a most useful critique of the manuscript and gave me the additional benefit of his expertise in philosophical and ideological backgrounds. My assistant, Carol J. Bergen, was both a valued critic and a helpful editor. The spontaneous and frank reactions of my students and lecture audiences in this country and Great Britain were of positive assistance. My mother, Louise N. Trueblood, helped in many ways in the earlier stages; my friends Dorothea B. Withington, Madeleine Clément, and Ineke Van Dongen and my student Mary E. Lemire in the later. Special thanks go, finally, to Ann Louise McLaughlin of Harvard University Press, for her sharp eye and ear and for her constant editorial assistance.

A final word in regard to the arrangement of this book.

The Spanish texts follow the order in which Machado placed them in the last edition of his complete works whose publication he supervised (1936). They respect the numerous departures from strict chronological order which the poet saw fit to make. The sixty-four groupings of poems, indicated by Arabic numerals, correspond to groupings Machado himself established. He designated them by Roman numerals, sometimes placing under a given Roman head a single poem, sometimes a few, sometimes more. The numerals themselves do not coincide (Machado's went to CLXXVI); a concordance establishes equivalences. The Spanish texts are taken from the definitive edition of the poetry by Oreste Macrì. I have also followed Macrì's practice in placing at the end in rough chronological order my selection of compositions never published by Machado in editions of his complete works. In keeping with the stress I have laid on the poet's unbroken development, as with my wish to afford an overview of his work, I have preferred not to break the poems into subsections corresponding to Machado's separate published books of verse.

A.S.T.

Little Compton, Rhode Island
February 1982

# Contents

*Introduction*  1

*Selected Poems*

1   *En el entierro de un amigo*   70
    *At the Burial of a Friend*   71

2   Fue una clara tarde, triste y soñolienta   70
    The clear afternoon was drowsy and sad   71

3   El limonero lánguido suspende   74
    Listless the lemon tree suspends   75

4   Yo escucho los cantos   76
    I follow the songs   77

5   Yo voy soñando caminos   78
    I dream my way   79

6   *Horizonte*   80
    *Horizon*   81

7   Sobre la tierra amarga   80
    Upon the bitter land   81

8   Crece en la plaza en sombra   80
    Moss grows in the shadows of the square   81

9   Al borde del sendero un día nos sentamos   82
    We settle down one day beside the path   83

10   Oh, dime, noche amiga, amada vieja   82
    Oh tell me, friendly night, so long beloved   83

11   *La noria*   84
    *The Waterwheel*   85

12   *El cadalso*   86
    *The Gallows*   87

13  Las moscas    86
    Flies    87
14  Glosa    88
    Gloss    89
15  Anoche cuando dormía    90
    Last night I had a dream    91
16  ¿Mi corazón se ha dormido?    92
    Has my heart gone to sleep?    93
17  Desgarrada la nube; el arco iris    92
    A rent in the clouds    93
18  Y era el demonio de mi sueño, el ángel    94
    And the devil in my dream    95
19  ¡Oh tarde luminosa!    94
    Oh lightstruck evening!    95
20  Es una tarde cenicienta y mustia    96
    This withered, ashen afternoon    97
21  Y ha de morir contigo el mundo mago    98
    And is the magic world to die with you    99
22  Tal vez la mano, en sueños    98
    Idling once in a dream    99
23  Y podrás conocerte, recordando    98
    And you can know yourself if you'll recall    99
24  Retrato    100
    Portrait    101
25  A orillas del Duero    102
    Along the Duero    103
26  El Dios ibero    106
    The Iberian God    107
27  Orillas del Duero    108
    Along the Duero    109
28  Eres tú, Guadarrama, viejo amigo    112
    Guadarrama, is it you, old friend    113
29  Campos de Soria    112
    The Soria Country    113
30  En estos campos de la tierra mía    120
    Back in the landscape of my native soil    121
31  A José María Palacio    122
    To José María Palacio    123
32  Poema de un día. Meditaciones rurales    124
    One Day's Poem. Rural Reflections    125

33  Los olivos    134
    The Olive Trees    135
34  Proverbios y cantares    140
    Proverbs and Song-Verse    141
35  Parábolas    144
    Parables    145
36  A don Francisco Giner de los Ríos    152
    To Don Francisco Giner de los Ríos    153
37  Apuntes    154
    Jottings    155
38  Galerías    158
    Passageways    159
39  Canciones de tierras altas    162
    Highland Songs    163
40  Canciones    168
    Songs    169
41  Proverbios y cantares    176
    Proverbs and Song-Verse    177
42  Los ojos    204
    The Eyes    205
43  Esto soñé    206
    This Was My Dream    207
44  Al escultor Emiliano Barral    206
    To the Sculptor Emiliano Barral    207
45  Los sueños dialogados    208
    Dreams in Dialogue    209
46  De mi cartera    212
    From My Portfolio    213
47  Sonetos    214
    Sonnets    215
48  Viejas canciones    216
    Old Songs    217
49  Rosa de fuego    220
    The Flaming Rose    221
50  Al gran Cero    222
    To the Great Nought    223
51  Ultimas lamentaciones de Abel Martín    222
    Last Lamentations of Abel Martín    223
52  Siesta. En memoria de Abel Martín    226
    Siesta. In Memory of Abel Martín    227

**53**  *Recuerdos de sueño, fiebre y duermivela*    *226*
       *Memories of Dreaming, Fever, and Dozing*    *227*
**54**  *Canciones a Guiomar*    *240*
       *Songs for Guiomar*    *241*
**55**  *Otras canciones a Guiomar*    *244*
       *Other Songs for Guiomar*    *245*
**56**  *Muerte de Abel Martín*    *250*
       *The Death of Abel Martín*    *251*
**57**  *Otro clima*    *254*
       *Another Climate*    *255*
**58**  En dónde, sobre piedra aborrascada    *256*
       Where have I seen you, heaped    *257*
**59**  *Otras coplas*    *258*
       *Further Lines*    *259*
**60**  *Apunte de sierra*    *258*
       *Mountain Note*    *259*
**61**  *Recuerdo infantil (de Juan de Mairena)*    *260*
       *Childhood Memory (of Juan de Mairena)*    *261*
**62**  *El poeta recuerda las tierras de Soria*    *260*
       *The Poet Remembers the Soria Country*    *261*
**63**  *Meditación*    *262*
       *Meditation*    *263*
**64**  *El crimen fue en Granada*    *262*
       *The Crime Was in Granada*    *263*


Notes to the Introduction    *269*
Notes to the Poems    *279*
Key to Poem Numbers    *305*
Index of First Lines    *307*

# Introduction

S OME HUNDRED YEARS after his birth and some forty
since his death, Antonio Machado y Ruiz
(1875–1939) has not achieved outside the Spanish-speaking world the standing accorded him in his homeland, where he is usually considered the foremost poet of
Spain since the seventeenth century. The predominantly
quiet tone of his verse, the reflective manner, not easy to re-
capture in translation, have made him less known than com-
patriots like Unamuno, Juan Ramón Jiménez, and Lorca. Less
inclined to self-dramatization, less assertive than Unamuno,
Machado reflects a similarly broad range of ethical and metaphysical concerns. Less self-important than Juan Ramón
Jiménez, he shows no less refinement of aesthetic perception,
and his lyricism is richer in spiritual overtones. Less dazzling
and intense than Lorca, he reaches equal depths of intuitive
vision, while his tragic outlook often carries an added tem-
pering of irony.

A Sevillian, Machado was born in July 1875 in the vast Palacio de las Dueñas, seat of the Duke of Alba in that city on
the banks of the Guadalquivir River in western Andalusia.
His father, a lawyer more inclined to letters than to the law,
was living with his family in one of the apartments into
which the old mansion had been subdivided, serving the
Duke as superintendent. There the first eight years of Machado's life were spent, in surroundings that were to leave a
lasting impression.

On both sides Machado's ancestry is marked, as far back
as the early 1800s, by a succession of free-thinking patriots,
teachers, men of scholarly and philosophical bent who so-

journed or traveled abroad at a time when this was more the exception than the rule among Spaniards. Although he himself would never leave Spain except for two brief sojourns in Paris and a final exodus en route to his death in 1939, his heritage of cosmopolitan liberalism is revealed in the poet's consistent openness of mind and in the humaneness of his outlook. From the first, beyond the Spanish horizons of his mind and sensibility, one glimpses those of Europe.

In 1883 the family moved to Madrid, where the paternal grandfather, head of the household, had been named to a University chair in natural sciences. For the next seven years the moral and cultural atmosphere of the home was supplemented for Machado by attendance at a highly innovative independent school (also then a rarity in Spain) founded a few years previously: the Institución Libre de Enseñanza, which Salvador de Madariaga, thinking of the developments which led to the Second Spanish Republic of the 1930s, called "the true nursery of contemporary Spain."[1]

Of lucid intelligence but no studious disposition, not until 1900, ten years after leaving the Institución Libre, did Machado acquire a state degree, the *bachillerato*, analogous to the French *baccalauréat*. He was still living with his family—his independent development never required an act of emancipation from this congenial milieu—taking on literary or editorial assignments as they came along.[2] Work on a French-Spanish dictionary took him to Paris for the first time for five months in 1899, but the impact of the "city of the Dreyfus affair in politics, of Symbolism in poetry, of Impressionism in painting, of elegant skepticism in criticism" was not decisive.[3] Much more so, ultimately, for Machado's artistic development was the crisis in Spanish national life brought on by the brief war of 1898 with the United States.

In these years Machado was beginning to compose the verse that would appear in 1903 in his first published volume, *Soledades* (Solitude), a work that would be much expanded in its second edition, *Soledades. Galerías. Otros poemas* (Solitude. Passageways. Other Poems), in 1907. In these volumes the intimate post-Symbolist mood of the turn of the century prevails, and one catches echoes of Verlaine in motifs and musical effects. Inwardness leads to the exploration of the "passageways" of memory, fantasy, and dream in pursuit of subtle movements of the psyche and the elusive stimuli which reach the self from without.

The need for a steady income (neither the poet nor his family were ever in easy circumstances) led Machado to qualify himself in 1907 through state examination to teach French in the secondary school system. (In 1917 he would become qualified to teach Spanish literature as well.) He was posted to Soria, a small city in the highlands of Old Castile, where in September he began what was to be a five-year stay. With no very strong pedagogic vocation, at least within the antiquated secondary establishment of the day, he would derive from teaching a modicum of livelihood and security that allowed him to write and would faithfully pursue for the next thirty years the career of a "modest teacher in a country school."[4]

With characteristic restraint Machado in 1917 sums up in a sentence his outer and inner experience of Soria: "Five years in the Soria country, now sacred to me—I married there and there I lost my wife, whom I adored—oriented my eyes and heart toward the quintessentially Castilian."[5] Machado's love for the child-wife whom he married in 1909, the fifteen-year-old Leonor Izquierdo, daughter of a retired sergeant of the rural constabulary—the family ran the pension where he lived—blended postadolescent idolizing (one thinks of Poe's Leonore) and paternal tenderness.

A government grant enabled Machado in January 1911 to attend one of the last of the famous lecture series of Henri Bergson at the Collège de France in Paris, an experience that helped to crystallize his own aesthetic. Leonor, though in no position to share her husband's intellectual and artistic pursuits, accompanied him, but the precarious state of her health forced a return to Soria in September. Her death the following August devastated Machado and he fled the city. Only the striking success of *Campos de Castilla* (The Castilian Country), his second volume of verse, which had just appeared, mitigated his despondency. Reflecting the "quintessentially Castilian" experience of Soria, it brought him national renown. He resisted suicide, Machado wrote Juan Ramón Jiménez, with the thought "that if there was some constructive power in me, I had no right to annihilate it."[6]

The poet requested a transfer and was posted to Baeza, a

small city in the mountainous country of eastern Andalusia near the crusty rim of the Mediterranean basin. Finding at first little companionship or intellectual stimulus there, thrown on his own resources in the need to solace his grief, he began in no very systematic way to seek out philosophical formulations of questions that had frequently underlaid his artistic expression. From Baeza he enrolled as a "free" degree candidate in the Faculty of Philosophy and Letters of the University of Madrid, where in 1917, with Ortega y Gasset as a member of the examining board, he was awarded the equivalent of a master's degree in philosophy.

Transferred at his request to Segovia in 1919, Machado soon found there a group of kindred spirits, some of them fellow-teachers of literature or philosophy, others active in other arts. The transfer to Segovia also brought him into closer touch with the movement of ideas in the capital, one hour away, where he spent every weekend. The increasing diversity of Machado's mature interests is reflected in the comprehensive but nonspecific title—*Nuevas canciones* (New Songs)—which he chose for the volume he published in 1924. It contained poems from the final Baeza years and from the earlier Segovia period.

In the later Segovia years a new love-interest in the person of "Guiomar" appeared in Machado's life after years of widowerhood and a few shadowy allusions to other attractions. Guiomar was Pilar de Valderrama, a minor Madrid poet whom Machado had met when she was sojourning with her husband in Segovia in 1928. With her Machado struggled with reciprocated feelings, whose consummation was forestalled by circumstances—until the battlelines of the Civil War raised an insurmountable barrier.

Machado published no new volumes of verse after *New Songs*, contenting himself with adding new sections to successive editions of *Poesías completas* (Complete Poems) and rearranging earlier sections. During the Segovia years, as he continued to be drawn by philosophical speculation, a pair of apocryphal poet-philosophers, Abel Martín and Juan de Mairena, who would serve to voice his reflections, first made their appearance. They are projections of himself in the direction of the philosopher he might have become, had his

penchant for philosophical thought not been offset by his
distrust of systematic abstraction.

Machado was still at Segovia in April 1931, when the mon-
archy fell and the Second Spanish Republic was proclaimed.
The following year he was transferred to a newly created
school in Madrid and went to live in the capital with the
family of José, a younger brother whose household was to be
his home throughout his final years.

Despite a profound conviction that poetry should remain
apolitical and that the artist's integrity required that he keep
his distance from centers of power, Machado now found
himself drawn into the mainstream of events.[7] He accepted
unhesitatingly the role of spokesman, first for the cause then
for the defense of Spanish liberalism, his dispassionate yet
committed voice appearing in the Madrid press under the by-
line of "Juan de Mairena" in wide-ranging commentaries on
cultural, political, and social matters. A handful of poems
dates from 1936 to 1939, with the war present in the foreground or background.[8] At the instance of the Republican
government, Machado and his brother's family took up residence in Rocafort, outside Valencia (November 1936–April
1938) when the capital was threatened. In April 1938 they
abandoned Valencia for Barcelona; in January 1939 they
joined the exodus into southern France, which culminated in
Machado's death at Collioure (Roussillon), February 27, 1939.

At heart a Romantic in his need to discover a place for the
affective and imaginative self in a world that can no longer
offer it sure bearings, Machado moves beyond Romantic solipsism as he grows aware of the perplexities of the inner
world. He attempts "to come to terms with otherness—within
himself, within other people, within nature," a tendency that
has, with some justice, been seen as existentialist.[9] He seeks
forms of reintegration through dialogue and communion with
his fellow-man, his society, his age, and, more broadly, in
speculations on a scheme of things from which God has
withdrawn.

Put this way, Machado's evolution appears more clear-cut
and orderly than it was. In fact, throwbacks to earlier han-

dlings of favorite themes alternate or overlap with later treatments, while developments to come are often foreshadowed. The slim volume of his first work—the *Soledades* of 1903, with its forty-two brief pieces—carries, in the plural of the Spanish title, suggestions of personal states of welcomed aloneness or of disturbing loneliness, as well as intimations of a surrounding emptiness—states of mind that would never be wholly transcended.[10] At the same time, in these first *Soledades* and in the expanded edition of 1907, one senses restiveness, a groping toward the concerns of the later verse, a reaching for otherness, objectivity of vision, and, occasionally, a transcending of self-absorption through a reflex of irony.

But Machado's *soledades*, more often loneliness than self-fulfillment, will never quite be left behind, however much circumstances may eventually draw him into the forefront of events. An inclination to stand somewhat apart was not only a matter of temperament; it reflected an independent intellectual outlook and indifference to literary modes. On the one hand, Machado stops short of fin-de-siècle decadentism; on the other, he is not tempted by free verse or avant-garde poetics.[11]

Salient elements in Machado's poetic expression are constantly evolving over the years: the perception of landscape, a temporal aesthetic, receptiveness to folklore, to traditional verse and song, the operative role of memory and dream, the apprehension of otherness, the ironic overlay. The depth and allusive power of Machado's poetry are the result of the continued reworking of a limited range of symbols and motifs of constantly expanding expressive power; they do not come from expansion of thematic or verbal resources. The polysemic character of a few favorite signifiers, the open-endedness of Machado's symbols—the ease with which a landscape may double as an ars poetica, for instance, or a dream have a metaphysical dimension—mark him as an artist reconciled to the approximativeness of poetic language, not haunted by it. He settles for simplicity and allows meaning to gather in context within the single composition, or to accrue from one composition to another, to develop through manipulation of tone and tempo rather than by setting out in pursuit of verbal exactitude. Machado's most characteristic poems begin casually, grope forward, suddenly catch hold in brief epiphanies, then quietly subside.

It was presumably the encounter with Bergsonian *durée* which helped Machado to put in words very early a predisposition to view poetry as "neither hard and timeless marble, / nor painting nor music, / but the word in time."[12] In 1924 we find him expanding in his notebook on the concept of temporality in art: "The work of art evidently aspires toward an ideal present, toward the nontemporal. But in no way does this mean that a sense of the temporal [*el sentimiento de lo temporal*] can be excluded from art. The lyric, for example, without abandoning its claim to the nontemporal, must give us the aesthetic sensation of the flowing of time; the flux of time is actually one of the lyric motifs that poetry tries to save from time, which poetry seeks to take out of time [*intemporalizar*]." Later he will find for the same thought the unusual formulation: "The poet is a fisherman . . . of fish capable of staying alive after being hauled out."[13]

In a retrospective consideration of his *Soledades* of 1903 Machado emphasizes corollaries to temporality which he calls "spiritual." These carry him beyond Parnassian, Symbolist, and post-Symbolist aesthetics, and their coalescence in Hispanic *modernismo* through the assimilative powers of the brilliant Nicaraguan, Rubén Darío, in a direction quite his own: "I thought that the poetic element was not the word in its phonic value, nor color, nor line, nor a complex of sensations, but a deep pulsing of spirit: what the soul supplies, if it does supply anything; or what it says, if it says anything, when aroused to response by contact with the world."[14]

Pulsation, with its suggestion of rhythmic recurrence and of vitality, here becomes in addition a manifestation of spirit and an impulse toward dialogue. If we add Machado's perception of "intuition—in the Bergsonian sense of an intimate revelation of life—as the essential thing in the work of art," and note that the aspiration "toward an ideal present" implicitly allows the conceptual a role in the ordering of the poem, we will have described the basis of a poetics from which, despite shifts of emphasis and direction, Machado will not deviate.[15] The ever-sensed presence of the stream of time, into whose depths the poet dips intuitively, will give water imagery in many forms—fountains, springs, rivers, sea, waterwheels—what more than once he calls, in a phrase of St. Teresa's, "the very living waters of life," a central symbolic role.[16]

> All of the imagery
> that has not sprung from the river—
> call it poor trinketry

he will declare.

Machado's self-reliance stems from the independent cultural formation he enjoyed (along with a select minority of his generation) in a country where neither the standard educational establishment nor the movement of ideas offered adequate stimulus for the unfolding of his talents. Though paradoxically the social and cultural deficiencies of late-nineteenth- and twentieth-century Spain would assure its preoccupying presence in his poetic world (much as Ireland would haunt Yeats), Machado escapes their restrictive effects. In the family milieu of his childhood and youth a Romantic heritage is still alive, an idealistic commitment to humanity that complements a still unproblematical trust in the primacy of affective experience. A cult of *Naturpoesie* with its zeal for popular poetry and traditions, particularly evident in the generation immediately preceding Machado's, will leave decisive traces in the form and substance of his own work. Machado will be the beneficiary of his father's avocation: the compiling of collections of popular riddles, enigmas, and traditions, of Spanish folksongs and *cante jondo*.

The effect of seven years at the Institución Libre de Enseñanza was to be similarly enduring. Founded in 1876 by Francisco Giner de los Ríos with the help of other liberals who, like himself, had lost their chairs in the University of Madrid with the fall of the First Republic (1868–1874), the Institución pioneered in replacing rote learning by an integrated development of the young person's total nature.[17] The guiding educational philosophy, derived from that of a German thinker, Karl C-J. Krause, stressed liberty of conscience, freedom of discussion, objective research, and a pervasive pantheistic spirituality.[18] Machado would remain to the end marked by its ethic of social commitment and almost ascetic personal austerity. Its spirit of optimism and confidence would provide a counterweight to melancholy and pessimism, and its ecumenical view of philosophy as a reconciliation of the most diverse doctrines, a wedding of reason and spirit at once Socratic and evangelical, would suit the eclectic trend of his own thinking. Machado's tribute (No. 36) to Giner de los Ríos on his death in 1915 catches in the simple restraint of the voice and the downplaying of the self, as well as in the values actually articulated, the spirit of Giner and the Institución and their legacy of "goodness" to himself and others of his generation.

The Institución fostered the fundamental good sense and the quiet self-assurance that made Machado permanently shy of both artistic and intellectual fads, while clear-headed and unhesitant in moral commitment. Even the omnipresence in his poetic cosmos of such a feature as the *camino*—the road as physical presence, as a phenomenon embodied in the walker, as an existential symbol coterminous and consubstantial with him, or simply as self-propelling mobility incorporated into the movement of verse—reveals the lasting effect of the un-Spanish practice of "footing" inculcated in Institución days.[19] This practice helps explain as well why Machado's landscapes, besides being contemplated, so often seem tactilely experienced, entered into almost bodily, in his words "told" as well as "sung."

The national crisis provoked by the War of 1898 with the United States reinforced in certain respects the effects of Machado's Institución schooling. The war tore away the final shreds of overseas empire—Cuba, Puerto Rico, the Philippines—to which the mother country had been clinging since the Spanish-American wars of independence early in the century and accelerated a process of national soul-searching already underway. As events redirected attention homeward and inward, the national scene—not only society, institutions, and traditions, but landscapes and countryside as physical presences, particularly those of the heartland, Castile, mistress of imperial destinies since the time of Queen Isabella—became an object of scrutiny and rediscovery for the writers and thinkers who would become known as the Generation of 1898. The sensitivity to natural and social surroundings which Machado's education had fostered was thus reinforced by the historical conjuncture. His responsiveness to the spirit of place will make landscape and physical settings permanent presences in his poetic cosmos.[20] These at first often function as emblems of otherness in problematical interaction with the self, then also in their own right as human habitat and historical locale. For a while, too, the vision of landscape becomes inseparable from the "problem of Spain," itself intensified by the crisis in values the country was undergoing. In Machado's prose the fatherland would remain an often painful concern to the end. In the verse of his second collection, *The Castilian Country* of 1912, the critique of rural or provincial types observed becomes unsparing; the assessment of the Spanish or Castilian state of mind, its role in history, its present predicament, is bleak.

Yet by this time, the residence of five years at Soria had aroused deep responses to the spirit and atmosphere of Old Castile. The stark highlands around the city located near the Aragonese border, lands situated, Machado says, somewhere between earth and moon, and "so sad, they have a soul," brought out the brooding spirituality of his own nature and added deeper resonances to his writing.[21]

Not that Machado did not sometimes find wearing the enforced residence—it would be twenty-five years in all—in the three provincial cities where he taught. "I have now had eight years of exile," he wrote from Baeza to Juan Ramón Jiménez in 1915. "I feel the weight of this provincial life in which one ends by devouring oneself. Often I think of giving up my chair and going off on my own to live by my writing. But that would mean poverty again."[22]

Restive and dispirited as Machado felt at times, he could always be distracted by the specimens of humanity, the social phenomena, and the natural spectacles, great or small, that caught his eye. True, his absorption never becomes immersion; he remains the reflective observer. Though the self-revelation necessarily involved in poetic viewing is not sidestepped, the self is not intrusive. Nothing prevents his sensitivity to the genius loci from registering the distinctive "feel" of different landscapes: catching their seasonal cycles, noting the human presence on the land, the works and days of man's georgic activity.

This responsiveness was undoubtedly sharpened by the inherent diversity of the Spanish regions he knew best: the sunlit Lower Andalusia of his Sevillian childhood, occasionally revisited—the broad and rich Guadalquivir Valley, with the salt of the Atlantic in the air; Madrid and New Castile—dusty, chalky terra cotta; the bare, high Duero Valley amidst the gaunt plains and mountains of Old Castile around Soria; the high Guadalquivir Valley of Upper Andalusia around Baeza, with its undulating terrain covered by olive groves, its highlands pungent with Mediterranean vegetation; Roman, Romanesque, and Renaissance Segovia, north of Madrid—not to mention other places experienced in travel or on the road to exile. Ultimately these successive landscapes are interiorized, stored away and blended or contrasted in the memory to reemerge in a complex play of recollection, nostalgia, and reelaboration. Soria and Upper Castile continue to figure after he leaves them in 1912, recreated from a distance in an imagined present of converted into dreamlike presences, the memory of them often interspersed with more recent experiences of other places.[23]

The play of these phenomena in Machado's poetics was undoubtedly both spurred and reinforced by early contact with Bergson, with the latter's pursuit of the "immediate data of consciousness," his stress on the nonanalytical, on the intuitive nature of thought and the nonconceptual character of poetic language, the primacy he gave to temporality, with the famous distinction between *durée pure* and *durée homogène*. This, though Machado would move beyond Bergson in seeking to reconcile the lyric impulse and the world of ideas.[24]

Nor could Bergson be of much help to Machado when it came to matters of religious belief. The need for a sustaining faith became urgent with Leonor's death. The spiritual conflicts aroused are patent in a letter to Unamuno: "I felt adoration for her, but over and above love is pity. I would have preferred dying myself a thousand times to watching her die . . . I don't think there is anything extraordinary about this feeling. There is something immortal in us that wants to die with whatever dies. Perhaps that is why God came into the world. This thought is some consolation, at times I feel hopeful. A negative faith is absurd too . . . Well, today she is more than ever alive in me and sometimes I firmly believe I shall recover her."[25]

Leonor, who while alive does not figure in Machado's

verse, will find a permanent place in his writing once she is removed from him. This experience of loss will contribute eventually to a view of love as an emotion compatible with solitude and nourished mainly on absence.

Machado's will to believe was destined never to be satisfied. Poem No. 15, published five years after Leonor's death, in 1917, records a dream in which the sensation of an immanent faith appears in three different guises, leading finally directly to the indwelling God, only to be recorded each time as a "blessed illusion." It has been plausibly suggested that the attraction of philosophy, and especially of metaphysics, which now begins to be felt, is a partial sublimation of the need for faith.[26] (Later Machado will veer strikingly away from his present rejection of the idea of a negative faith.) The philosophical questions he begins to ponder are centered on the issue of the one and the many: subject and object, self and other; the character of reality and the means and extent of man's knowledge of it; logic versus insight; immanence versus transcendence. Questions of human communion and communication and of art in historical, critical, and theoretical perspectives increasingly preoccupy him.

Out of such ruminations and from the activities and associations of everyday life, Machado begins to make poetry less reflective than that of *The Castilian Country* of the larger generational concerns of the 1898 writers (though these remain an undercurrent) and less attuned to the inner movements of the psyche than that of *Solitude. Passageways. Other Poems.* "One Day's Poem" (No. 32), written early at Baeza, suggests in its casual run-on rhythms and recurring reflections a day-to-day routine in a particular social and agricultural setting. It offers a glimpse into the life of the mind and spirit that made the routine bearable.

In these years it is the Greeks first of all—the pre-Socratics, Plato, and Aristotle—and then Descartes, Kant, Leibniz, Schopenhauer, and Nietzsche whom we find Machado mulling over in his prose writing and in the jottings of his notebooks, and recalling occasionally in his verse.[27] As emblems of universal process and flux and of cosmic harmony, Heraclitus' river and fire and Pythagoras' lyre will figure in his verse as something more than set metaphors inherited from nineteenth-century France or the *modernismo* of Rubén Darío.

The ethical preoccupations already evident in the Baeza years come increasingly to the fore after the move to Segovia in 1919 and the regular visits to Madrid that ensued. The artistic atmosphere of the city in 1919 was buoyant. Neutrality had spared Spain the horrors of the Great War; the aftermath of disillusionment and spiritual exhaustion scarcely touched the capital, which was feeling the impact of European avantgarde movements. Nevertheless, even during the Baeza years, Machado appears keenly aware of the crisis European civilization is undergoing and sees a need for a new beginning in human brotherhood. His attention was drawn more and more to political and social problems beyond the national sphere and we find him looking with idealistic admiration toward Russia, seeing in the Bolshevik revolution as well as in Tolstoyism Europe's best hope for salvation.[28] In Segovia he played an active role in the formation of the *Universidad Popular*, an innovatory free institution created especially for persons inadmissible by reason of poverty or working-class status into the regular educational establishments.

The *New Songs* of 1924 reflect the widening range of Machado's interests, and the increasingly diversified experience of regions of Spain which underlies his poetry of the land and of the earth. The renewed Segovian experience of Castile, superimposed on recollections of Soria, blends, sometimes in a single composition or a single sequence, with that of eastern Andalusia, itself both felt at first hand and reelaborated in memory. The properly Andalusian content consists mostly of brief landscape pieces and short verse reminiscent in form and manner of traditional spoken and sung lyrics: the two-line distichs, three-line *soleares* (the term is a popular Andalusian version of *soledades*), four-line *coplas*, and the brief sequences of octosyllabic ballad lines. The snatches of gnomic, aphoristic utterance which had made a first appearance in 1909 and been included as "Proverbs and Song-Verse" in *The Castilian Country* in 1912 now occupy a larger place. They reflect not only popular tradition and folk wisdom but also Machado's philosophical musings. Although they have sometimes been viewed as a desertion of the aesthetic of temporality and intuition, this aesthetic in fact still underlies the lyric intensity and pregnancy of image deriving from the popular manner which they cultivate. Moreover, the "song-verse" which stands out amid the flashes of ingenuity and cryptic wit retains an essentially temporal musicality. Even those other, longer compositions in which a more properly philosophical undergirding is perceptible represent an enrichment, not an abandonment, of Machado's native lyricism.

Though he several times formulated distinctions between the poet's and the philosopher's ways of thinking, Machado, somewhat like T. S. Eliot when he espoused the aesthetic of the English metaphysicals and observed that "their mode of feeling was directly and freshly altered by their reading and thought," found ways of wedding philosophical concerns with a fundamental lyricism.[29] Though the blend of strong feeling and intense thought characteristic of the English metaphysicals (with whom he had no acquaintance) is not so immediately apparent in Machado, nor does he have their casual and easy way with metaphysical contexts, his images are often similarly functional as nerve-centers for entire compositions, and a similarly keen intelligence is on the alert despite the affective temper traceable to a Romantic heritage which Machado never felt the need to disown.

His later work manifests a prolonged effort to reconcile an inborn lyric impulse with a conceptualizing bent of his mind. "The poet's ideas," he was to write in 1931, "are not formal categories, logical capsules, but direct intuitions of being in the process of becoming, of his own existence." Already in 1923 his notebook records the notion that "the poet's metaphysics need not necessarily be that which expresses the basis of his thought, as thinker, as philosopher, that is, as a man with a passion for truth, but that which suits his poetry."[30] The fact that in *New Songs* we find Machado first seriously cultivating the sonnet (at a time when it was elsewhere being superseded in favor of more flexible forms) is indicative of a new interest in formal schemes correlated with conceptual substructures. In his handling of the sonnet Machado manages to retain suppleness and mobility despite the fixity of the frame.

The increased prominence in *New Songs* of compositions in which the poet's individual voice seeks attunement to the collective voice of popular poetry, Andalusian or Castilian, is symptomatic of a continuing search for forms of expression facilitating communion with others and, more broadly, of a search for some meeting ground with the otherness of the world. The ongoing inner dialogue had of course never ceased:

> I talk with the man who is always at my side—
> one who talks to himself hopes to talk to God sometime—
> soliloquizing is speaking with this good friend
> who has shown me the way to love of humankind.

So Machado had written in the "Portrait" (No. 24) dating from 1908, with which he subsequently introduced the seemingly outgoing phase of *The Castilian Country* (1912). But amid the groping for the other within oneself, God or fellow-man, which these words convey, there is a curious hesitancy between soliloquy and dialogue, noticeable a few lines earlier, when Machado writes: "I've learned to tell the voices from the echoes / and of all the voices listen to only one."

In the most characteristic compositions of *The Castilian Country* a solo voice predominates, talking to itself audibly, as it were, as it surveys the local and national scene across time and space. Five years later Machado has listened more attentively and persistently to the play of voices within. In 1917 he observes: "A state of feeling [*sentimiento*] is something created by the individual subject out of materials from the outer world made over in one's heart. There is always in it a collaboration of a *you*, that is to say, of other subjects. One cannot settle for this simple formula: My heart, face to face with the landscape, produces feeling. Once produced, I communicate it by means of language to my fellow-man. Face to face with the landscape my heart would scarcely even be capable of feeling cosmic terror because even this elemental feeling needs, for its production, the distress of other frightened hearts amid a nature not understood. My feeling in the face of external nature, which I here call landscape, does not arise without an atmosphere of fellow-feeling. In short, my feeling is not exclusively mine, but *ours*. Without emerging from myself, I note that in my feeling other feelings are pulsating and that my heart always sings in chorus although its voice is for me the best-tempered one. The problem of lyric expression is to make it such for others as well."[31]

Affinities between such reflections, the *Ich und Du* of Martin Buber (1923) and the aesthetic aspects of Jung's collective unconscious with its upsurgings of atavistic voices within the individual poetic voice, have not escaped critical notice. Characteristically, however, Machado's formulation of the ideas in question seems largely his own, though the ideas themselves may have reached him through interpreters of European thought in Spain, especially Unamuno and Ortega. He is perfectly aware, as he goes on to note, that language, which one has to acquire from others, is even less one's own than is a given feeling, and in this he may even be said to be anticipating modern semiotics and *Rezeptionsästhetik.*

From *New Songs* on, an increasingly characteristic poetic stance is that of wonder—not the bated breath which greeted the delicate early moments of epiphany, but wonder openly exclamatory or compressed into poetry of simple statement, notation of the existence of things. Wonder, that is, that anything should exist at all in the face of nothingness. Such wonder runs the gamut from curiosity and perplexity to amazement, astonishment, joy, and disbelief. It pervades even the love-poetry addressed to Guiomar. The wonder of this love's very existence finds expression against a backdrop of absence, separation, make-believe, and, ultimately, disbelief. Guiomar could not reconcile herself to infidelity, while Machado was haunted by doubts about the possibility of transcending the bounds of self in a love of mutual self-surrender. Convinced of love's inevitable shortcoming, he explicitly came to view it as above all a sensation of something missing, as a presence of the beloved in absence. Love for Guiomar in the end only reinforced the solitude embraced and chafed at all his life.

With the invention of Abel Martín and Juan de Mairena during the Segovia years, Machado fashions for himself expressive outlets geared to the increasing complexity and subtlety of his mature thinking. An enlarged edition of the *Complete Poems*, published in 1928, contains a final section, "Abel Martín," in subsequent editions additionally entitled "From an Apocryphal Songbook," some thirty pages dating from a

few years earlier. They present a selection of the poems of
Abel Martín, a Sevillian philosopher and poet (1840–1889),
set in a a running exposition of his poetics and metaphysics.[32] There are neither sharp distinctions nor set correlations
between the discursive ruminations of Machado in verse or
prose and those of his two apocryphal mouthpieces. Although the latter no doubt provided a protective covering for
his sense of professional inadequacy as a philosopher, his relation to them often became an ironical one. It freed him to
voice or play speculatively with views he did not need precisely to espouse, allowed him to challenge and undermine
his own assertions. One of Machado's most understanding
critics has called Abel Martín "the scapegoat who assumes
the burden of the sin of thought" and has remarked that if
Juan de Mairena comes into existence not long after his master, it is because the fundamentally dialectical nature of
thinking, as Machado viewed it, made it inevitable that any
concept or idea entertained would in due course generate an
answering one.[33] In practice, however, the relationship between the two apocryphal voices is usually closer to complementarity than to dialectical opposition, despite the critical or
humorous reservations which Mairena on occasion expresses
toward his master, reservations which amount to a new invo-
lution of Machadian irony.

Well before the move to Madrid, Machado's fidelity to his
post-Romantic aesthetic, his penchant for philosophical speculation, and his growing commitment to a social role for art
had made him an increasingly isolated figure amidst the
avant-garde poetic movements of the twenties and thirties.
Politely but firmly he expressed his lack of sympathy for
"pure poetry," for a "sportive" or ludic aesthetic, for "the
higher algebra of metaphor" and the "dehumanization of art"
(phrases coined by Ortega), for the poetics of abstraction and
the poetics of irrationalism—in short, for what he considered
the new baroque tendencies which crystallized about the ter-
centenary of Góngora in 1927.

On the other hand, Machado is more than ever a presence
in the Madrid press in these years, in commentaries embrac-
ing a broad range of cultural, political, and social matters. In
November 1934 Juan de Mairena is revived in the first of a
cycle of fifty installments that ends in June 1936, just before

the outbreak of war, and is then collected in book form as *Juan de Mairena (Sayings, Witticisms, Notes, and Recollections of an Apocryphal Professor)*. In these "agile, good-humored and profound notes," often based upon unpublished materials dating from much earlier, which shed incidental light on the verse Machado was writing, Mairena appears as "an informal teacher conversing, 'hands in pockets,' with his young students . . . or jotting down ideas and anecdotes in the conversational tone of a dialogue in a café."[34] Among the many subjects that come up for comment are: Christianity and Christ, with the latter's exaltation of human dignity favored over the former, except in its fraternal Russian form; Marx, whose materialism is deplored; the bourgeoisie, criticized, and the common people, exalted. The brilliant miscellany includes a brief dramatic skit, imagined dialogues, interpolated verse; reflections on literary texts, on language and usage, dissections of commonplaces; considerations of figures of past and present from Agamemnon to Nietzsche, from Phillip II to Freud, Heraclitus to Heidegger; thoughts on childhood, on national character, all of this sometimes protracted, sometimes pithy and aphoristic, usually seasoned with ironical understatement.[35]

After the Civil War began, Mairena continued to figure in a monthly series of out-and-out topical reflections on circumstances of the struggle. An earnest, eloquent voice that never descended to vituperation or abuse championed the liberal values of which Machado saw the Republic as the best hope, whatever misgivings he may have felt about the use it had made of its opportunities. This voice was still heard during the final months in Barcelona, but by then Machado's activity as a poet had ceased.

Although Machado never felt constrained to exclude the "hateful" self from his poetic cosmos, as Symbolist aesthetics at its purest had prescribed, it is in the earliest work that the self evidently looms largest. The processes and phenomena of memory and dream, down to the finest overlapping nuances of daydreaming and the recollecting of dreams, are sensitive areas in the exploration of the inner world since they are the keys to what is most authentically one's own.

"Dreams are complementary to our waking hours," Machado
will write to Guiomar, "and one who does not remember his
dreams does not even know himself."[36] Still, the pursuit of
the core of the self, which marks Machado's early period, inevitably ends up in frustration and bewilderment. Subsequently there will be moments of strong reaction against a
poet's "exploration of the more or less subterranean city of
his dreams" and times when Machado, rather than welcom-
ing, as he usually does, the syncretic and reelaborative character of memory, will decry it.[37] "Memory is unfaithful: not
only does it erase and blur but at times it invents and throws
us off," he will remark in passing as late as 1938.[38] As for
dreams, he will declare in 1935: "Only in his lazy moments
may a poet devote himself to interpreting dreams and seeking in them elements to be used in his poems."[39] But three
years later we find him avowing: "I have always been a man
very attentive to his own dreams, because they reveal to us
our deepest disquietudes, those which do not always reach
the surface of our waking consciousness."[40] (The cast of this
remark reflects Machado's curiosity about Freudian psychol-
ogy.) The enterprise of inner exploration, in abeyance for
longer or shorter periods, is never abandoned altogether; it is
simply interwoven with new preoccupations—sociohistorical,
philosophical, and psychological.

In later years Machado formulated an ingenious conception of the "plasticity of the past," its capacity for being
transformed into a "true creation" of the subject. Mairena, in
speaking to his students in 1935 of this "apocryphal past,
something alive in one's memory and insofar as it is active in
one's consciousness, incorporated thereby into a present and
constantly in function of the future," and recommending its
cultivation in preference to an inert "irreparable" past of historical fact, is thinking in ethical, philosophical, and even political terms.[41] But the passage has undoubted aesthetic overtones and sums up admirably the crucial function of memory
and dream, particularly in Machado's early work. There is a
certain resemblance to the Proustian resuscitation and revivi-
fying of the past in its fullness, with the intensification
achieved by placing the processes of memory at the service
of art. But Machado did not identify Proust's attitude to time
with the plasticity of his own "apocryphal past." In Proust's

novel he saw a "Romantic poem . . . in the decadent manner
. . . *Le temps perdu* is, in truth, the author's century, seen as a
past that cannot be converted into a future and that is irrepa-
rably lost, if it is not remembered."[42] Machado's malleable
handling of memory and of dream immerses them more
deliberately in the onflowing current of time, then draws
them momentarily out of it, but with the traces of temporality retained. Memory for him is less a well than a reservoir,
constantly renewed by inflowing and outflowing waters.

Yet even such a statement cannot be absolute because Machado feels perfectly free to manipulate memory as lyric occasions determine. At times it does act like a well in which
things may not only be held but be lost (see Poem 17, ending). One is reminded of Augustine's query: "When . . . the
memory loses something . . . where are we to look for it except in the memory itself?"[43] And at times the subject seems
to collaborate, with different degrees of effort, in the process
of remembering, so that one can hardly say to what extent
recall is voluntary, to what extent involuntary (Poems 3, 20).
On occasion it is obviously involuntary (Poem 17, again), on
occasion quite deliberate, at least in theory—as in Poem 23,
where memory appears to be a "storehouse," to use Augustine's term. But one notes that the same poem speaks of what
is to be remembered as the *turbios lienzos* (hazy pictures) of
past dreams. However deliberate the process of recall, time
will have been at work on what is recalled. We are thus
brought back to the characteristic Machadian emphasis on
the transforming action of memory.

Present and past are inextricably interwoven in Poem 17
(1904), which not only presents an experience recovered
through a cluster of highlighted sensations, but records a process of involuntary sensory recall occurring within the more
or less modifying medium of a dream. More tranquilly, less
fleetingly in Poem 3 (1903), the past is made to reemerge
through sensory recall, partly induced, partly involuntary, in
the context of a return to the patio of the Palacio de las
Dueñas, probably in 1903, where the speaker rediscovers the
prelapsarian world of childhood, held magically intact in fragrance and reflection.[44]

A more deliberate plunge into the self, set off by an urge
to probe a mood which Machado, many years later, will see

as anticipating Heideggerian sorge and angst, occurs in Poem 20. After a false start and subsequent gropings, the speaker sees his way clear and eventually uncovers, in a memory of childhood distress, a correlative for present anxiety, in some sense allaying the anxiety by distancing it.

The brief Poem 23 (1907) speaks for itself as a classic statement of the experiences variously combined in the poems in which memory and dreaming are channels to self-knowledge and provide a way of turning the loneliness of *soledad* into fulfillment. Poem 7 (1903), focused concretely on the world of dreams, follows a similar movement from bitterness to reconciliation and in the intervening range of moods touches on recurrent symbols, images, and motifs of Machado's poetic world.

In almost all these poems there are traces of a *tú*, a second person, but in No. 20 this is either a rhetorical vocative (as in the address to the *dolor*), or marks only a fleeting appearance of a second person external to the self; the latter is the case with No. 17 as well. Poem 23, however, with its displacement of a first-person voice by a second, a characteristic stance of the early Machado, does convey one side of an authentic inner dialogue. The effect is similar in Poem 3; the address to the afternoon moves palpably from remembrance to recognition, though here the silent "you" is appealed to more as witness than as interlocutor.

This poem leads to other characteristic ones in which an actual dialogue is externalized in exchanges, sometimes reassuring, sometimes disquieting, with phenomena of nature or figments of the poet's fantasy: evening, the wind, a wraithlike fin-de-siècle figure, a voice, or even silence. In the present selection, the dialogues with the fountain (No. 2), with the devil in the speaker's dream (No. 18), and with the night (No. 10) represent this Machadian manner. They coincide in ending inconclusively or in an ultimate failure of dialogue, expressing with different nuances the final inaccessibility of the self. In another poem, No. 5, Machado makes us strongly aware of an absolute absence of dialogue.

In Poem 2 (1903), the most patently Romantic of this group in its affective underscoring, an innocent retrospective impulse ends by resurrecting a painful "historical" past. This the speaker's memory had recreated "apocryphally" by soft-

ening bitterness through distantiation into bittersweet daydreaming. The dialogue with the voice of the fountain ends
in an impasse of silent frustration. With a more characteristic
sobriety, Poem 18, dating also from 1903, equates the inner
space of a dream with the "deep vault of the soul." Again,
both advancing, penetrating motion and inner dialogue
express the irresistibility of psychic exploration as well as the
danger of ultimate revelations.

In the purely dialogic situation of the protracted exchange
with the night, No. 10 (1903), the result is unknowability: the
self disintegrates into a "blurred labyrinth of mirrors," a
multiplicity of possible identities. In the impasse between authenticity and inauthenticity of feeling, or between the affective state and its expression, it becomes impossible to sort
out "voices" from "echoes."

But in Poem 6, "Horizon" (1903), one already senses restiveness within the "tedious" confinement of this impasse. A
series of mirror effects here figures forth the speaker's attempt to transcend the self. Although the "thousand tall
shadows," presumably those of trees lining a road, are felt as
vague projections of somber dreams haunting the speaker,
the burst of light and color from the sunset totally absorbs
them and refracts them out of sight. The speaker, lifted out
of himself, senses a new beginning beyond the range of his
own reverberating footsteps.

With Poem 5 (1906), a somewhat similar situation of
"dreaming" one's way "down evening roads" is handled less
effusively; mirrors are abandoned altogether, and one is even more
aware of an impending change of direction. The movement of
the poem is more frankly outward, away from a self here
taken for granted and toward the otherness that surrounds it.

Nearly thirty years later (1935) Machado will write in *Juan
de Mairena*: "It is in the solitude of the countryside that man
ceases to live among mirrors" and will speak of the poet's
"intuiting rhythms there which are not in accord with the
flowing of his own blood and are, in general, slower."[45] In
Poem 5 the solo voice ringing out and the landscape in which
it moves along go their own ways, each at its own pace, coex-
isting without interacting. Yet the otherness of the land, felt
with particular keenness at the midpoint as it withdraws into
its "ingathered" stillness, is devoid of the disquieting or

alienating overtones remarked on previously, and frequent later in similar existential contexts. The distinct strands within the poem are interwoven through a skillful interplay of focusing and loss of focus, one already implicit in Poem 3 and peculiarly characteristic of Machado's art.[46]

In the *copla*, the interpolated song, Machado is stylizing a traditional folk-motif in keeping with a long-standing tradition which, in Spain, continues to favor interaction between cultivated and popular art strains. In Machado's poem the singer, for a moment at least, in able to subsume his own into the communal voice, bypassing problems of echoes and individual authenticity of expression.

As the landscape here withdraws to meditate, so a process of transference, as observed in Poem 6, frequently endows objects or phenomena external to the psyche with the property of dreaming that characterizes its inner life; the lemons dreaming on deep in the fountain of Poem 3 are another example, while in other poems we will find water, rocks (more commonly symbols of inert otherness), the land itself dreaming, and flowers sources of "dream honey."

Nevertheless, such transference will henceforth usually signify moving away from a subjective dream world and out toward a world directly observed, whatever aura of epiphanic magic or post-Symbolist incantation may still be retained in the early period. Poem 19 (1907) is transitional in this regard: the air is spellbound, the swallows dream and soar, yet the focus grows sharper and sharper as the eye follows first the single swallow, then the stork to their roosting places, as if the speaker were steadying himself against the impact of too luminous a vision. The grotesque humor with which the stork is caught at the end marks a reflex of irony symptomatic of future trends, one which belittles the "dark corner" emblematic of the withdrawn self.[47]

This poem initiates, then blunts, an early impulse toward what Machado will later speak of as the *vuelo de altura*, the verse of "soaring flight," which he contrasts to poetry that plunges into the tunnels and "dark corners" of the psyche.[48] Such an urge toward transcendence—intermittent, impaired, but enduring—is perceptible as well behind the Pythagoreanism of Poem 22 (1907), in effect a brief ars poetica. Eschewing simple acquiescence in a cult of the turn of the century, the poem appropriates this cult to express the speaker's private awareness that his restrained utterance and sparseness of diction are in effect verbal links in an expanding chain of correspondences binding the phenomenal to the noumenal.

Before this brief yet total statement, two earlier compositions, both of 1903, exemplify the unceasing meditation on poetic art which would find outlets in verse or in prose to the end. Poem 4, entitled "Children's Songs" on its original appearance in the first *Soledades*, reveals how well Machado's ear is attuned from the start, no doubt in consequence of his father's active interest in folklore, to the communal voice in poetry and song. A listener here, rather than an interlocutor, Machado combines motifs and materials found in poems already glanced at, such as the singing fountain and the popular song, in a lyric that functions as an aesthetic creed. Writing in his notebook nearly twenty years later, Machado saw this poem as "proscribing the anecdotal" and proclaiming the right of the lyric to relate (*contar*) only feeling (*emoción*), effacing the human story in its entirety.[49] The human story, but not the narrative voice. For it is implicit in the temporal basis of his aesthetic that an action of some kind, however inward or understated, is always unfolding, moving toward some culmination (which may evidently never be reached). Even when, as later, he will pen what he calls "jottings," the poems will not be static notations of moods. Feeling, to be communicated, must be "told," that is to say, informed with the temporal sequentiality that also characterizes narration. Mere transcription of sensation is not sufficient. "The lyric has always been a transcription of feeling [*sentimiento*], which contains sensation, not the other way round," Machado will tell Guiomar.[50] He will deplore what he considers the *symboliste* reduction of emotion to sensation or "a complex of sensations" and disdain Verlaine's proclaimed reduction of lyricism to musicality.[51]

With a different emphasis from "Children's Songs," one of the earlier noted "Jottings," which Machado in 1924 dates back to 1902, also observes that:

Poetry is song and telling.
A live story is sung
when the melody is told.                              (Poem 46, II)

Musicality and narration, rather than interchangeable, as in this crisp formulation, are more subtly fused in "Children's Songs," each modifying the other in the direction of the shared "monotone" of a timeless present. Unlike the monotony of the similarly "singing" and "telling" fountain of Poem 2, however, this monotone carries no heavy emotional charge, only a pure distillation of feeling, "serene pain," an affective aura which has gathered about these products of the communal muse in the course of time. The two contemporaneous poems formulate for the future the alternatives of a poetics grounded in personal recall and one drawing on collective memory.

Poem 11, "The Waterwheel," the other early ars poetica, concentrates on the consolatory and compensatory role of poetry in a manner which half bridges the gap between Poem 2 and Poem 4. The inwardness emblematized in the blindfolding suggests a "godlike" gift of personal creativity, yet what the water sings is a "workaday tune"; the water is also a collective voice of traditional song, one capable of supplementing the activity not only of games, as in Poem 4, but of work, thereby alleviating the weary toilsomeness of existence. The humble mule is here a symbol both of personal creativity and of the audience that absorbs it and makes it its own.

Not that Machado is to be free henceforth of afterthoughts regarding the ultimate adequacy of whatever compensation and consolation the gift of creation affords. Poem 21 (1907) raises with great delicacy the question that will never cease to haunt him: what if it all comes to nothing in the end? By contemplating such doubts, the poet achieves at least some temporary displacement of them.

Besides these explorations and these questionings of the function of the poet and his art, there is, finally, in Machado's early work an "objective" vein, here exemplified in two poems—No. 12, "The Gallows," and No. 13, "Flies"—which, with the poem just examined, comprise a subsection called "The Great Inventions." The title confers on all three a touch of ironic or sardonic humor not otherwise apparent in the poem just examined, but evident in "Flies." To glance first, however, at a more sober poem in this realistic vein: in No. 1, "At the Burial of a Friend" (1907), only the reverberat-

ing impact of the "brutal" of the opening line betrays the
speaker's tensely withheld feelings as he etches exact details
of setting, atmosphere, and event. The harshness of a world
unprotected by dreaming is squarely faced. In "The Gallows," on the other hand, an earlier poem (1903), Machado
appears to be experimenting a bit heavy-handedly with the
opposite technique, a grotesquely overstated expressionism.
Nevertheless, the poem marks an early instance of his attention to the grim realities of life in backward areas of rural
Spain.

In "Flies" the speaker deliberately provokes, through the
agency of the omnipresent insects, a train of reminiscences
that encapsulate the stages of a lifetime. The combination of
capriciousness in choice of agent and order in recall—comprehensive, cumulative, and accelerating—makes for a humorous sort of evenhandedness. The appeal of the "soaring
flight" receives passing acknowledgment in "flying is all that
counts."

No losses, no setback, no disillusionment—at least not
until the Republican cause turned hopeless during the final
two years in Valencia and Barcelona—would ever permanently check this upward impulse. It is plainly in evidence in
1912 in *The Castilian Country*, though Machado's critical eye
and broad-ranging awareness keep it well controlled. In the
fullest sense the impulse to the "soaring flight" corresponds
to widening spheres of concern—from self to society, nation,
mankind, and philosophical transcendence.[52] This idealizing
tendency is manifest at times in poetry of contemplation and
reflection; at times it is mediated in accounts of upward
movement in pursuit of broader vision—ascents of hills,
flights of birds.

Unquestionably, in the poetry centered on Castile, whether
written on the spot or during the early Baeza years, it is the
direct view of the face of the land that most forcefully strikes
the reader, a view not merely of landscape, but a georgic vision, alert to the human presence. Moreover, attunement to
the genius loci makes Machado particularly sensitive to the
presence of what he calls "spirit" (*alma*), a word he invests
with a variety of overtones—historical, personal, supraper-
sonal. In 1932, twenty years after *The Castilian Country* first ap-

peared, he writes: "Soria is, probably, the most spiritual part
of spiritual Castile, in its turn spirit of all Spain. There is
nothing overpowering in it, nothing flashy or boisterous,
everything there is simple, modest, plain . . . It always in-
vites us to be what we are, and only that . . . Soria is an ad-
mirable school of humanism, of democracy, and of dignity."[53]

Machado's vision was not at all times so positive. Yet his
words not only reveal how his concerns radiated outward
from Soria; they point also to the deep affinities with his own
nature sensed in the spirit of Castile—the land, the people,
the way of life, the values. "Landscapes of Soria, / . . . you
have found your way to my heart— / or were you already
there?" he wonders at the end of "The Soria Country" (No.
29, ix). Speaking of Castile is still a way of speaking of himself—all the more so when, with time and absence, the vision
of Castile recedes inward and must be recaptured in the
transforming medium of memory.

Writing in 1917 about *The Castilian Country*, Machado has
begun to pose the question of the reciprocity between inner
and outer worlds more problematically in terms of selfhood
and otherness: "We are, I thought, victims of a double mi-
rage. If we look outward and attempt to penetrate into things,
our outer world loses solidity and ends up dissolving before
our eyes, as we come to believe that it exists because of us,
not in its own right. But, if, convinced of an intimate reality,
we look inward, then everything seems to come from without
and it is our inner world, ourselves, that fades out. What to
do then? Weave the thread we are given, dream our dream,
live."[54]

He turns away from the dilemma, still sees hope in dreaming, and, especially, settles for "living" in preference to cogitation. In the more outward-looking poetry of the Soria and
early Baeza years, though dreams occasionally hover on the
face of the land and the landscape at times may turn inward
or seem about to, it is the observant eye that predominates,
as well as an ear attuned to the voices of other men—fellow-
Spaniards, other human beings. Years later, when Juan de
Mairena formulates successive definitions of poetry as "the
dialogue of man with time" and "the dialogue of man, of a
man with his time,"[55] it may be legitimate to see in the

changed wording an intention to encompass more than "the poet's vital time with its own pulsation," to leave room for the time in which he lives, his epoch, for a "dialogue of man" that admits human interlocutors.[56] Four selections in this book represent the direct vision of Castile: two long poems written during the Soria years— "Along the Duero" (No. 25) and the sequence entitled "The Soria Country" (No. 29)—and two dating from shortly after—"The Iberian God" (No. 26), first published in 1913, and a second poem entitled "Along the Duero" (No. 27) that appeared only in 1917, in the expanded *Castilian Country* included in the first edition of *Complete Poems*.[57] In all, the role of memory and dream is a minor one and scarcely distinguishes the poetry written after leaving Soria from that composed during the Soria years.

"Along the Duero," in recounting the ascent of a hill overlooking Soria, moves from spatial to temporal coordinates, from a sweeping visual panorama to a long view of history. The crucial hinge comes just before the midpoint, in lines carefully set apart from those preceding and following:

> Castile's, Iberia's, oaken heart is spanned
> by the Duero.                                        (Poem 25)

This flash of insight from the hilltop, not quite so sudden as it seems, in changing the river from a presence in the landscape to an emblem of the flow of Spanish history catalyzes a view of the martial past which has been accumulating as a metaphorical overlay on the panoramic vision.[58] The prospect from the summit, reducing the scale of the sparsely inhabited scene below while highlighting the presence of the river, constancy in flux, slowly unblocks vistas of a glorious past and of an inglorious present shot through with a sense of that past enduring as absence, decline, abandonment. Moods of melancholy, anger, and perplexity follow one another, states of mind characteristic of the Generation of 1898. After scorn has run its course, the harshness of the immediate scene is softened by the coming-on of evening, but the speaker's mood remains grave. The somber concluding vista divulges a barren, shapeless future, the inevitable

sequel to a present marked, when one looks closely, by depopulation, degeneracy, and disintegration of the sustaining
patterns of popular culture.

*Campos de Castilla* contains other poems, not included here,
in which the mood is equally somber and the vision of present and past as unsparing. More characteristic, however, are
the poems in which indignation is softened by sympathy and
some degree of hopefulness. This is the case with "The
Iberian God," even though Machado knows that the savagery
he observes in the Spanish peasant has the weight of cen-
turies behind it. There comes through, in the peasant's
prayer, an undercurrect of sympathy for the tough endurance
of a peasantry who refuse to prostrate themselves before a
God whose incomprehensible ways govern both the harshness of nature and the injustice of man. Sympathy turns to
admiration for the accomplishments of a faith on which this
blasphemy does not encroach in the least. The reassurance to
the "men of Spain" that the old energies are waiting to be
tapped again is not merely glib or rhetorical. The final
stanzas reflect confidence in the "plasticity of the past." Machado holds out a challenge to consider nothing irredeemable
and nothing foreclosed and looks to a leader—Unamuno?—
prepared to meet the challenge.

In "Along the Duero" (No. 27), removal from Castile
allows for as encompassing a vision of the high tablelands as
in the earlier poem of the same name, but the necessary inwardness of the recollective process, as it endows with *alma*
what was simply given before—the physical presence of the
land—makes the personal voice more prominent and softens
the harshness of the historical vision.[59]

Despite the stress on Soria's humbleness at the beginning,
the initial vastness of the spatial setting presages the ascending movement of the first part toward a culminating evocation of the spirit of an entire region. In this part one can
sense the speaker resisting the temptation to interiorize the
landscape as he recreates its bittersweet savor. Then specific
sensory recall takes over for awhile, initiating the downward
movement of the second part, with the Duero once again a
presence in the landscape—successively physical, legendary,
and historical. By the end the poem can be seen to be oscil-

lating between cyclic renewal and decline as possibilities inherent in the on-running river of time.

"The Soria Country" is a product of meditation in situ, though the last section must mark a temporary departure from the city. The cycle of nature is dwelt upon: April and the hesitant advance of spring in I and II; autumn and winter by IV and V, with anticipations of a new spring; autumn again in VIII, with glances backward and forward to spring. The ongoing cycle of human life is interwoven with that of nature: new life in IV; life and death, old age and childhood, in V; young love always renewed in VIII. Yet the remaining sections, removed from seasonal time, point toward the lasting essence of the Castilian spirit—in an outburst of color in III, coinciding with the characteristic ascending movement:

> But if you climb a hill and view the scene
> from heights where eagles live,

and in a new upsurge echoed at the end of IV. The stark and eerie presentation of the town in VI seems to revert to Machado's most implacably critical manner, but by the end the lunar lighting dispels the mightmarish vision and the apostrophe to "Cold Soria"—ostensibly a reference to climate—captures something cool and quintessential.

Minutely observed details of the activities of man and nature on the land are set off throughout the poem by occasional projections of dream into the landscape. In the end affective and aesthetic impulses prevail over the critical, emerging particularly in the repeated enumerative series of VII and IX, which, in Wordsworthian fashion, mark an effort to impress a particular spirit of place on the speaker's sensibility more and more deeply, to store it away for future recollection. With the concluding vision of the country people the mood shifts from pensiveness to buoyancy in the familiar rising movement.

As Machado recalls Soria in the Baeza years and afterward, the figure of Leonor, the child-wife buried in the graveyard at the top of *El Espino* (Hawthorn Hill) acquires the relief lacking when her presence in his life could be taken for granted. The loss of what at a distance appears a paradise or a "child's bright dream of Arcady" (No. 29, II) has at its core his personal loss. The finest of the earlier group of poems centering on Leonor—the verse-letter to José María Palacio (No. 31) dated Baeza, 29 March 1913—must be read retrospectively from the allusion to Leonor in the final lines if the delicate contraposition of renewal and definitive loss is to be caught. The tentativeness with which the poem proceeds, through questions and imaginative suppositions, keeps remembered details accumulating in easy succession without rhetorical strain as the speaker gropes for a precise point of the upland spring's brief advance appropriate to the mission he asks his friend to discharge.

Among poems of this anthology, Leonor will be present in a passing but poignant allusion in "One Day's Poem" (No. 32), another product of the early Baeza years. In *New Songs*, to anticipate for a moment, she will be a focal point for the first of the "Dreams in Dialogue" (No. 45), and her memory will inform other sonnets of that collection. As for the Soria country, the "Highland Songs" (No. 39) of *New Songs* will be characterized by an interplay between recollections of that region and others, while Poem 38, "Passageways," of the same collection will carry it along with all the rest of Machado's remembered landscapes to their highest point of fusion.

Returning to the Baeza years, one may note that the contrast between the new Andalusian settings and the one left behind, added to the numbing effect of the loss of his wife, appears at first to have proved unhinging, inducing fears of creative sterility. One sees as much in the poem beginning "Back in the landscape of my native soil" (No. 30), dated 4 April 1913 at Lora del Río, a town on the lower Guadalquivir between Cordova and Seville. Machado finds himself back in the setting of his native Lower Andalusia, but the surrounding presence of what had existed only in the afterlife of childhood memories has an inhibiting effect and the burden of the poem is the failure of the creative process to take hold. Symbols fertile in earlier verse turn barren now, for all their sensory sharpness. It is not merely that the memory of Castile has intervened: "the thread that binds the memory to the heart / is missing, the anchor on its brink" (lines 29–30). For such binding to occur, distancing, in space as well as in time, is essential. In "Back in the landscape of my native soil" the

interval which, like Wordsworth, Machado needed for creative reelaboration has been suddenly effaced and with it the
links to the inner world. Significantly, it is contrasting imagery of temporal flow, the deep river that draws the past in-
sensibly into the present, that appears at the end as an alternative to the present sterility.

By way of contrast, all sense of strain disappears when a
present experience unblocks channels of association with
similar ones of the past. There is a clue in this to the "thousand Guadarramas" and the "thousand suns" of the poem
(No. 28) written in 1911, when the poet, coming upon the
Guadarrama Mountains afresh after a long interval, finds the
experience becoming overlaid by past visions of them and
thus paradoxically lifting itself out of the current of time.

In Baeza, Machado's alertness to his new surroundings,
and the stimulus to his creative imagination of more intense
contact with philosophy, replenished his poetic energies,
overcoming apprehensions of sterility. Although he is still
drawn to continued pursuit of earlier lines of poetic exploration, his production from this time on branches out from
them increasingly, sometimes in surprising directions.

Some poems of the earlier Baeza years carry into the new
eastern Andalusian setting the georgic concerns, the keen responsiveness to locality of the Castilian poetry. Again hopefulness alternates with bitter pessimism in the face of social,
cultural, and economic realities.

His ruminations on philosophical issues are reflected in
Machado's poetic expression in several forms: they produce
overt "parables"; they are condensed into the already mentioned "proverbs" and "song-verse," in which the learned
and the popular, the whimsical and the sardonic, the topical
and the personal mingle; finally, they energize longer compositions, shaping structure and controlling form. It is the last
which provide the most impressive, though not the most accessible development in Machado's later work. The enigmas
and obscurities of all this poetry are neither obscurantist nor
willful. They result from the effort to confront fundamental,
often anguishing, perplexities, dilemmas of existence and of
mortality.

Machado's thinking, though unsystematic and tentative, is
associative and, in this sense, integrative. In the later produc-

tion, aesthetic, erotic, phenomenological, and metaphysical concerns tend to merge; a purely conceptual composition such as "To the Great Nought" (No. 50) is exceptional. Thus, the group of love poems to Guiomar is as much a prolongation of speculations engaged in elsewhere on the impossiblity or unreality of love, on time, on memory, even on the nature of art, as a direct tribute.

The "cinematographic" unraveling that marks the form of the "Memories of Dreaming, Fever, and Dozing" (No. 53) brings together the most varied preoccupations of a lifetime—political, social, and artistic, as well as psychic, metaphysical, phenomenological. All of this later poetry inevitably appears under the aegis of aging, mingles retrospection, summing-up, renunciation, *déjà vu*, and compassion. The melancholy of the advancing years, which have brought neither certainties nor deliverance from solitude, breaks through in unexpected places, though never insistently; sometimes it hangs cloudily over longer compositions. Inevitably, the mood grows more somber in the poetry written during the Civil War: "Meditation," 1937 (No. 63), the final recollection of Soria in the sonnet of 1938 (No. 62). It flares into tragic anger in the elegy to Lorca, 1936 (No. 64).

In "One Day's Poem: Rural Reflections" (No. 32), written in early 1913, shortly after Machado took up his teaching duties in Baeza, we find the poet training his glance on himself in his new circumstances with a sustained dispassionateness foreign to the earlier intimate poetry. An uneasy sense of detachment, existentialist at heart, runs through the rambling, yet coherent lines. With a note of disbelief the poet surveys his situation at the outset, and at the end he drifts back from routine social intercourse to problematical solitude. In between, he reaches out sporadically in imaginative attempts at identification or dialogue with persons and things outside the self: people of the land—farmers and farm hands; Unamuno, Chancellor of the University of Salamanca; the rain itself; the group conversing at the druggist's, day in, day out, month in, month out, on the same subjects. The backdrop is once more the cycle of seasons and crops, variable yet repetitive, just as the foreground is the ticking of the clock. The cyclical pattern, when the ultimate "vanity of vanities" is warded off, as it mostly is by the speaker, comes closer for him to giving a sense to things than does the Bergsonian homogeneity of time segmented by the clock—time maddeningly, meaninglessly monotonous. Only occasionally do the hope and despair of a personalized psychic time break through: in the upsurge of fellow-feeling for Unamuno's campaign for a moral regeneration of Spain, in the bitter fissures of personal loss and lack of faith. For the rest, the trivia of existence and inconclusive ruminations on ultimate philosophical issues and more immediate ones occupy the speaker. The trend of the reflections shows how Machado's thought (as one also gathers from notebook jottings of the Baeza years) is moving beyond Bergson's excessive subjectivism and making concessions to Kantian ethics and rationality.[60] Concessions will be made to Platonic idealism as well.

The regional setting surrounding the small-town milieu of "One Day's Poem" becomes the center of the visual field in "The Olive Trees" (No. 33), with the tone rising to a climax of enthusiasm by the end of the first part, dropping abruptly as the second opens, and sinking to utter pessimism by the end. The swings of mood correspond to the disparity between the sweeping vision of nature in a beautifully ordered landscape and a close-up view of the disorderliness of institutionalized communal life on the same land. The poem blends pure landscape poetry—the gathering momentum and the patterning of the rhythms convey both a total panorama and a range of particular lightings and atmospheres—with a georgic tradition and one of social critique. In the first part Machado works up to an enthusiastic vision of a mutually supportive relation between the land and those who toil on it, indeed of a stable social order in which gentry and peasantry, bandits and smugglers, all find a secure niche.

One may speculate that the two parts of the poem were of independent genesis. The journey of part II has in fact been pinned down to June 1915.[61] Their juxtaposition and the effect of falling away it produces, a recurrent one in Machado's later work, is crucial, however. In turning the tables, it upsets much more than a fancied social order. It is not only the failure of man and his institutions in the face of the goodness of the earth, but the painfulness of the human condition, of consciousness itself, that the spectacle before him stirs up in the poet.

The "Parables" (No. 35), which span the period from 1912 to 1917, play up the "telling" aspect of poetry and play down, without eliminating it, the "singing."[62]

Noticeable in these compositions is the increasing impact on Machado of Unamuno, long an object of reverential admiration. It is visible in his responsiveness to Unamuno's call for reactivation of the latent spiritual, moral, and emotional energies of Spain, a summons Machado credited with helping to liberate him from the subjectivism of his early verse.[63] The one-sided dialogue with Unamuno in "One Day's Poem" (No. 32) reflects the actual one begun earlier in correspondence that grew more active during the Baeza years and soon extended to fundamental questions of faith and knowledge. Unlike Unamuno, Machado will never be able to talk himself into nourishing faith on doubt; his metaphysical speculations are inevitably tinged with skepticism and irony. In stimulating Machado, Unamuno also pushes him into awareness of divergences from him.

Thus, the ending of the first parable (1915)—"Perhaps he woke up—who knows!"—strikes a very different note from a statement written under the impact of Unamuno's *Niebla* in a letter to him the same year: "We are asleep, are we? Very well. And we dream, do we? Granted. But there can be awakening, hope, doubting with faith."[64] Something close to free-floating whimsy hangs over the equally balanced alternatives of the "advice" of the fourth parable (originally called a "whim"), a far cry from Unamuno's activism. The whimsy has vanished in the sixth, one of the latest (1917), in which skepticism is compounded by the irony of the allusion to the triune God of Catholic orthodoxy. The vague echoes of Unamuno's thought sensed here are much clearer in the earlier fifth parable—his definition of faith as "creating what we do not see" and of God as the creature of man's need as much as vice versa—even though in Machado the poem is less a profession of faith than a "doubting with faith."[65]

The remaining parables (excepting the third) highlight in various tones one aspect or another of the fundamental dilemma which Machado elsewhere formulates as that of two forms of consciousness: one light, the other patience.[66] These appear, with a certain flippancy, as reason and feeling in VII; as conceptualization and creativity, somewhat sardonically, in VIII; as ratiocination and dreaming in II, the least schematic and most impressive of the parables. Here the thinker ends up with nothing but a sense of divorce from life in time (akin to the lifeless abstractions dealt in by the I-figure of the final parable), while the dreamer, though he closes off the immediate perceptual brightness, is carried by it into the eternal present of myth and attains a new illumination. But it remains the illumination—the illusion?—of a dream. In these poems dreaming is oriented no longer toward the individual psyche but toward the surrounding world. Metaphysical, not psychic, its aim is insight (and so it will remain) though attainment seems no closer than before.

As far back as 1909 Machado had turned to the brief forms of traditional anonymous verse as vehicles for the wide-ranging reflections and the insights which he would soon begin to record at greater length in his notebooks. In this strain of his production, if in part he is cultivating the gnomic, aphoristic, and epigrammatic forms of a more or less philosophical poetry, he is also stylizing a popular poetry rooted in folklore and regional traditions.[67] Although there is no sharp dividing line, Machado emphatically understands "folklore" in no collector's or archaeologist's sense. Years later, in 1935, he will explain, apropos of Juan de Mairena's interest in the subject: "For him folklore was not a study of reminiscences of old cultures, of dead elements that the soul of the common people unconsciously transmits in its language, in its practices, in its customs, etc. . . . Mairena thought that folklore was the live, creative culture of a common people from whom there was a great deal to be learned so as to be able to teach the moneyed classes properly . . . 'Among us,' Mairena is quoted as saying, 'university knowledge cannot compete with folklore, popular knowledge.' "[68]

The attraction of *el saber popular* came naturally as a family heritage. In addition, it offered a way of reaching out to blend the individual voice with that of the collectivity. In these series we run the gamut of Machadian tones from the ludic to the melancholic. The personal voice sometimes insistently prevails over the sought impersonality; the folk aphorism sometimes acquires "learned" overtones. When there is a regional flavor, it sometimes suggests an immediate impression, especially when Andalusian. Sometimes it is resurrected from memory; this is usually the case with Castile.

In a first series of "Proverbs and Song-Verse" (No. 34), brought together in *The Castilian Country* in 1912, although the pithiness is not as marked, one already finds compact, sometimes enigmatic, formulations which are frequently cynical, occasionally even bitter in tone. In *New Songs* (1924), a further series similarly entitled is noticeably more philosophical in orientation, more subtly ironical; its tone is mellower.[69] It echoes in brief certain themes of the "Parables" and takes up new themes. Composition corresponds to the first five Segovia years, though an occasional verse is probably earlier; the ninety-nine brief compositions are not arranged in any discernible order. The peculiar interaction between the personal and the collective voices is acknowledged by Machado when he writes in 1920, in answer to an inquiry: "At present, I am doing nothing but folklore, *autofolklore* or folklore of myself. My new book [*New Songs*] will, in large part, be one of *coplas* which do not claim to imitate the folk manner—one which cannot be imitated or improved upon, whatever the teachers of rhetoric may think—but *coplas* containing everything within me that I share with the spirit that sings and thinks in the common people. In this way, I believe I am continuing on my way without changing course."[70]

A pair of verses sums up the relationship of the personal and the traditional. Poem 41, LXXI advises: "Give your verse double lighting / for reading straight on / and sideways." But if such irony is smoothed away in the course of circulation, one need not be disturbed, we are at once told in LXXII, because wide currency is precisely the goal. The same symbolism attaches to the coin of LXXVIII which, in preference to the jewel, is to receive the artist-craftsman's finest attention; there is to be no cult of the exquisite at the expense of the ideal of wide accessibility. The key to XIX and XX, which in the guise of the popular enigma ask the meaning of the small earthenware jug never removed from the springside, is Machado's conviction that utilitarianism and artistry are perfectly reconcilable.

In a remark in the 1920 text just cited, Machado takes issue with the Kantian view of art as the "pure form of pur-

posefulness," that is, as "purposefulness without a purpose,"
a kind of "supreme game." "The first man who made a vessel out of a piece of clay was a supreme artist, even though
his fellow-man might drink out of that vessel."[71] Later in the
same statement, with his usual proneness to second thoughts,
Machado will observe that the traditional need not be re-
stricted to the utilitarian: "May a poet sing of roses and lilies,
while other men, and even he himself, struggle for bread or
justice? Certainly. Roses and lilies are not worn rhetoric: they
are produced every spring."

The apparent impersonality of tone of the "Proverbs and
Song-Verse" is easily penetrated when one sets them in the
full context of Machado's thought and literary creation in
these years. Because Machado is at no pains always to main-
tain such a tone, the compositions offer incidental glimpses
of his mind at work, of the sensibility that pervades his
thinking. Conceptualization is often simply the obverse side
of lyricism in this verse:

> A concept that's chemically pure
> is generally an empty husk;
> it can be a red-hot cauldron.                    (Poem 41, LXXX)

In more familiar fashion, pregnant poetic thought is valued
above mental enlightenment:

> Not the sun but the bell,
> when it wakes you up,
> is the best part of morning.                    (Poem 41, LXXXII)

Though some of these poems have an aphoristic dryness
and are as terse as epigrams, one keeps encountering others
whose resonances are those of Machado's familiar lyric
world. The dominant strains in the series relate to self and
other, to personal artistic and aesthetic values, to the stream
of time and its effects on what necessarily exists within it.
The tone, though sometimes disabused, is rarely cynical.
When it is playful and whimsical, something more than
whimsy is usually involved.

The vision of self is only occasionally sardonic. Machado's
early pursuit of one among many inner voices has grown into

a sense of their complementary character. He acknowledges
an otherness within as well as without. The self becomes
many-sided, extensible, resisting delimitation:

> Never set down your limits
> nor fuss with your profile:
> they're only externals.                     (Poem 41, XIV)

> Look for your counterpart
> who's always alongside you,
> and is usually your opposite.               (Poem 41, XV)

Narcissistic solipsism, with its treasuring of what is unique to
the self, is repeatedly eschewed (III, VI, XVII, LXVI, LXXXV). Personal truths are not truths at all; one must seek *the* truth (XVII
and LXXXV). The other that one seeks in the mirror may be
that part of the self that is stirred to fellow-feeling with
others (IV, XXXIX), although at the same time Machado recognizes "the essential heterogeneousness of being,"[72] the distinctness of its every manifestation, never to be overcome,
even in love (XL). This fundamental otherness (I), if it ultimately circumscribes the attempt to transcend the personal
self, at the same time makes dialogue the fundamental manifestation of human intercourse.

Although the opening emphasis of the series is on otherness, Machado follows it up immediately (II) by pointing the
way to dialogue: ask and then listen. The inadequacy of the
Bergsonian *moi fondamental,* on whose uniqueness Machado
had still fallen back at the end of "One Day's Poem," is apparent when he writes:

> It's not the basic I
> that the poet is after
> but the essential you.                      (Poem 41, XXXVI)

The dialogue—indeed the dialectic—between self and others
is recurrent. Pursuit through art of the essential you, he acknowledges ruefully at one point, may only lead back to self:

> That you in my song
> doesn't go for you, friend.
> That you is me.                             (Poem 41, L)

On the other hand, the appeal of the ethic of the Christ of the Gospels, for Machado so much stronger than that of the dogmas of the Church, like the attraction of Plato and later of Cervantes, lies in an assumption of reciprocity in love between essentially distinct subjects: "In Christ's dialogues it is not reasons that are sought but forms and acts of affective communion," Machado will write in *Juan de Mairena*.[73] He will also remark: "The whole [nineteenth] century was, at heart, a monstrous reaction against the essential themes of Western culture, which are—would anyone doubt it?—that of Socratic dialectic, which invents human reason, the mental communion of a plurality of subjects in transcendental ideas, and that of the other, more subtle dialectic of Christ, which reveals the object in terms of feeling and establishes the brotherhood of men, emancipated from bonds of blood." These remarks help clarify the significance of the otherness viewed as implicit in Christ's teachings in XLII and XLIII, and the "divine" character attributed to the spoken word as it breaks through the noisiness and the dumbness of the world in XLIV. Even the whimsical gypsy humor of LVI and LXXV is cast in conversational form.

The sudden objective and ironic glance at the self, still isolated in spite of everything, is, I suspect, behind the cricket singing away in his cage of XXIII, the little old man chuckling away of LXXXIII, the uproarious laughter of LIX, the self-canceling advice of XCIV. This last, however, is followed by a reminder (XCV) that since the advice may in fact be self-directed (a *"you"* being really a *"me"*), it might well be borne in mind after all. An "I" may also be contained in the "he" of LXIX and LXX, written, one would suppose, to exorcise the demon of subjectivism in self as well as in others. Indeed the few actual verses of undisguised self-revelation, with barriers of irony down, such as LII and LVIII, attenuate the distinctively personal note, despite the first person, because the succinctness of their *solear* form depersonalizes the "I."

Machado is rarely truly self-deprecatory, and it is in self-affirmation, not self-pity, that he recognizes in LIV the unmodishness of his "poetry of the heart" in the avant-garde atmosphere of the early twenties. He looses his own shafts at the "pure," the conceptualistic, the self-propagating and self-sufficing "creationist," poetic manners that in his view draw more on previously elaborated art than on life. In explanation of XVI, he observes in 1920, after quoting it, that the artist does not copy nature but sips or drinks from it: "I call nature all that isn't art, and I include in it the heart of a man." Decadent art merely seeks to "sweeten the honey or, as Shakespeare said, 'to throw a perfume on the violet.' "[74] The bee imagery recurs even more compactly in LXVII, the primacy of the natural in application to fragrances in XC. Similar convictions underlie the Pythagorean "Don't roast what's been boiled" (XXII), the preference for voices over echoes (XXIX), the eschewing of dissonance (XXX). If modern artifice is decried, so, in LXXXVIII, is the earlier artifice of the baroque proper, against which Juan de Mairena will later inveigh at length, though as usual Machado allows concessive afterthoughts (LXXXIX). For Machado, perhaps the main appeal of popular art, wisdom, and song is its freshness, the seeming spontaneity it retains as a thing constantly immersed in, yet always emergent from, the stream of time. Hence the preference expressed, even within the area of folklore (in LXXIX), for children's songs (subject of the ars poetica of Poem No. 4) over old ballads, a preference attributable to the more active role played by song-music in carrying words out of a distant past and keeping them fresh in the listener's present. The mature Machadian experience of *temps durée* is crystallized in the concluding reference to "yesterdays that still are." (The spring, the jug, and the water of XIX and XX allude more generally to the endless power of renewal of popular art forms.)

In contrast, how inadequate the pedantry is which forgets that "today always is still" (XXXVIII), the insight already enunciated by itself (VIII) which echoes endlessly through Machado's later work, grafting youthfulness of spirit upon a ripe awareness of permanence. Hence his receptiveness to "old words" (XLI), like those bringing variations on the same message out of diverse ethical and spiritual traditions—Pythagoras, Buddha, Christ—whose "time's not up yet" (LXV). Conversely, Machado eschews novelty as a cult in itself (XXXIV, with its echoes of D'Annunzio; XXXI and XXXII, alluding hostilely to Nietzsche) and shows skepticism regarding the turning-over of new leaves in history.

It is in connection with such skepticism that Machado's favorite imagery for the flowing-on of time—running water—

first appears in the series, in VII; it becomes dominant in the succeeding four poems, which, in consequence, are closer to the brief lyrics of a personal voice than to epigrams or proverbs. In the short span of this series, water, perceived directly, metaphorically, symbolically, acquires an extraordinary range of overtones. It would be difficult to say from how far back the "water in the live rock of my heart" takes its flow—surely from beyond even the calm, clear "springs that feed my verse" of the frontispiece to *The Castilian Country* (No. 24). The series shows with particular clarity that the shifts from outer scene to inner landscape and back again are never absolute breaks in Machado.

In LXXXVII, perhaps dating, like the second of the "Parables," from 1915, this interaction seems quite straightforward. Yet here again the river flowing in time—the time of nature and that of history as well as the time of a human life—appears emblematic of a whole nexus of permanent Machadian concerns. And in XCIII, where the question posed is of a more sweeping and ultimate nature, while "the river flowing by" is surely that of Heraclitus, and the anchor possibly Bergsonian, the dreaming sailor must be a persona of the poet.[75] One senses that Machado's lifelong fascination with the running water of rivers—his expeditions to the sources of the Duero and the Guadalquivir, his surveying of a sweep of the Duero from a hilltop, and his following the whole course of the Guadalquivir downstream—is inseparable from his total perception of human existence in time and his ponderings on history and on timeless being itself.

It is impossible to do justice to the scattering of other notes and tones found in "Proverbs and Song-Verse": skepticism as to the possibility of action (XXVI); variations on the relativity of truth and lying, with fantasy falling somewhere in between (XLVI, XLIX); sheer humor (XXIV, XXV); moments of cynicism in regard to human motivation (LX), to religious faith as a genuine refuge (LVII), to the chances of the young (XLV, XCVI, XCVII), to slogans such as "renewal from above" (XCI). The topical edge of much of this verse is perhaps sharpest in the casual reference to the fates of Kaiser and Czar (LXXXIII). Personal attitudes toward the experience of aging (Machado is in his late forties) show through occasionally: unsureness as to what it teaches in LXI; the futility of trying to hold on to what age takes away (LXII).

The last two poems sum up values underlying the whole varied series. The deep roots of Machado's social convictions underlie XCVIII, which looks forward to a poetry of broad social resonance. The brief dialogue on art in the concluding poem seems to fuse pros and cons voiced throughout. The symbol with which we are left at the end, the glowing coal with its overtones of Heraclitean fire, points (like its counterparts in LVIII, LXXX, and LXXXIX) to the possibility of an art in which the lyrical and the conceptual are vitalized by fusion.

Although in the section of *New Songs* originally entitled "Folklore" (that is, "folklore of myself"), Machado includes only one of the several series of "Jottings" and "Songs"—shorter sequences somewhat less capriciously assembled than the "Proverbs and Song-Verse"—his designation "folklore" applies to all, for in all these series the personal voice is more or less audible through the impersonal manner.

The brief verse forms of popular traditions—*soleares* and *coplas*—still predominate. In "Jottings" (No. 37), the first of these series, Machado compresses into brief lines the sparest of notations, catching in a few essential strokes Upper Andalusian scenes between Baeza and Cordova. One can draw no easy distinction between impressions recalled and impressions freshly received. Place-names are specific, but the aim is less to pin down than to take in sweepingly, quintessentially—as in the owl's eye view. Machado gives a whimsical twist to the popular tradition of its diabolic character—as a creature of darkness, it drinks up the oil of the New Light—by making it behave like Noah's dove.[76] In IX, however, the mood suddenly shifts. The speaker recoils, as if surfeited with clarity of light and line, with spatial vastness, and a dejected personal voice emerges.

The landscapes of "Highland Songs" (No. 39) are evidently drawn from remoter recesses of memory. The lines in the original still fall into the metrical patterns of popular poetry: ballad and *copla*. The first nine compositions of this series (the tenth and last requires consideration in another context) fit easily into the formula "folklore of myself."[77] More melodic than the simple jottings just examined, more clearly "songs that sing and tell," their more personal tonality is elegiac and nostalgic. The settings throughout (sometimes framed in a Lower Andalusian present) are those of Soria, except for the last two, evidently Segovian; with them the technique is closer to that of the "Jottings." Familiar sensory effects acquire additional nuances and new personal overtones. The purple tonalities range from violet and mauve to lavender, the dark air carries not only the sound but the "bitter song" of water. Recollected from the lowlands, the landscapes turn lunar.

Memory for once operates not so much to blend as to replace present impressions with past ones. At the mouth of the Guadalquivir (VII) Machado turns back to the source of the Duero. The situation is that of years earlier (No. 30, "Back in the landscape of my native soil"), but the poetic voice now sings of what is absent rather than lamenting the inability to sing of what lies close at hand.

The particular series of short compositions in this selection, which was originally placed under the rubric "Folklore" (No. 40, "Songs"), is the one in which the "autofolkloric" voice most easily blends with the popular. Its original title, "Songs of Various Places," reveals the variety of locales: nights of Málaga as well as Castile, the Roman aqueduct of Segovia, the little town square of Soria (its reappearance will not be the last), the Sorian church of Santo Domingo, and other inland or coastal places not located specifically. There is a wide range of manners as well: the "proverbs" and enigmas of "Proverbs and Song-Verse" turn up in XI and in the little earthen jug of XIII; the then-current mode of the Japanese haiku blends with the three-line Spanish *solear* in II, IV, and IX; more specifically Machadian symbols—bees and honeycomb evocative of the activity of artistic creation—are touched upon playfully in I and V.

Even when the first person points to a clearly individual recollection, as in XII, the "I" easily merges with the communal "I" present in VI, X, XIII, or in XIV, where it makes no difference whether the heart is sliipping away from the mouth of the Guadalquivir or the Argentine pampas. The tone is light-hearted, without brooding nostalgia. The harsh early vision in "Along the Duero" (No. 25), of a Castile and Iberia peopled by "boors that gape but cannot dance or sing" and depopulated by emigration, also has mellowed. In this particular "autofolkloric" mood Machado achieves a happy personal stylization of popular verse, song, dance, custom, and tradition. The last of these poems was in fact written, like the words for Manuel de Falla's "Seven Popular Spanish Songs," to be set to music.[78]

The remaining series, "Old Songs" (No. 48), in which Machado is apparently looking back to Baeza from Segovia, still makes use of popular verse forms—*coplas, soleares,* ballad meter—but the handling is more markedly individualistic, with no attempt to cultivate a concomitant brevity of style or manner.[79] The popular tradition of the bandit-hero is worked into the second and third poems through the speaker's assumption of a bandit identity. The first and the last sections of the series point to Machado's developing proclivity for the "soaring flight," an indication of the importance that sharpened seeing and breadth of vision assume as he seeks to emerge from self and focus on the surrounding world, the world shared with others, making himself accessible to a wider range of readers.

Poetry, Juan de Mairena will write, is "always an act of seeing, of affirming an absolute truth, because the poet always believes in what he sees, no matter what eyes he looks at it with. The poet and the man. His experience of life . . . has taught him that there is no living without seeing, that only vision is evidence, and that one never doubts what one sees, only what one thinks."[80]

Intelligence, too, needs to recover its eyes, Machado had written earlier, reacting against the anti-intellectualism of the Symbolists and the intuitionism of Bergson, envisaging a possible resurgence of a Platonic type of idealism, and consequently a role for "ideas" in poetry.[81] "Today, just as yesterday, the mission of the eyes, the eyes of the head and those of the mind, is to see."[82] Since one can no longer take seriously a view of the world as the narcissistic reflection of one's own consciousness, however inaccessible the absolute may remain, "my relation with the real is also real. Is this not equivalent to an awakening?"[83]—an awakening after the long post-Romantic somnolence in which "the poet ex-

plor[ed] the more or less subterranean city of his dreams
[and] . . . descend[ed] into his own hells, renouncing all
soaring flight."[84]

Foreshadowings of these tendencies mark the earlier production: the soaring, though still dreaming, swallows in the
light-struck evening of No. 19, and the ascensional movements that come in *The Castilian Country*—most obviously the
ascent of the hill and the far vision of No. 25, "Along the
Duero," but also the marked shift of perspective from earth-
bound to eagle's-eye view in the third section of "The Soria
Country" (No. 29): "But if you climb a hill and view the
scene / from heights where eagles live." The high-flying
birds are natural agents of this expansion of the visionary
field. The shift of perspective just noted occurs more subtly
later in "Jottings" (No. 37), in the second of which one is first
looking up at the owl "flying and flying" and the next moment sharing the vision of its sharp eyes over broad stretches
of country.[85] No longer sinister, this bird is rather the emblem of Athena's wisdom.

The first section of the "Old Songs" (No. 48) superbly
catches the upward surge expressive in Machado of aspira-
tions unrealizable but irrepressible: the emerging peaks; the
larks climbing into invisibility; the "feathering" of the fields,
giving wings to earth; finally the eagle higher than all else,
seeing further and further. "To sink back on the blue of sky
/ as the eagle settles on the wind / . . . trusting to wings and
breath" will be the ultimate sigh of Abel Martín in his "Last
Lamentations" (No. 51), while in the "Memories of Dreaming, Fever, and Dozing" (No. 53) fantasies on the ease of flying will acquire a sardonic edge in VII and VIII before the
plunge downward abruptly ends them.

Earlier signs that probing the underground world of
dreams has become less appealing are noted in 1917: when
Machado incorporates into the first edition of his *Complete
Poems* a definitive version of the *Solitude. Passageways. Other
Poems* of 1907, he adds at the end of the section entitled "Soledades" a composition (No. 16) renouncing dreams as a
means to knowledge and a path to creation. Their place is
taken by wakefulness—the watchfulness of wide-open eyes
and the attentiveness of a heart listening to silence, not
within but beyond. This addition corresponds to the already

noted orientation of dreaming in the "Parables" of
1912–1917.

Still, as we know, Machado will never lose his fascination
with dreaming and dream worlds. The very insistence on vigilance is symptomatic of the pull of dreaming. Especially
when the poet falls in love with Guiomar in the late 1920s
will he be led to acknowledge the extent to which dreams,
daydreaming, and fantasy more or less indistinguishably
work themselves into the fabric of experienced feeling.

In the end we shall find him playing down the distinctness
of dreams from the world of everyday, as the problematical
character of material and experiential reality grows on him.
The ultimate sense of waking up may pertain to awakening
from the dream—or nightmare—of life itself. Behind Machado's repeated calls for waking and staying wide awake
undoubtably also lies a need increasingly felt to put every
faculty at his command to use in order to contend with the
world as it is.

There are other ways of breaking through the solipsism of
the dream: "dreams in dialogue"; dreams pinned down, recorded, rather than spun out and pondered over; nightmares
and nightmarish visions faced up to. Several of the proverbs
of "Proverbs and Song-Verse" (No. 41)—V, LIII, LXXXI, LXIV—
play upon these gradations in Machado's attitudes:

> If it's good to live
> it's better to dream,
> and the best thing of all
> is waking up.                              (Poem 41, LXXXI)

In LXIV dreaming is seen as a mere by-product of hope or
fear.

The appearance of the series of four sonnets, "Dreams in
Dialogue" (No. 45) in *New Songs* (the second dates back to
Seville, 1919), signals an attempt to hold on to the dream, yet
attentuate its solipsistic character. The title is ambiguous; one
does not know whether these sonnets originated in actual
dreams, which were "dreamt in dialogue." Yet the title is less
paradoxical than it seems, for, though an interlocutor is assumed—more than one sometimes—only one voice of the dialogue is audible and it is the same voice throughout. It is

just this consistency of the speaking voice that makes these sonnets in some sense a sequence. In the first the speaker is heard at the beginning, recounting the almost cinematographic action of memory as it "obediently" subserves his art and brings back a sought-after scene. Only then does the figure of Leonor, evoked at the outset, emerge as a silent interlocutor whose presence lends the recalled scene the immediacy of primary experience. The interlocutors are much more shadowy and rhetorical in the second sonnet, in which—as on other occasions, such as No. 30 and No. 39, VII—we find memory operating in a moment not of fusion, but of substitution, without the intervention of dream. At the end the child-wife, far from being an interlocutor, is only an oblique allusion.

The "Lady" addressed and rejected in the third sonnet is just as shadowy, serving as little more than a frame within which to expose a state of emotional turmoil through expressionistic description of a nightmarish mountain setting. The natural sequel in the fourth is an interlocutor who ironically turns out to be solitude herself—as muse, as mystery, and, it will appear later, as death.[86] Machado vividly projects the very sound of a voice we just miss hearing, a voice emanating not from within the self but from an unattainable other.

The strain of dreaming operative in Machado's poetic cosmos to the end will interact with memory in the familiar way as part of the poetic process, acquire visionary or nightmarish proportions, point clairvoyantly beyond the life of man. Setting off this strain is a group of compositions in which not closed but open eyes are the means to apprehension of the world, as if in obedience to an injunction of Juan de Mairena "to keep the eyes wide open in order to see things as they are."[87]

A poem significantly entitled "The Eyes" (No. 42) figures among those which Machado included in the section of *New Songs* originally entitled "Folklore." Despite its third-person narrative form, this "folklore" is predominantly "folklore of myself," in all likelihood involving an allusion to Leonor. Here neither the mirror, nor recollection or pondering in solitude, but a direct, if chance, visual contact brings home the truth quite uncomplicatedly.

That it may in fact be hard to sustain the vision of a truth, especially when it is that of the self, is evident from the far more subtle and intense poem (No. 44) to the sculptor Emiliano Barral, Machado's Segovian *confrère*. Here the self, as it emerges through the eyes of someone else and in the mirror of his art, turns into the other. Compounding the painfulness of what the eye must look upon in the world, the disturbing effect of such self-estrangement accounts for the bitter note of the end.

The last of the "Highland Songs" (No. 39, x [1923]) is likewise fundamentally a disquieting poem of private seeing, though the bitterness is more subdued. The rare sight of a rainbow at night, of which the other passengers on the train apparently take no notice, leads the speaker to visualize concretely the thoughts of the sleeping child and the indigent mother, while those of the "tragic passenger" with the piercing eyes, visions of strange things, can only be surmised. The mountain setting leads his own thoughts back to visions of other mountains, those of Soria, inevitably—whence perhaps the placing in the series of "Highland Songs." The ultimate question of seeing, its manifold relation to God, is masterfully raised in the final lines.

Machado's most sustained attempt at open-eyed vision is the poem "Passageways" (No. 38) of *New Songs*. The title originally carried the significant addendum "Jottings for a Lyric Stereoscope." "Passageways" might be seen as fulfilling the recommendation of Juan de Mairena not only "to keep the eyes wide open in order to see things as they are," but to open them "wider still to see things other than they are; even wider to see them better than they are."[88]

Although the passageways in which the views originate are, as of old, those of memory, our awareness of this origin is diminished by extraordinarily vivid effects of direct visual impact. It turns out that what we have been seeing is a series of views through a "lyric" stereoscope. "Stereoscopic" manipulation has led to a much more deliberate and vigilant handling of memory than in Machado's early verse. The resultant views have the sharpness of outline, the broadened and deepened visual field, the three-dimensional effect produced by the bifocal mechanism of the stereoscope, which in fact improves upon the vision of the naked eye. The views succeed one another abruptly, without blurring or fade-out. This enhancement of vision, this seeing things "other than they are," does facilitate the reader's access to these once private memories. It could be shown as well that the actually composite character of the particular views works to the same effect.[89]

But "Passageways," as its final section reveals, is more than a succession of vivid views bound together by the controlling metaphor of the lyric stereoscope. It is also an attempt to see things "better than they are"—manifestly to extend the range of ideas beyond that of sensation in an avowedly non-Symbolist manner. The attempt must inevitably fail, yet it accords with deep impulses of Machado's nature, here carried by two of those figures which he elsewhere characterized as among the "great" metaphors common to philosophical and poetic vision: the Pythagorean lyre and Heraclitean fire.[90] These figures, expressly articulated in the last section, undergird the poem as a whole. Behind the lightning of the third section lies the Heraclitean view, elsewhere recalled by Machado, that lightning—that is, fire—forever flaring up and dying back is the governing force of the universe.[91] A cyclical movement involving the further Heraclitean notions of ascending and descending phases, decline and rebirth, conflict between fire and water, binds together the several discrete sections of the poem. The Heraclitean view that out of conflict harmony arises links this movement to the presence of the other controlling metaphor, the Pythagorean lyre, most evident in its chromatic manifestations: the harmonic pulsations of "the seven strings of the sun's lyre" (the rainbow) in the fourth section of the poem, and in the spectrumlike unfolding of color in the sixth. "Passageways" thus becomes an attempt to accede to a noumenal order, to reach the vision of a harmonic cosmos by penetrating intently observed phenomena of this world. The poem is visionary in the fullest sense of the term.

Though the attempt cannot be sustained in the end, the persona who appears in the final section, seemingly dazed by the effort, succeeds in isolating momentarily in its purest form an effect—an illusion—of ideal harmony that outlasts the phenomena through which it had earlier been intuited:

In the silence,
Pythagoras' lyre goes on vibrating,
the rainbow in the light.                    (Poem 38, VII)

But only for a moment. As Valverde has noted, the very con-
tinuity of the pulsations of the Pythagorean lyre makes their
harmony, the harmony of the spheres, inaudible; similarly,
the chromatic harmony of the rainbow is lost in flooding
light.[92] Platonic-Pythagorean ideas quickly subside into pure
lifeless abstractions, in terms of the other "great" metaphor,
into the blinding ash of the Heraclitean fire, leaving a world
of pure nothingness—mute, unseeing, and with the transparency of emptiness.

In imagery, technique, and themes "Passageways" brings
together aspects of Machado's art highlighted in a number of
poems remaining to be considered. The Heraclitean fire reappears in a remarkable sonnet, "This Was My Dream" (No.
43); a conscious manipulation of memory characterizes another group of sonnets (No. 47); and the ultimate vision, that
of nothingness, becomes more and more prevalent in other
poems, displacing intimations of harmony.

In "This Was My Dream," the dream-state affords a way
of holding the vision that could not be sustained with eyes
open in "Passageways." The vision is of an order of being in
which vitality and ideality are one, of an ashless Heraclitean
fire. Dream-logic allows access to the vision by steps that
would scarcely provide it in a waking world: existence in
time; art conditioned by such existence, yet not ultimately
timebound; time and mortality overcome. One presumes a
link between this "glowing coal of life" and the "glowing
coals" present or implicit in the four proverbs and song-verse
of No. 41 alluded to earlier, in which the symbolism embraces the vital, the conceptual, and the aesthetic.[93]

This sonnet is exceptional in achieving an ultramundane
perspective on existence. In the series of four entitled simply
"Sonnets" (No. 47),[94] the speaker is back within the world
and the retrospective view is that of memory—alternately
comprehensive recollection and specific recall—induced by a
sense of age closing in as Machado approaches fifty. The recollective process itself is the subject of the first sonnet, an indication of the greater control now sought over the action of

memory. The earlier metaphors, whose ground is a movement of dispersal and recall, find a natural extension in the
image of the activity of bees, the familiar figure for the transforming action of recollection as a means to artistic creation.
Here the presentness of the past is inevitably transfused by
the melancholy of the present.

The second sonnet, on the other hand, is pure vivid recall,
as if through a "lyric stereoscope"—induced undoubtedly by
the rediscovery of a first draft dated 1902, which identifies
the city as León and makes the road to Compostela not solely
one of dream.[95] It must be Leonor who is addressed in the
frame of the third sonnet which, like the first, surveys the
past—the emotional life this time—in a long perspective and
writes a new variation, almost naïvely apologetic, on the
image so often encountered of life and love at their origin as
clear springs, and in their development as increasingly turbid
waters.

The masterpiece of this series is the fourth sonnet. The de-
monstrative with which it opens focuses on light as the cata-
lytic link with the past; the poem appears induced by a later
return to the Palacio de las Dueñas of Machado's Sevillian
childhood. Nowhere has he so perfectly conveyed the indi-
visibility of past, present, and future ("today always is still")
or so effectively set "the word in time" as here through the
imaginative empathy which draws his own present back into
a specific scene out of his past, a "moving picture" of his father in a present of his own suspended between a further
past and the apprehension of a future—Machado's present.

It is evident that as Machado grows older, his pursuit of
poetry of broader appeal must vie with the obscurity that
arises from the struggle to express ultimate personal concerns. This is particularly true of the poetry that follows *New
Songs* and it even affects both series of love songs addressed
to Guiomar. Whatever their immediate occasion, as earlier
suggested they soon involve speculation on the possibility of
love, on whether self and solitude can be transcended and
otherness reached, whether the image of the beloved corresponds to her actuality or to the lover's needs and fantasies—
subjects on which Juan de Mairena also speculates at length
in prose.[96] These ponderings are reduced to crisp "autofolk-

loric" formulations in a series of enigmatic jottings that open the "Other Songs for Guiomar" (No. 55 [1936]).

Such enigmas, less tersely formulated, pervade the first "Songs for Guiomar" (No. 54 [1929]) as well. The current of time as the medium of love is a leitmotif of all three. The first presents a chain of queries as to what love may offer. Time may promise fulfillment, or may not; it may bring some semblance of fruition or nourish a fantasy of it, may even produce a true epiphany to dispel a long train of loneliness. In the second poem time collaborates in a sort of confluence of life-streams; self and other blend, but only in the lover's solitary dream, which, moreover, ends by denying itself. The coda can only bravely reassert the capacity of love, illusory or not, to intensify all phenomena.

In the third poem, the motion of the train carrying the poet back to Segovia from Madrid and Guiomar induces a fantasy of flight with her (the "goddess and her lover"), pursuit, and escape. In the second part of this third poem, which could well have been a fourth, written in the solitude of the poet's Segovia lodgings, distance and absence set the imagination free. The memory of Guiomar becomes a catalyst for a magical personal revelation. One senses affinities with "Passageways"—rainbow, harmony, transparency—but it is the river, not the fire, of Heraclitus that figures here. The current of time which brings the revelation has a new and reassuring buoyancy; the familiar pattern of "today—or yesterday—always is still" achieves one more memorable configuration. Instead of exposing a void, the transparency of this April afternoon lets through the light of yesterday. Time seems to stop even as it flows, and the dawns and dusks dispersed throughout the other two songs come together in a single chorus of time fulfilled, a mature return to a Bergsonian conception of memory as an accumulation of past experiences overlaying a current one.

Such expressions of plenitude are rare in Machado's later work. The "Other Songs for Guiomar" (No. 55), written "in the manner of Abel Martín and Juan de Mairena,"[97] comprise Machado's fullest expression in verse of the active role forgetting plays in the love relationship and ultimately in the creative process.[98] The first six parts of this series had in fact appeared in 1935 as examples cited in an exposition by Juan de Mairena of the thought of Abel Martín on the vital role of forgetting in creation.[99] They begin (I) with a set of disjoined images of Guiomar, alternately projected against the speaker's present (and future) solitude and recalled as fragmentary memories of past moments with her. At this stage, love is obsessive haunting by a specific "historical" past.

Yet since the beloved is already being proclaimed a creation of the lover (line 22), the inability asserted in the final line to transcend the stage of forgetting is not a permanent trauma. In II the speaker has already moved beyond and is proclaiming love to be pure fantasy. Juan de Mairena writes in a résumé of the thinking of his master, Abel Martín: "Thanks to the capacity for forgetting, the poet . . . can pull up the roots of his spirit, buried in the soil of the anecdotal and trivial, in order to sink them deeper down in the subsoil or live rock of feeling, which ceases to be the evoker and becomes—at least in appearance—the illuminator of new forms. Because only impassioned creation wins out over forgetting."[100]

The last phrase suggests that in his thinking on forgetting Machado-Mairena-Martín is turning a liability of timebound human nature, particularly bewailed by the Romantics and their successors, into an asset, showing, as part VII of the present poem will reveal more fully, why it is not enough to fantasize.

Parts III, IV, V, and VI play lightly on the thought expressed in the round in II. Part VII, however, suddenly turns deeply earnest. Even smoke, not to mention ash, is impurity, whether it clouds the flame of Heraclitean fire or the glow from live coals of deep human feeling. The transcendent lyricism, Machado is saying, is one of anonymity, in which the personal is, so to speak, burned away and concept bears feeling infused. The authenticity of the original emotion, alone surviving the stage of forgetting, is the sole warranty of the intensity which will add power to the poet's verse. Machado's aesthetic is much more classic than Romantic here.[101]

Part VIII finally reworks and expands in more dramatic, not to say more lurid, terms the contrast between the *turbia escoria* (turbid slag) of line 56 and the *limpio metal* (shiny metal) of line 57 of VII. The "flowers of evil" Machado might seem to be speaking of here are not such in any moral sense; he is simply suggesting an analogy between the role of forgetting in the creation of art and that of nature's indifference to particular forms of life in her creation of new ones. The achievement of such reconciliation with the ways of nature is rare in the mature Machado. The sonnet "The Flaming Rose" (No. 49), one of the "erotic rhymes" of Abel Martín, offers one more example in its concentration on youthful vitality, with only faint hints of a shadowy future.[102] More characteristic is a shift of focus in which the possibility of ultimate nothingness that already looms in the later love poetry is faced more and more squarely, not to say abstractly, though one continues to sense at times an ironic tone that persists in spite of Machado's often expressed willingness to accept the need for man, as a rational and social being, to engage in conceptualized thinking.

Two short poems, Abel Martín's sonnet "To the Great Nought" (No. 50) and Juan de Mairena's lines entitled "Siesta" (No. 52), focus closely and abstractly on the concept of nothingness.[103] Abel Martín's remarks on the first of these sonnets make it plain that the "human thought" in question is not poetic thought but ratiocination—"homogenizing thought"—which the poet, as a specifically *human* being, cannot dispense with, even though it "cannot even by chance coincide with the pure heterogeneousness of being"—that is, with the disparateness of single phenomena. This thought "needs nothingness in order to think what is; because in reality, it thinks of it as *not being.*"[104] Its premise is thus the negating character inherent in the abstractive process which is the basis of cognitive thought. Machado, like Hegel, needs to move through this stage to reach affirmative insight. As Nancy A. Newton puts it: "Machado, too, draws strength from what denies and limits him . . . The negative constitutes . . . an essential step in the acquisition of the ideal 'integral awareness,' " a step Abel Martín calls "the integral nought." The image of the emptied egg "represents man's act of thinking, which negates the universe's substance but provides a boundary around that created void . . . the necessary delimitation that is thought's crutch."[105]

"Siesta" places the principles of negativity and rationality in a more tangible and nuanced setting than that of the son-

net's "witty parody of the Creation story."[106] In an appro-
priately formal garden only the mobile fish and the cicada
with its pulsating song point—limitedly—to a world beyond
that of the God of nothingness. The ensuing paean to this
God moves progressively away from the sensory and the immediate, extolling somewhat equivocally gifts symbolic of
man's ability to detach himself from the bewildering "omnipresence" of disparate phenomena by means of alternatives
that allow him his own abstractions: darkness, silence, distance and absence, conceptuality as an anchor in the flux of
existence, theoretical lines to delimit and orientate his
thought.

In the longer poems from the writing of Martín-Machado,
abstraction contends with the circumstantiality and affective
aura of retrospection in a melancholy, disabused, sometimes
anguishing process that exposes the nakedness of the self in
the face of the irretrievable, the unknowable, the void ("Last
Lamentations of Abel Martín," No. 51; "The Death of Abel
Martín," No. 56), while looking ahead subjects it to hallucinatory visions ("Another Climate," No. 57).[107]

In "Last Lamentations of Abel Martín," Machado returns
via a dream to the familiar world of time. Retrospect and
prospect, youth and age, hope and disillusionment, meet in
an unlimited present, the "today" with which the poem
opens. The passageways of memory lead back once more to
the lemon garden, the Sevillian patio; but a new note of anguish hangs over the garden, troubling its magic as the
speaker half-rediscovers, half-projects backward, childhood
apprehensions of a "terrifying" future. (The transformation
earlier worked in the mirror's depths anticipates those apprehensions.) The shift in lighting obliterates the possibility of
poetic expression as a capturing of life in time and projects
awareness of death as culmination—or, rather, annihilation.
Nothingness reenters, not as a philosophical concept, but as
angst. In the rest of the poem recollection gives way to renunciation of past dreams and present challenges, and in the
end death as annihilation of consciousness is the only resolution.

A tone of melancholy resignation keeps the angst within
bounds in these lamentations; it becomes almost unbearable
when Machado-Mairena describes Martín's death, his con-

frontation with the ultimate solitude, with nothingness. Recollection and recapitulation here are oppressive and jarring. (The occasional ironic tone of the speaking voice does not dispel the tenseness of mood.) Even in his solipsistic withdrawal Martín cannot shut out the disorderly clamor of the world's "omnipresence," an inner as well as an external clamor. Dust and smoke suggest a blurred and painful vision of past, present, and future. Initiating a process of disengagement that will end in his death, Martín turns toward alternatives of absolute negativity: distance, absence, forgetting, the cipher itself, the shadow that shields vision from blinding light. But he foresees that death will remove this protection, as indeed happens in the end.

Man is caught between bitter alternatives: jarring omnipresence of the world, obliterating loss of selfhood. After the somewhat equivocal encounter with the angel, the muse of solitude appears and proves to be the muse of death. Is death then to be seen as at once the original fountainhead of art and the ultimate solitude?

In the fourth section the imminence of death leads Martín to articulate, in new form, familiar Machadian dilemmas: alternatives of creation or cogitation, purposefulness or contemplation, vigilance or dreaming. The last section supplies the physical dimensions of actual and existential agony, a state of mind, body, and soul conveyed with almost painful acuity. But the "serenity" with which Abel Martín offers the final toast with the shadow-filled glass—a subtle indication that he is at last out of mortality's reach—explains the calm gesture with which Juan de Mairena lifts a similar glass in his master's memory in "Siesta." The sureness of Machado's mature touch is revealed in this mere hint of a state of consciousness which, like that of the mystic at the end of his journey, is inherently inexpressible—and, to the modern mind, unknowable. Though this poem, unlike most earlier ones, is necessarily written from the viewpoint of an omniscient narrator, the limits of his omniscience are respected. The poem, perhaps the most difficult of any Machado wrote, offers no resolution of the increasingly acute dilemmas and heightened paradoxes into which his mind and sensibility were leading him.

"Another Climate" reads like an epilogue to "The Death of

Abel Martín," or an alternative version of it. In Martín's final words, spoken now with more detachment and less anguish, time lived in as a dimension of personal history recedes from the speaker's consciousness, giving way to tentative visions of the broader course of a nonpersonal history, that of the world and of the cosmos. The connecting thread of the poem is the suggestion of a cyclical process in history, prompted in part by classical antecedents, in part by Machado's strong sense that an era was ending and another dawning in his own day, conceivably also by hints of Nietzsche's "eternal return." Upon this thread Machado manages to string in curious, yet not clashing, promixity his social progressivism, his skepticism with regard to dogmatic Christianity, his fascination with negativity, the "soaring flight" (the final vision "from the summit"), and an occasional sardonic reflex—the chilling gust that momentarily puts down humanism. The view of the cyclic process is fundamentally Heraclitean, one of worlds dying and being reborn, with the balance tipped slightly in favor of social renewal in the end.

The "Memories of Dreaming, Fever, and Dozing" (No. 53 [1931]) belong, like "Another Climate," to the last decade of Machado's life, although an unpublished prose "Fragment of a Nightmare," dated 1914, sheds some light on its fourth episode.[108] These "Memories" constitute a "motley sequence of visions and hallucinatory dialogues, in a folkloric tone."[109] In the absence of the coherence found in "Another Climate," the links between the different sections grow slack and sometimes disappear, although some parts of the series are noticeably interconnected. While the technique recalls that of the sets of "Jottings" and "Songs" in *New Songs*—one detects specific reminiscences—the fragmented structure reproduces the discontinuities and non-sequiturs, truncations, and inconclusiveness of a fevered border zone between waking and sleeping. Despite the sudden shifts and juxtapositions and the obsessively recurrent motifs, Machado's technique is not surrealistic. It does not reflect the random associativeness, the clashing imagery, the cultivated irrationalities, in short, the liberated subconscious of the Surrealists.[110] It still "sings and tells."

The title points to an irrational state, not provoked but suffered through and even combatted. The harsh summons to wake up that repeatedly breaks through the nightmare, however hostile in tone, reflects the urge to face the world with wide-open eyes. The vantage point reached by the end—two plus two equals four—is a fundamental one, despite the irony.

Writing to Guiomar around this time, Machado sees dreams as states in which "our images are forced upon us rather than chosen," in which the usual "miraculous power" to select and replace them at will is lost.[111] The poem is presented as a jotting down, as if by way of exorcism, of what can be remembered of a nightmare; it is not an exercise in automatic writing, much less in "pure poetry." Valverde sees the poem as "an extreme attempt to pour out the very depths of his solitude," which cured Machado of subsequent cultivation of dream-states.[112]

The poem may ultimately have autobiographical roots—some slightly delirious fevered state that brought to the surface distressing memories, motifs and snatches from Machado's own writings, and obsessive concerns including, inevitably, haunting thoughts of death, all exacerbated by inevitable solitude. A protective coating of irony relieves the rawness of the material, however. The tone is varyingly gay, sardonic, satirical. The lively interplay in the dialogue sections may be savage or, like the whole poem, marked by buoyant humor and fantasy. Where voices have not jelled into dialogue, the speaking voice may slip from one role to the next with the casualness characteristic of dreaming. In one exceptional section, the sixth, Machado felt impelled to break into the nightmare with an ars poetica in the form of a pure parable—which we may imagine as a tranquil dream, if we wish. It echoes other expressions in verse and prose reconciling creativity with utility.

Certain strains keep recurring, some of them originating in the opening section: persecution and inquisitorial trial, youth and age coalescing, love as sexual drive ("they're all the same," lines 19-20) and as a dream of fulfillment—the memory, of Leonor, presumably, tentatively emerges out of forgetfulness, then is lost again (iii). Grotesque fantasies of trial and execution at dawn by different methods, appropriate and inappropriate, appear in iv. In the fifth section, the spreading light of the dawn hour captures our attention in its own right, shifting the locus of persecution to hare and hunting dogs. The reference in IV to the "plain old gallows," with its suggestion of dangling suspension, is the point of departure for the grotesque developments on "wingless" flying in VII and VIII, which give the old impulse toward "soaring flight" a bizarre twist.

The plunge to dark depths that occupies the rest of the poem seems an inevitable countermovement. Valverde notes that the figure of Charon, from Dante and Vergil, "obsessed the poet's dreams for a number of years." One wonders if Machado is not also updating the flippancy of Lucian's "Voyage to the Underworld."[113] As if affected by Lucian's tone, Machado, in this strange underworld of his own, focuses not on the darker impulses and passions, but on a tangled skein of disillusionments. The decor recalls an elaborate Spanish graveyard full of mausoleums, as well as the intricate labyrinthine streets of once Moorish quarters in old Spanish cities like Seville and Ubeda. In the "Square of the Greatest Disillusion" the poet looks up to see a figure evoking death— a physical death—waxen, but neither mysterious nor horrifying. Could death, herself mortal, be the greatest disappointment of all, the end point of a train of deaths of one love after another (beginning of XII)? In a more prosaic key, the intuition of the sonnet "This Was My Dream" (No. 43) reappears: death as a human dream simply. More chilling, in any case, is the transformation of the popular song figure of Lola, the "Manola" of the final lines, from one who does not sleep alone to one who now does—in death. From her the poet and his companion beat a quick retreat.

Two selections remain to be discussed: the elegy to Lorca (No. 64) and the nocturne "Meditation" (No. 63). They belong to the period of Machado's residence in Rocafort outside Valencia during the Civil War and are dated 1936 and 1937. With the brutal execution of Federico García Lorca, Machado sees grimly realized in the person of the most brilliant of a new generation of poets the prospect haunting his own dreams and fantasies. The sobering effect is evident in "The Crime Was in Granada," especially in the first section, an account of the crime, where the starkness of the expression allows inexpressible shock and indignation to show through.

His own long cultivation of the muse of solitude and his later intuition of her mystery as that of death led Machado to imagine the ultimate solitary promenade of Lorca with death, his final courting of her, in a brilliant evocation of the death motif that runs throughout Lorca's work. The backdrop of spreading sunlight and sounding forges echoes only faintly, almost ironically, the trust in the building of a better future which pervaded the 1915 elegy to Giner de los Ríos (No. 36). The movement in the final section toward reconciliation with grief, traditional in the elegy, is not allowed to prevail over the anger that flares up again at the end.

The elegiac mood of "Meditation," as the title suggests, is quieter and more diffuse. The atmosphere of the night carries the poet prophetically away from the soothing sensations of hour and setting and overrides fantasies of the war's illusoriness. In the last stanza, more is presaged than the familiar playback of memory and dream from an anticipated future: nothing less than the impending eclipse of Machado's Spain.

The passage from poetic expression to philosophical speculation and back again characteristic of Machado's maturity is summed up in a phrase of Mairena's, who in 1935 calls his master's philosophy "a constant meditation on poetic activity."[114] Machado's metaphysics may thus be seen as originating in a pursuit of analogies between poetic creation and that of the universe. His ethics, in part at least, grew out of a concern for the poet's relationship with those to or for whom he speaks and those whom he thinks of as speaking in or through him. The concern for otherness and the urge to overcome solipsism through "love of humankind" or love of woman—agape or eros—arise from the poet's instinctive sense of the reality, independent of his own, of everything his eyes light upon. There are moments when the effort to see appears to represent a conviction, as Machado puts it, that "with sensation we are partly in things themselves,"[115] a belief that by looking hard enough the poet will be able to see *into* things, see through them and beyond them "into the seeds of time," and in the process grasp the nature of their reality and what lies beyond it.[116]

But the question of time is not quite so easily disposed of.

It lies at the heart of Machado's philosophical dilemma, as it does of his poetics. In the very act of looking, the object of vision becomes ungraspable because this object, existing in time just as the act of looking at it occurs in time, ceases to be what it was. [117] The river of Heraclitus, meditated upon unceasingly, has cut channels deep into Machado's sensibility. It is forever undermining mental constructs and causing "a flood of questions that increases in force with the years."[118] And not only mental constructs, but psychic ones as well: "In the flowing of natural thought . . . and, in a certain sense, of poetic thought—it is not pure intellect that is moving discursively, but the psychic block as a whole, and logical forms are never pontoons anchored in the river of Heraclitus but actual waves of its current."[119]

So much for logic. Deep aspirational affinities draw Machado toward those who had broken through the dilemma in other ways. Those, first, who from Pythagoras and Plato onward had found a transcendent grasp on reality in supreme harmonies and supreme ideas. How well they had exorcised the darker spirits of solitude.[120] "Platonic faith in transcendent ideas saved Greece from the *solus ipse* within which sophistry would have confined it."[121] Machado recognizes how indispensable to human discourse such breathtaking visions of order are. Very early he had moved beyond Verlaine and made his choice between the cosmic harmonies of Pythagoras and the former's dissonantal *musique avant toute chose*, the product, so he thought, of a "lyric sick with subjectivity."[122] Undoubtedly he felt the enchantment of earthly music, but for him it lay in temporal flow, in a "constant ceasing that never ceases."[123]

Looking closely, one can find traces of similar sympathy for the mystics, for "Teresa, fiery soul [and] John of the Cross, flaming spirit" (No. 34, III). Machado accuses Abel Martín of treating them with "grave injustice" and "scant understanding."[124] He calls St. John of the Cross "perhaps the deepest of the Spanish lyric poets," and in just a few lines displays extraordinary insight into the dynamics of his poetic-spiritual expression.[125] The impact of the mystic way is apparent in a poem described earlier (No. 15) which stands out strikingly in regularity of formal contour and systematic handling of traditional mystic imagery when inserted into *So-ledades* for the first time in the *Poesías completas* of 1917. "Last night I had a dream" uses with great delicacy traditional metaphors for mystic revelation—water, bees, the sun as a fiery hearth—images at the same time authentically Machadian—only to insist on their ultimate illusoriness.

In the end Machado can embrace neither the vision of Platonic idealism nor that of mysticism through any means other than the most benevolent imaginative participation. He grasps them ludically, one might say, rather than viscerally: ideas as a beautiful and necessary myth, mysticism as a compensatory illusion. Can one say the same of the long fascination with metaphysical speculation pure and simple, with "its greatest feat of all . . . conceiving being out of time, essence apart from existence, as it were, the fish live and dry and the water of rivers as an illusion of fishes"?[126] Machado's later poems, like his prose, record the struggle of his apocryphal thinkers to rest upon just such metaphysical premises—and their inability to do so. The river of Heraclitus is not to be stopped up.

What then, finally, of the *via negativa*, and what are we to make of certain cryptic statements, clearly not uttered perversely, however pronounced the irony of the contexts in which they are found? "For the poet there is only *seeing and going blind* [*ver y cegar*], *a seeing that sees itself,* pure evidence, which is being itself, and a creative act, necessarily negative, which is simply nothingness."[127] The parallel between the poet and the God whose supreme creation is not what is, but what is not, is striking. "Seeing aware of itself seeing," as we might paraphrase, describes the basis of the poetics of wonder of Machado's later period, to which he has just alluded in the context in question in emphasizing that even the most bitter and negative poetry is *un acto vidente* (at once "an act of seeing" and "a visionary act") "and that one never doubts what one sees, only what one thinks."

Machado's poetry of wonder, in the act of re-creating what is, finds a raison d'être that obviates any need to question what it is doing. It has an invulnerable self-sufficiency. One could perhaps see the "going blind," the "necessarily negative creative act, which is simply nothingness," as referring to an alternative poetics, not of re-creation but of creation understood as unconditioned making (*poiesis*) on a par with that of God, in contrast to a poetics of mimesis.[128]

The fascination with nothingness records in any case a supreme urge of the imagination toward purity, its impulse to overcome the power of attraction and monopolization normally exercised upon it by the created world. In this mood the vision of existence as a blemish on the face of nonbeing carries Machado beyond Romantic Platonism—as seen, for example, in Shelley's famous "Life, like a dome of many-colored glass, / stains the white radiance of eternity"—to a more abstract cosmic detachment in which he is able, quoting Valéry, to conceive "Que l'univers est un défaut / dans la pureté du non-être."[129]

But it is impossible to overlook the devitalized, programmatic character and the noncommittal irony of the poetry which seeks to demonstrate or celebrate creation ex nihilo. Machado saw, if he had ever had any doubts, that his creative gifts—and with them his allegiance—lay elsewhere—within the world of time:

> Once again my attention
> is bound by water—
> but water in the live
> rock of my heart.                                     (Poem 41, xi)

If in Poem 15 the waters of faith flowing in the heart are only the blessed illusion of a dream, there is nothing illusory about these waters heard flowing within. They are those of the river of Heraclitus and they place the solitary poet existentially face to face with his own timebound being. If time's corollary, mortality, inevitably introduces anxiety into *soledad* of this kind, it is precisely such uneasiness, inherent in human consciousness, that the poet draws upon in all his creative activity. "Would the poet sing without his anguish about time?" Machado asks in 1934. "Insofar as our life coincides with our consciousness, time is the ultimate reality, refractory to the power of logic, irreducible, inevitable, fatal. Living is devouring time."[130] Only in intellectual sophistication does this formulation differ from what he had written presciently nearly thirty years before (1907):

We settle down one day beside the path.
Our life is time now and our only care
assuming desperate postures while we wait . . .
But She'll not miss the rendezvous.    (Poem 9)

Now Machado feels it urgent to spell out in prose the phe-
nomenology of the poet's anguish in his confrontation with
time, and to record it unsparingly in verse. A result included
in the same 1934 context of *Juan de Mairena* to which I have
been referring is "Childhood Memory (of Juan de Mairena)"
(Poem 61).[131] Here the heightening of awareness contingent
upon a child's confinement in a dark room, which makes the
most minute sensations triggers of anxiety, is read retrospectively as the poet's anguish in his "showdown" with time,
with his "vital time with its own pulsation," as Mairena had
put it a few years earlier,[132] with the distress caused by "conversing with the humming of his own ears, which," as he
now puts it, "is the most elemental sonic materialization of
temporal flux."[133]

Insofar as Machado can be said to have come to rest in a
philosophical position, it is not suprising to find him drawn
to a Heideggerian ontology of existence after he discovers
this philosophy in the late 1930s: "Are we [Spanish] somewhat Heideggerian without realizing it?" he asks in 1937.[134]
He reads back into the *vieja angustia* (old distress) of Poem 20
(1907), which the speaker had professed himself unable
"even vaguely to understand," the sorge and ultimately the
angst of Heidegger.[135] The first of these, Machado says, is the
fundamental a-priori "existential uneasiness . . . the fear or
alarm which the ordinary anonymous man (*das Man*) calms
by trivializing it, converting it into everyday tedium." The
second is "incurable anguish in the face of man's infinite
helplessness . . . together with a vision of the totality of our
existence and a reflection on its end and conclusion: death."

Conceivably this Heideggerian line of thought provided
Machado with something of the sustaining power he saw as
its goal: "Because it is from the existential interpretation of
death—death as a borderline, in itself nothing—that we are
to draw the strength to face it." In any case, it would only
have complemented those reserves of moral strength he already possessed: "There is no avoiding the fact that our

thought is sad. And it would be much more so if our faith went with it, if it enjoyed our most intimate allegiance. That—never!"[136]

So Machado wrote in May 1936, shortly before the outbreak of civil war. Whatever the inner doubts raised by his ruminations, they did not inhibit his acting nor diminish his capacity for moral hegemony. He did not live long enough to be disabused by Soviet Russia of his idealization of the fraternal values of the Russian people and the ethical values of Russian literature. His faith in the common people of Spain never faltered. But in the end the poetic corpus that stands as his definitive achievement best reflects the double integrity of his world view. His poetic work is integral at once in its coherence and in its truthfulness. Rather than an imposed or arranged coherence, it exhibits slow organic growth, expansive enough eventually to allow for inconsistencies and to accommodate several strata of irony.

The truthfulness is, in the first place, aesthetic: sobriety of expression; a preference, especially in later years, for long intervals of meditative silence over writing variations on himself out of some dubious need of the man of letters to remain in the public eye. It is also ethical honesty, that disconcertingly proud Hispanic rectitude quite devoid of sanctimoniousness which startles the late-twentieth-century reader as much as it refreshes him:

> . . . I only hope
> that the verse I leave behind, like the captain's sword,
> may be remembered, not for its maker's art,
> but for the virile hand that gripped it once.    (Poem 24)

As one gains one's bearings in this poetic world, how multidimensional and interconnected its simplest features become. It is veined with fire and water, the early symbolic force of which reaches ultimate plenitude in the cyclic Heraclitean fire and the on-flowing Heraclitean river. The secret of the omnipresent, multivalent "glowing coals" is that they, too, vibrate with the rhythms of life, brightening and dimming. In them the Heraclitean fire still flares up and dies down, and the resultant pulsation links them with the "deep

pulsing of the spirit" that is at the core of Machado's poetics.
The hard diamond retains in its sparkle the "planetary fire"
out of which it evolved.[137] It, too, has its past that "always is
still," reflected in the polish of the finished work of art or in
the compact density of classic form.

But there is much "planetary sadness" in Machado, melancholy emanating ultimately from that sadness within, which
he tries so hard to belittle.[138] It hangs over the brooding
"mountains of ash and lead" that loom as symbols of human
limitation, as massive barriers to aspiration. Their mineral in-
ertness weighs upon the spirit. With the fires of life long
since extinct, only the passing fire of the zenith or the reflected glow of sunset is able to revive them momentarily and
bring passing relief to the poet's spirit. Only the "soaring
flight" counteracts their oppressiveness; however much they
may check its upward impulse, they can never quite break it.

In the end they must cede to the waters. If the

> Stone claws of the cold
> mountain range
> reach into the river                              (Poem 60)

in the contest of "water on stone," water ultimately prevails:

> Like you, then, River Duero, and forever,
> shall Castile run downward to the sea?            (Poem 27)

For water has the power to work its will upon the mineral
masses long abandoned by the life of fire, to convert them
into needed confines for its own channeled purposes—for
those of human will and human art, insofar as they can be
adjusted to the flux of the river of Heracltus:

> The spirit casts up it banks,
> mountains of ash and lead,
> spring garden groves.                             (Poem 46, III)

Only subdued traces remain in Machado of the old Heraclitean struggle between fire and water. In these latter days it is
no longer a battle to the finish and the victorious water is

content to coexist with the live or dead pockets of its old adversary.

The "very waters of life" that so deeply impressed Machado in St. Teresa's springs and fountains, in the rivers of Manrique, and ultimately in the unending flow of Heraclitus—waters, respectively, of eternal life, of mortal life, and of universal life in time—are more than complementary to fire as sources of vitality, as powerful sources of renewal as well, in Machado's poetic cosmos. One senses them—hears rather than sees them—everywhere on the move, often in confluence, sometimes overlapping, but with the eternal flux of Heraclitus prevailing in the end.

This within the realm of the flowing. Beyond, where Machado's Heracliteanism no longer suffices,[139] where the rivers are swallowed up in Manrique's "sea of dying," Machado attempts to fall back again on Heidegger: "this new—new?—philosophy which to the essential question of metaphysics—What is being?—gives the answer: Investigate it in human existence. (*Das Dasein ist das Sein des Menschen.*) And to penetrate into being, the only chink is man's existence, being in the world and in time . . . That is the profoundly lyrical note which will draw poets to the philosophy of Heidegger like moths to the flame."[140]

Perhaps only to burn their wings, as might have been the case with Machado had he lived, since it is hard to conceive of his finding ultimate satisfaction within the limitations of a purely existential outlook. There would have remained the doubt of which he was writing at the same time (during the Civil War), not "doubt after the manner of philosophers . . . but poetic doubt, which is human doubt, that of a man solitary and uncertain of his path, among many paths. Among paths which lead nowhere"[141]—the paths of the wayfarer whom he had addressed in a poem many years earlier:

Wayfarer, there is no way—
only foam trails in the sea.

Selected Poems

## 1 *En el entierro de un amigo*

Tierra le dieron una tarde horrible
del mes de julio, bajo el sol de fuego.
   A un paso de la abierta sepultura,
había rosas de podridos pétalos,
entre geranios de áspera fragancia
y roja flor. El cielo
puro y azul. Corría
un aire fuerte y seco.
   De los gruesos cordeles suspendido,
pesadamente, descender hicieron                     10
el ataúd al fondo de la fosa
los dos sepultureros . . .
   Y al reposar sonó con recio golpe,
solemne, en el silencio.
   Un golpe de ataúd en tierra es algo
perfectamente serio.
   Sobre la negra caja se rompían
los pesados terrones polvorientos . . .
   El aire se llevaba
de la honda fosa el blanquecino aliento.          20
   —Y tú, sin sombra ya, duerme y reposa,
larga paz a tus huesos . . .
   Definitivamente,
duerme un sueño tranquilo y verdadero.


## 2

   Fue una clara tarde, triste y soñolienta
tarde de verano. La hiedra asomaba
al muro del parque, negra y polvorienta . . .
            La fuente sonaba.
   Rechinó en la vieja cancela mi llave;
con agrio ruido abrióse la puerta
de hierro mohoso y, al cerrarse, grave
golpeó el silencio de la tarde muerta.

# 1 *At the Burial of a Friend*

They put him in the ground one brutal afternoon
of scorching sun, in July.
   Close to the open grave were roses
with petals going bad
and geraniums with their acrid smell
and scarlet blooms. The sky
cloudless and blue.
A stiff, dry breeze was blowing.
   Steadying thick ropes
above the open grave,                                          10
two gravediggers eased
the heavy coffin down . . .
   The thud when it touched bottom
rang out in the silence solemnly.
   A coffin striking earth
is indisputably something serious.
   Against the black casket
the heavy dusty clods kept breaking open . . .
   The whitish breath from the grave's depths
was taken by the wind.—                                        20
   And you, without a shadow now, sleep and rest,
a long peace to your bones . . .
   Sleep most decidedly
a true, unbroken sleep.


# 2

   The clear afternoon was drowsy and sad,
a summer afternoon. Ivy strands dangled
dusty and black, from the garden wall . . .
      A fountain was splashing.
   With a grating noise my key turned the lock.
The rusty old gate on its strident hinge
slowly gave way, then swung heavily to
and struck the silence of the dead afternoon.

En el solitario parque, la sonora
copla borbollante del agua cantora                    10
me guió a la fuente. La fuente vertía
sobre el blanco mármol su monotonía.
La fuente cantaba: ¿Te recuerda, hermano,
un sueño lejano mi canto presente?
Fue una tarde lenta del lento verano.
Respondí a la fuente:
No recuerdo, hermana,
mas sé que tu copla presente es lejana.
Fue esta misma tarde: mi cristal vertía
como hoy sobre el mármol su monotonía.              20
¿Recuerdas, hermano? . . . Los mirtos talares,
que ves, sombreaban los claros cantares
que escuchas. Del rubio color de la llama,
el fruto maduro pendía en la rama,
lo mismo que ahora. ¿Recuerdas, hermano? . . .
Fue esta misma lenta tarde de verano.
—No sé qué me dice tu copla riente
de ensueños lejanos, hermana la fuente.
Yo sé que tu claro cristal de alegría
ya supo del árbol la fruta bermeja;                  30
yo sé que es lejana la amargura mía
que sueña en la tarde de verano vieja.
Yo sé que tus bellos espejos cantores
copiaron antiguos delirios de amores:
mas cuéntame, fuente de lengua encantada,
cuéntame mi alegre leyenda olvidada.
—Yo no sé leyendas de antigua alegría,
sino historias viejas de melancolía.
Fue una clara tarde del lento verano . . .
Tú venías solo con tu pena, hermano;                40
tus labios besaron mi linfa serena,
y en la clara tarde, dijeron tu pena.
Dijeron tu pena tus labios que ardían;
la sed que ahora tienen, entonces tenían.
—Adiós para siempre la fuente sonora,
del parque dormido eterna cantora.
Adiós para siempre, tu monotonía,
fuente, es más amarga que la pena mía.

Through the empty garden the gurgling sound
of the water singing its run-on lines                                    10
led me to the fountain. The fountain was dripping
monotony down on the white marble slab.
  The fountain sang: "Does it all come back,
the faraway dream, on my present song?
The slow afternoon in the summer's slow time . . ."
  I answered the fountain:
"It does not come back
but your singing, I know, has a faraway sound."
  "This was the very afternoon. Just as now
my water streamed down                                                   20
and spread its monotony over the marble.
Don't you remember? These long-cassocked myrtles
you see now were shading clear songs
you now hear. Ripe flame-colored fruit
hung down from the branch
as it hangs today. Don't you remember? . . .
It was this same slow summer afternoon."
  "These faraway daydreams—what can they be,
that your laughing verse keeps recalling to me?
  I know your bright water with its joyous sound                         30
once tasted the flame-colored fruit of the tree,
and I know my bitterness is a distant thing
dreaming the old summer afternoon away.
  I know your mirrors as they sang their song
reflected raptures of yesterday's love
but tell me, fountain of enchanted tongue,
my happy legend forgotten so long."
  "I have no joyous old legends to tell:
old melancholy times are all I recall.
  One bright afternoon in the summer's slow time . . .                   40
alone with your suffering you sought out my rhyme.
Your lips pressed down to my tranquil flow;
in the bright afternoon they related your woe.
  Your burning lips related your pain.
Thirsty they were then, thirsty they remain."
  "Goodbye forever, fountain of song,
the sleepy old garden's eternal tongue.
Goodbye forever—your monotone
is bitterer far than this pain of my own."

Rechinó en la vieja cancela mi llave;
con agrio ruido abrióse la puerta                                    50
de hierro mohoso y, al cerrarse, grave
sonó en el silencio de la tarde muerta.


# 3

El limonero lánguido suspende
una pálida rama polvorienta,
sobre el encanto de la fuente limpia,
y allá en el fondo sueñan
los frutos de oro . . .
                    Es una tarde clara,
casi de primavera,
tibia tarde de marzo,
que el hálito de abril cercano lleva;
y estoy solo, en el patio silencioso,
buscando una ilusión cándida y vieja:                                10
alguna sombra sobre el blanco muro,
algún recuerdo, en el pretil de piedra
de la fuente dormido, o, en el aire,
algún vagar de túnica ligera.
    En el ambiente de la tarde flota
ese aroma de ausencia,
que dice al alma luminosa: nunca,
y al corazón: espera.
    Ese aroma que evoca los fantasmas
de las fragancias vírgenes y muertas.                                20
    Sí, te recuerdo, tarde alegre y clara,
casi de primavera,
tarde sin flores, cuando me traías
el buen perfume de la hierbabuena,
y de la buena albahaca,
que tenía mi madre en sus macetas.
    Que tú me viste hundir mis manos puras
en el agua serena,

With a grating noise my key turned the lock.                    50
The rusty old gate on its strident hinge
slowly gave way, then swung heavily to
and rang through the silence of the dead afternoon.


# 3

Listless the lemon tree suspends
one pale and dusty branch
over the clear fountain's spell
and deep inside, dreaming,
the gold fruit appears . . .

                              The afternoon is bright,
with spring in the air,
a mild March afternoon,
with a breath of April stirring.
I am alone in the quiet patio
looking for some old untried illusion—            10
some shadow on the whiteness of the wall,
some memory asleep
on the stone rim of the fountain,
perhaps in the air
the light swish of some trailing gown.
    The afternoon gives off
that scent of absence
that tells the glistening spirit: never,
and asks the heart to wait.
    The scent that summons back the ghosts         20
of maiden fragrances long dead.
    Yes, I recall you, bright and happy afternoon
with spring in the air,
and no flowers in bloom,
how you used to bring
the good sweet scent of mint,
the scent of good sweet basil
that my mother kept in earthen pots.
    You saw me dip my innocent hands
into the limpid water                              30

para alcanzar los frutos encantados
que hoy en el fondo de la fuente sueñan . . .     30
   Sí, te conozco, tarde alegre y clara,
casi de primavera.


# 4

   Yo escucho los cantos
de viejas cadencias,
que los niños cantan
cuando en coro juegan,
y vierten en coro
sus almas que sueñan,
cual vierten sus aguas
las fuentes de piedra:
con monotonías
de risas eternas,                                  10
que no son alegres,
con lágrimas viejas,
que no son amargas
y dicen tristezas,
tristezas de amores
de antiguas leyendas.
   En los labios niños
las canciones llevan
confusa la historia
y clara la pena;                                    20
como clara el agua
lleva su conseja
de viejos amores,
que nunca se cuentan.
   Jugando a la sombra
de una plaza vieja,
los niños cantaban . . .
   La fuente de piedra
vertía su eterno
cristal de leyenda.                                 30

to reach the magic fruit
that dreams on now in the fountain's depths . . .
    Ah yes, I know you, bright and happy afternoon,
with spring in the air.


# 4

    I follow the songs
of children at play
intoning old airs
in their singing games,
pouring forth in song
their fondest dreams,
the way stone fountains
pour waters forth:
in a monotone
of age-old laughter                                    10
empty of joy,
in the mournful tones
of sadness lingering,
bitterness gone,
the sadness of love
in ancient legend.
    On children's lips
the singing carries
a tale confused
but pain still clear,                                  20
the way clear water
carries a strain
of love long past
and leaves it unsaid.
    Playing in the shade
of an old village square,
the children were singing . . .
    The old stone fountain
poured forth its unceasing
water of legend.                                       30

Cantaban los niños
canciones ingenuas,
de un algo que pasa
y que nunca llega:
la historia confusa
y clara la pena.
    Seguía su cuento
la fuente serena;
borrada la historia,
contaba la pena.                                    40

# 5

    Yo voy soñando caminos
de la tarde. ¡Las colinas
doradas, los verdes pinos,
las polvorientas encinas!...
¿Adónde el camino irá?
Yo voy cantando, viajero
a lo largo del sendero...
—La tarde cayendo está—.
"En el corazón tenía
la espina de una pasión;                            10
logré arrancármela un día:
ya no siento el corazón."
    Y todo el campo un momento
se queda, mudo y sombrío,
meditando. Suena el viento
en los álamos del rio.
    La tarde más se obscurece;
y el camino que serpea
y débilmente blanquea,
se enturbia y desaparece.                           20
    Mi cantar vuelve a plañir:
"Aguda espina dorada,
quién te pudiera sentir
en el corazón clavada."

The children sang
ingenuous songs
of things going on
and never concluding.
The tale was confused
and the pain was clear.
  Serenely the fountain
went on with its tale;
the story effaced,
it related the pain.                                40


# 5

  I dream my way
down evening roads.
Gold hills, green pines,
and dusty oaks . . .
Where can the road be leading?
I sing my way along,
the road stretches away,
evening is coming on.
"Love pierced my heart
with its thorn.                                     10
One day I got it out—
now the heart is numb."
  And the land all about
grows dim and still,
ingathered for a moment.
There are sounds of wind
in the river poplars.
  The dusk begins to gather
and the twisting road,
still glimmering faintly,                           20
blurs over and is gone.
  My song laments once more:
"Sharp golden thorn,
if only I could feel you
piercing my heart."

## 6   Horizonte

En una tarde clara y amplia como el hastío,
cuando su lanza blande el tórrido verano,
copiaban el fantasma de un grave sueño mío
mil sombras en teoría, enhiestas sobre el llano.
La gloria del ocaso era un purpúreo espejo,
era un cristal de llamas, que al infinito viejo
iba arrojando el grave soñar en la llanura . . .
Y yo sentí la espuela sonora de mi paso
repercutir lejana en el sangriento ocaso,
y más allá, la alegre canción de un alba pura.            10

## 7

Sobre la tierra amarga,
caminos tiene el sueño
laberínticos, sendas tortuosas,
parques en flor y en sombra y en silencio;
    criptas hondas, escalas sobre estrellas;
retablos de esperanzas y recuerdos.
Figurillas que pasan y sonríen
—juguetes melancólicos de viejo—;
    imágenes amigas,
a la vuelta florida del sendero,                            10
y quimeras rosadas
que hacen camino . . . lejos . . .

## 8

Crece en la plaza en sombra
el musgo, y en la piedra vieja y santa
de la iglesia. En el atrio hay un mendigo . . .
Más vieja que la iglesia tiene el alma.

## 6  *Horizon*

On a bright evening, vast as tedium,
beneath the swinging sword of the summer's heat
a thousand tall shadows were lined up in the plain,
copying the phantom of my somber dream.
The sunset's splendor was a purple mirror,
flaming glass relaying toward infinity
the somber dreaming on the plain.
And I heard my footsteps ring out like a spur
and ricochet far off on the blood-stained west
and farther off a pure dawn's joyous song.                    10

## 7

Upon the bitter land
dreams set a maze of roads,
tangles of paths, gardens in bloom,
in shadow, silent,
    deep vaults, steps to scale the stars,
puppet shows of hopes and recollections.
Small shapes that pass and smile—
an old man's wistful toys—
    well-wishing images
where the path turns and flowers,                    10
and rose-gowned fantasies
going their way . . . far off . . .

## 8

Moss grows in the shadows of the square
and on the church's old and sacred stone.
In the portico is a beggar . . .
His soul is older than the church.

Sube muy lento, en las mañanas frías,
por la marmórea grada,
hasta un rincón de piedra . . . Allí aparece
su mano seca entre la rota capa.
Con las órbitas huecas de sus ojos
ha visto cómo pasan                                           10
las blancas sombras, en los claros días,
las blancas sombras de las horas santas.


# 9

Al borde del sendero un día nos sentamos.
Ya nuestra vida es tiempo, y nuestra sola cuita
son las desesperantes posturas que tomamos
para aguardar . . . Mas Ella no faltará a la cita.


# 10

¡Oh, dime, noche amiga, amada vieja,
que me traes el retablo de mis sueños
siempre desierto y desolado, y sólo
con mi fantasma dentro,
mi pobre sombra triste
sobre la estepa y bajo el sol de fuego,
o soñando amarguras
en las voces de todos los misterios,
dime, si sabes, vieja amada, dime
si son mías las lágrimas que vierto!                          10
Me respondió la noche:
Jamás me revelaste tu secreto.
Yo nunca supe, amado,
si eras tú ese fantasma de tu sueño,
ni averigüé si era su voz la tuya,
o era la voz de un histrión grotesco.
Dije a la noche: Amada mentirosa,
tú sabes mi secreto;

On cold mornings he slowly makes his way
up the marble steps
to a nook of stone . . . There his bony hand
emerges from the tattered cape.
    Through the hollow orbits of his eyes
on bright days                                    10
he has watched white shadows pass,
white shadows of the holy hours.


# 9

    We settle down one day beside the path.
Our life is time now and our only care
assuming desperate postures while we wait . . .
But She'll not miss the rendezvous.


# 10

    Oh tell me, friendly night, so long beloved,
bringer of my puppet world of dreams,
bare, barren stage that holds
only my phantom inside,
my poor unhappy shadow
alone on the steppes under a scorching sun,
or dreaming up bitter things
in the voice of every mystery,
tell me, if you know, my old beloved:
are these tears I shed my own?              10
The night replied:
you never let me know your secret.
I could never tell, beloved,
whether that phantom in your dreams was you,
I never learned if that voice was yours
or the voice of a wretched actor overplaying.
    I said to the night: faithless mistress,
you know my secret;

tú has visto la honda gruta
donde fabrica su cristal mi sueño,                          20
y sabes que mis lágrimas son mías,
y sabes mi dolor, mi dolor viejo.
    ¡Oh! Yo no sé, dijo la noche, amado,
yo no sé tu secreto,
aunque he visto vagar ese, que dices
desolado fantasma, por tu sueño.
Yo me asomo a las almas cuando lloran
y escucho su hondo rezo,
humilde y solitario,
ese que llamas salmo verdadero;                             30
pero en las hondas bóvedas del alma
no sé si el llanto es una voz o un eco.
    Para escuchar tu queja de tus labios
yo te busqué en tu sueño.
y allí te vi vagando en un borroso
laberinto de espejos.


## 11 *La noria*

    La tarde caía
triste y polvorienta.
    El agua cantaba
su copla plebeya
en los cangilones
de la noria lenta.
    Soñaba la mula
¡pobre mula vieja!
al compás de sombra
que en el agua suena.                                       10
    La tarde caía
triste y polvorienta.
    Yo no sé qué noble,
divino poeta,
unió a la amargura
de la eterna rueda
    la dulce armonía

you have looked deep into the cavern
where the crystal of my dream is made,                    20
you know my tears belong to me,
you know my pain, my pain from so far back.
    Oh, the night said, I do not know, beloved,
I do not know your secret,
although I have seen that forlorn phantom
you speak of, roaming through your dream.
I look into the depths of souls that weep
and listen to their prayers,
humble, solitary,
prayers you speak of as true psalms,                      30
but in the deep recesses of the soul,
whether weeping is voice or echo
I do not know.
    To hear from your lips your lament
I sought you out in your dream,
and I saw you wandering there
in a blurred labyrinth of mirrors.


## 11  *The Waterwheel*

    Evening was falling,
dusty and sad.
    The water sang
its workaday tune
in the brimming scoops
of the slow-turning wheel.
    The old mule was dreaming,
poor worn-out mule,
keeping time with the shadowy
sound of the water.                                       10
    Evening was falling,
dusty and sad.
    I can't say what noble
and godlike poet
linked the soft accord
of the dreaming water
    to the bitter toil

del agua que sueña,
y vendó tus ojos,
¡pobre mula vieja! ...                                          20
    Mas sé que fue un noble,
divino poeta,
corazón maduro
de sombra y de ciencia.

## 12  *El cadalso*

    La aurora asomaba
lejana y siniestra.
    El lienzo de Oriente
sangraba tragedias,
pintarrajeadas
con nubes grotescas.
. . . . . . . . . .
    En la vieja plaza
de una vieja aldea,
erguía su horrible                                              10
pavura esquelética
el tosco patíbulo
de fresca madera ...
    La aurora asomaba
lejana y siniestra.

## 13  *Las moscas*

    Vosotras, las familiares,
inevitables golosas,
vosotras, moscas vulgares,
me evocáis todas las cosas.
    ¡Oh, viejas moscas voraces
como abejas en abril,
viejas moscas pertinaces
sobre mi calva infantil!

of the endless round
and blindfolded you,
poor worn-out mule . . .                    20
But that poet, I know,
was noble and godlike,
a heart steeped in shadow
and ripe with knowing.

## 12  *The Gallows*

Dawn was breaking,
distant, grim.
The canvas of the east
was dripping tragedies
slapped bloodily on
with bizarre clouds.
. . . . . . . . . . .
On the old square
of an old village,
brutally flaunting                          10
its skeletal dread,
was a gallows rough-hewn
of fresh wood . . .
Dawn was breaking,
distant, grim.

## 13  *Flies*

Old familiar flies,
greedy, unavoidable,
plain flies of everyday,
you bring back everything.
Old flies with appetites
as keen as April bees,
or running those tickly legs
over my infant scalp.

¡Moscas del primer hastío
en el salón familiar,                                    10
las claras tardes de estío
en que yo empecé a soñar!
    Y en la aborrecida escuela,
raudas moscas divertidas,
perseguidas
por amor de lo que vuela,
    —que todo es volar—sonoras,
rebotando en los cristales
en los días otoñales . . .
Moscas de todas las horas,                               20
    de infancia y adolescencia,
de mi juventud dorada;
de esta segunda inocencia,
que da en no creer en nada,
    de siempre . . . Moscas vulgares,
que de puro familiares
no tendréis digno cantor:
yo sé que os habéis posado
    sobre el juguete encantado,
sobre el librote cerrado,                                30
sobre la carta de amor,
sobre los párpados yertos
de los muertos.
    Inevitables golosas,
que ni labráis como abejas,
ni brilláis cual mariposas;
pequeñitas, revoltosas,
vosotras, amigas viejas,
me evocáis todas las cosas.


# 14 *Glosa*

*Nuestras vidas son los ríos*
*que van a dar a la mar,*
*que es el morir. ¡Gran cantar!*
    Entre los poetas míos
tiene Manrique un altar.

Flies of my first tedium
in the parlor of our house                                    10
on bright summer afternoons
when I first began to dream.
    And in the hated schoolroom,
funny zooming flies,
hounded from sheer delight
in everything that flew
        (flying is all that counts),
buzzing, bumping windowpanes
on autumn days . . .
Flies at every stage—                                         20
    babyhood and teenage,
golden days of youth,
and now this second innocence
with nothing to believe in,
    always flies . . . Plain old things,
you'll never find your singer—
you're far too commonplace:
I know that you've alighted
    on the charmed plaything,
on the shut schoolbook,                                       30
on the love letter,
and on the rigid lids
of the dead.
    Greedy, unavoidable,
you never work like bees,
nor glitter like a butterfly,
you tiny little gadabouts,
you're old friends just the same
and bring back everything.


## 14 Gloss

*Our lives are rivers
flowing on to the sea,
the sea of dying.* Matchless lines!
    Among all my poets
I worship Manrique most.

Dulce goce de vivir:
mala ciencia del pasar,
ciego huir a la mar.
Tras el pavor del morir
está el placer de llegar.                                    10
¡Gran placer!
Mas ¿y el horror de volver?
¡Gran pesar!


## ✳ 15

Anoche cuando dormía
soñé, ¡bendita ilusión!,
que una fontana fluía
dentro de mi corazón.
Di, ¿por qué acequia escondida,
agua, vienes hasta mí,
manantial de nueva vida
en donde nunca bebí?
Anoche cuando dormía
soñé, ¡bendita ilusión!,                                     10
que una colmena tenía
dentro de mi corazón;
y las doradas abejas
iban fabricando en él,
con las amarguras viejas,
blanca cera y dulce miel.
Anoche cuando dormía
soñé, ¡bendita ilusión!,
que un ardiente sol lucía
dentro de mi corazón.                                        20
Era ardiente porque daba
calores de rojo hogar,
y era sol porque alumbraba
y porque hacía llorar.

Sweet taste of being alive,
hard learning how things pass,
blind rushing to the sea.
    After the fright of dying,
the joy of having arrived.
    Boundless joy!                                    10
But—that dread of a return?
Endless pain!


## 15

    Last night I had a dream—
a blessed illusion it was—
I dreamt of a fountain flowing
deep down in my heart.
Water, by what hidden channels
have you come, tell me, to me,
welling up with new life
I never tasted before?
    Last night I had a dream—
a blessed illusion it was—                            10
I dreamt of a hive at work
deep down in my heart.
Within were the golden bees
straining out the bitter past
to make sweet-tasting honey,
and white honeycomb.
    Last night I had a dream—
a blessed illusion it was—
I dreamt of a hot sun shining
deep down in my heart.                                20
The heat was in the scorching
as from a fiery hearth;
the sun in the light it shed
and the tears it brought to the eyes.

Anoche cuando dormía
soñé, ¡bendita ilusión!,
que era Dios lo que tenía
dentro de mi corazón.

# 16

¿Mi corazón se ha dormido?
Colmenares de mis sueños
¿ya no labráis? ¿Está seca
la noria del pensamiento,
los cangilones vacíos,
girando, de sombra llenos?
No, mi corazón no duerme.
Está despierto, despierto.
Ni duerme ni sueña, mira,
los claros ojos abiertos,                                    10
señas lejanas y escucha
a orillas del gran silencio.

# 17

Desgarrada la nube; el arco iris
brillando ya en el cielo,
y en un fanal de lluvia
y sol el campo envuelto.
Desperté. ¿Quién enturbia
los mágicos cristales de mi sueño?
Mi corazón latía
atónito y disperso.
. . . ¡El limonar florido,
el cipresal del huerto,                                      10

Last night I had a dream—
a blessed illusion it was—
I dreamed it was God I'd found
deep down in my heart.

# 16

Has my heart gone to sleep?
Have the beehives of my dreams
stopped working, the waterwheel
of the mind run dry,
scoops turning empty,
only shadow inside?
   No, my heart is not asleep.
It is awake, wide awake.
Not asleep, not dreaming—
its eyes are opened wide                    10
watching distant signals, listening
on the rim of the vast silence.

# 17

A rent in the clouds,
the rainbow brightening in the sky;
glassing the landscape in,
a lantern of sun and rain.
   I woke. Who clouded over
the magic windows of my dream?
My heartbeats cast about,
bewildered.
   . . . The lemon grove in flower,
the cypress trees in the orchard,          10

el prado verde, el sol, el agua, el iris . . .
¡el agua en tus cabellos! . . .
    Y todo en la memoria se perdía
como una pompa de jabón al viento.


## 18

    Y era el demonio de mi sueño, el ángel
más hermoso. Brillaban
como aceros los ojos victoriosos,
y las sangrientas llamas
de su antorcha alumbraron
la honda cripta del alma.
    —¿Vendrás conmigo? —No, jamás; las tumbas
y los muertos me espantan.
Pero la férrea mano
mi diestra atenazaba.                                          10
    —Vendrás conmigo . . . Y avancé en mi sueño,
cegado por la roja luminaria.
Y en la cripta sentí sonar cadenas,
y rebullir de fieras enjauladas.


## 19

    ¡Oh tarde luminosa!
El aire está encantado.
La blanca cigüeña
dormita volando,
y las golondrinas se cruzan, tendidas
las alas agudas al viento dorado,
y en la tarde risueña se alejan
volando, soñando . . .

green meadow, wetness, rainbow, sun . . .
the wet against your hair! . . .
    And memory let it all slip off again
like a soap bubble in the wind.


# 18

    And the devil in my dream
was the fairest angel.
The swordpoints of his eyes
shot glints of triumph
and the blood-red fire of his flare
lit up the deep vault of the soul.
    "Will you come with me?" "No, never.
Tombs and dead men make me shudder."
But the iron grip
was fastened on my wrist.                          10
    "You will come with me . . ."
I moved on through my dream,
blinded by the crimson flare.
And in the vault I heard a clank of chains
and caged beasts stirring.


# 19

    Oh light-struck evening!
The air is spellbound.
The white stork
dozes in flight,
and the crisscrossing swallows,
spreading sharp wings to a gold wind,
move off in the smiling dusk
and dream and soar . . .

Y hay una que torna coma la saeta,
las alas agudas tendidas al aire sombrío,                    10
buscando su negro rincón del tejado.
   La blanca cigüeña,
como un garabato,
tranquila y disforme ¡tan disparatada!
sobre el campanario.


# 20

   Es una tarde cenicienta y mustia,
destartalada, como el alma mía;
y es esta vieja angustia
que habita mi usual hipocondría.
   La causa de esta angustia no consigo
ni vagamente comprender siquiera;
pero recuerdo y, recordando, digo:
—Sí, yo era niño, y tú, mi compañera.

   Y no es verdad, dolor, yo te conozco,
tú eres nostalgia de la vida buena                          10
y soledad de corazón sombrío,
de barco sin naufragio y sin estrella.
   Como perro olvidado que no tiene
huella ni olfato y yerra
por los caminos, sin camino, como
el niño que en la noche de una fiesta
   se pierde entre el gentío
y el aire polvoriento y las candelas
chispeantes, atónito, y asombra
su corazón de música y de pena,                             20
   así voy yo, borracho melancólico,
guitarrista lunático, poeta,
y pobre hombre en sueños,
siempre buscando a Dios entre la niebla.

And one comes streaking back,
sharp wings spread to shadowy air,                    10
seeking its dark corner of the eaves.
   The white stork,
perched like a pothook,
placid and ungainly, looking so queer
up there on the belfry!


# 20

   This withered, ashen afternoon:
a day in disarray, just like my spirits.
The old distress is back,
stirring inside the same old fancied ills.
   What causes this distress I can't pretend
even vaguely to understand.
But I go back—I think back and I say:
Ah yes, I was a boy and you a girl with me.

   But that's not it—pain, I know you better:
you are the longing for the happy days,               10
the loneliness that fills the somber heart,
that haunts the ship unfoundering and unstarred.
   Like a dog left behind without a trail
to sniff, straying this way and that,
no way his own, and like
a child on carnival night,
   lost in the crowd, the dusty air,
the spurting flares,
bewildered, his heart aching
with music and distress,                              20
   I go my way, a moody sort of drunk,
strumming a crazy tune—a poet,
a poor creature in a dream,
groping for God perpetually in the mist.

# 21

¿Y ha de morir contigo el mundo mago
donde guarda el recuerdo
los hálitos más puros de la vida,
la blanca sombra del amor primero,
    la voz que fue a tu corazón, la mano
que tú querías retener en sueños,
y todos los amores
que llegaron al alma, al hondo cielo?
    ¿Y ha de morir contigo el mundo tuyo,
la vieja vida en orden tuyo y nuevo?                  10
¿Los yunques y crisoles de tu alma
trabajan para el polvo y para el viento?

# 22

Tal vez la mano, en sueños,
del sembrador de estrellas,
hizo sonar la música olvidada
    como una nota de la lira inmensa,
y la ola humilde a nuestros labios vino
de unas pocas palabras verdaderas.

# 23

Y podrás conocerte, recordando
del pasado soñar los turbios lienzos,
en este día triste en que caminas
con los ojos abiertos.
    De toda la memoria, sólo vale
el don preclaro de evocar los sueños.

# 21

And is the magic world to die with you,
the world where memory keeps
life's purest breaths—
white shadow of first love,
    voice that went to your heart, hand
you wished in dreams to keep in yours
and all loved things
that touched the soul, the deeper sky?
    And is your world to die with you,
the old life you reshaped your way?                    10
Have the crucibles and anvils of your soul
been working for dust and for the wind?

# 22

Idling once in a dream,
the hand that sowed the stars
plucked a single string of the vast lyre.
    The long-forgotten music came to life
and a humble ripple ended at our lips,
carrying some few brief words of truth.

# 23

And you can know yourself if you'll recall
the hazy pictures of past dreams
on this sad day when you are going about
with open eyes.
    For this alone is memory to be prized,
this signal gift of calling back old dreams.

# 24 *Retrato*

Mi infancia son recuerdos de un patio de Sevilla,
y un huerto claro donde madura el limonero;
mi juventud, veinte años en tierra de Castilla;
mi historia, algunos casos que recordar no quiero.
Ni un seductor Mañara, ni un Bradomín he sido
—ya conocéis mi torpe aliño indumentario—,
mas recibí la flecha que me asignó Cupido,
y amé cuanto ellas pueden tener de hospitalario.
Hay en mis venas gotas de sangre jacobina,
pero mi verso brota de manantial sereno;                                    10
y, más que un hombre al uso que sabe su doctrina,
soy, en el buen sentido de la palabra, bueno.
Adoro la hermosura, y en la moderna estética
corté las viejas rosas del huerto de Ronsard;
mas no amo los afeites de la actual cosmética
ni soy un ave de esas del nuevo gay-trinar.
Desdeño las romanzas de los tenores huecos
y el coro de los grillos que cantan a la luna.
A distinguir me paro las voces de los ecos,
y escucho solamente, entre las voces, una.                                  20
¿Soy clásico o romántico? No sé. Dejar quisiera
mi verso, como deja el capitán su espada:
famosa por la mano viril que la blandiera,
no por el docto oficio del forjador preciada.
Converso con el hombre que siempre va conmigo
—quien habla solo espera hablar a Dios un día—;
mi soliloquio es plática con este buen amigo
que me enseñó el secreto de la filantropía.
Y al cabo, nada os debo; debéisme cuanto he escrito.
A mi trabajo acudo, con mi dinero pago                                       30
el traje que me cubre y la mansión que habito,
el pan que me alimenta y el lecho en donde yago.
Y cuando llegue el día del último viaje,
y esté al partir la nave que nunca ha de tornar,
me encontraréis a bordo ligero de equipaje,
casi desnudo, como los hijos de la mar.

# 24 Portrait

My childhood is memories of a patio in Seville
and a sunny yard with lemons turning ripe,
my youth twenty years in lands of Castile,
my story certain matters I don't care to recite.
  I never was a playboy or Don Juan—
you know how shabbily I always dress—
but one of Cupid's arrows came my way
and women found a lodging in my breast.
  The springs that feed my verse are calm and clear
for all my heritage of rebel blood;                            10
I'm neither doctrinaire nor worldly wise—
just call me in the best sense simply good.
  In my passion for beauty, out of modern aesthetics
I've cut old-fashioned roses in gardens of Ronsard,
but I've no great love for the latest in cosmetics
nor will you find me trilling the stylish airs.
  I'm not impressed by those puffed-up tenors' ballads
or the cricket chorus crooning to the moon.
I've learned to tell the voices from the echoes
and of all the voices listen to only one.                      20
  Call me romantic or classic—I only hope
that the verse I leave behind, like the captain's sword,
may be remembered, not for its maker's art,
but for the virile hand that gripped it once.
  I talk with the man who is always at my side—
one who talks to himself hopes to talk to God sometime—
soliloquizing is speaking with this good friend
who has shown me the way to love of humankind.
  In the end I owe you nothing—you owe me all I've written.
I go about my work, I pay in my own coin                       30
for the clothes upon my back, the roof over my head,
the bread that sustains my life, the bed where I lie down.
  And when the day for the final voyage is here
and the ship that does not return heads down the stream,
I'll be aboard, you'll find me traveling light
and nearly naked like children of the sea.

## 25 *A orillas del Duero*

Mediaba el mes de julio. Era un hermoso día.
Yo, solo, por las quiebras del pedregal subía,
buscando los recodos de sombra, lentamente.
A trechos me paraba para enjugar mi frente
y dar algún respiro al pecho jadeante;
o bien, ahincando el paso, el cuerpo hacia adelante
y hacia la mano diestra vencido y apoyado
en un bastón, a guisa de pastoril cayado,
trepaba por los cerros que habitan las rapaces
aves de altura, hollando las hierbas montaraces                    10
de fuerte olor—romero, tomillo, salvia, espliego—.
Sobre los agrios campos caía un sol de fuego.
Un buitre de anchas alas con majestuoso vuelo
cruzaba solitario el puro azul del cielo.
Yo divisaba, lejos, un monte alto y agudo,
y una redonda loma cual recamado escudo,
y cárdenos alcores sobre la parda tierra
—harapos esparcidos de un viejo arnés de guerra—,
las serrezuelas calvas por donde tuerce el Duero
para formar la corva ballesta de un arquero                        20
en torno a Soria. —Soria es una barbacana,
hacia Aragón, que tiene la torre castellana—.
Veía el horizonte cerrado por colinas
obscuras, coronadas de robles y de encinas;
desnudos peñascales, algún humilde prado
donde el merino pace y el toro, arrodillado
sobre la hierba, rumia; las márgenes del río
lucir sus verdes álamos al claro sol de estío,
y, silenciosamente, lejanos pasajeros,
¡tan diminutos! —carros, jinetes y arrieros—                       30
cruzar el largo puente, y bajo las arcadas
de piedra ensombrecerse las aguas plateadas
del Duero.
          El Duero cruza el corazón de roble
de Iberia y de Castilla.
                        ¡Oh, tierra triste y noble,
la de los altos llanos y yermos y roquedas,
de campos sin arados, regatos ni arboledas;

# 25  *Along the Duero*

It was mid-July and a splendid day.
Climbing through clefts in the rocks, I picked my way
slowly, seeking out pockets of shade.
I was alone and occasionally I made
a halt to wipe the moisture from my face
or give my heaving chest a breathing space.
Then, making sure of my footing, I strained on,
body thrust forward, grasping a cane
in my right hand—it was this that took
the bulk of my weight, like a shepherd's crook.                    10
Ascending heights where soaring birds of prey
make nests, I trampled, as I climbed,
on pungent mountain herbs along the way—
sage and lavender, rosemary and thyme.
A blazing sun beat down on the harsh land.
    On outspread wings a vulture went cruising by,
alone and lordly in the clear blue sky.
Far off I could see a mountain tall and pointed
and a rounded knoll like a breastplate firmly jointed,
livid hills strewn over the brownish ground                        20
like scraps of ancient armor cast around,
bare, stubby ranges whose contortions send
the Duero twisting in a crossbow bend
round Soria—Soria is a barbican
that towered Castile presents to Aragon.
I saw dark hills close off the sky's round rim
with stands of oak trees clustered at their brim,
bare spurs of rock, sometimes a meager field
where sheep were grazing or bulls kneeled
to ruminate. The sun raised a sheen                                30
on the poplars marking the river's course in green.
Crossing in silence the bridge's many spans,
I saw lines of tiny figures—muleteers
and men on horseback, carters with their vans
—so far away—and the Duero's glistening waters
darkening where they flowed past the old stone piers.
    Castile's, Iberia's oaken heart is spanned
by the Duero.
                Noble, sad Castilian land!
Country of high plateaus, of rocks and empty spaces,

decrépitas ciudades, caminos sin mesones,
y atónitos palurdos sin danzas ni canciones
que aún van, abandonando el mortecino hogar,
como tus largos ríos, Castilla, hacia la mar!    40
Castilla miserable, ayer dominadora,
envuelta en sus andrajos desprecia cuanto ignora.
¿Espera, duerme o sueña? ¿La sangre derramada
recuerda, cuando tuvo la fiebre de la espada?
Todo se mueve, fluye, discurre, corre o gira;
cambian la mar y el monte y el ojo que los mira.
¿Pasó? Sobre sus campos aún el fantasma yerra
de un pueblo que ponía a Dios sobre la guerra.
La madre en otro tiempo fecunda en capitanes
madrastra es hoy apenas de humildes ganapanes.    50
Castilla no es aquella tan generosa un día,
cuando Myo Cid Rodrigo el de Vivar volvía,
ufano de su nueva fortuna y su opulencia,
a regalar a Alfonso los huertos de Valencia;
o que, tras la aventura que acreditó sus bríos,
pedía la conquista de los inmensos ríos
indianos a la corte, la madre de soldados,
guerreros y adalides que han de tornar, cargados
de plata y oro, a España, en regios galeones,
para la presa cuervos, para la lid leones.    60
Filósofos nutridos de sopa de convento
contemplan impasibles el amplio firmamento;
y si les llega en sueños, como un rumor distante,
clamor de mercaderes de muelles de Levante,
no acudirán siquiera a preguntar ¿qué pasa?
Y ya la guerra ha abierto las puertas de su casa.
Castilla miserable, ayer dominadora,
envuelta en sus harapos desprecia cuanto ignora.
El sol va declinando. De la ciudad lejana
me llega un armonioso tañido de campana    70
—ya irán a su rosario las enlutadas viejas—.
De entre las peñas salen dos lindas comadrejas;
me miran y se alejan, huyendo, y aparecen
de nuevo ¡tan curiosas! . . . Los campos se obscurecen.
Hacia el camino blanco está el mesón abierto
al campo ensombrecido y al pedregal desierto.

of crumbling cities, roads without stopping-places,    40
of fields untouched by plow or shade or spring,
of boors that gape but cannot dance or sing,
who still, when hearth fires fail, can only flee
down the long river valleys to the sea.
    Wretched Castile, supreme once, now forlorn,
wrapped in her rags, closes her mind in scorn.
Does she dream or wait or sleep? What of the squandered
       blood?
Does it still remember thirsting for the sword?
Everything flows, moves on, revolves or rushes by.
Changing are sea and hills, changing the very eye . . .    50
Can all be over? A phantom yet walks abroad
of a race that fought for the glory of the Lord.
    Castile, the mother of captains long victorious
now brings forth drudges lowly and inglorious—
she, a great-hearted mother in an earlier day
when Rodrigo, the Cid, went his triumphant way
and then came back to place in Alfonso's hands
the pride of his spoils, Valencia's gardenlands;
the mother of pioneers in the great adventure
who begged the Crown to be sent to find more treasure,    60
conquering vast New World rivers, of the warrior race
that fought the world like lions, face to face,
or swooped like crows to plunder silver and gold
and bring home galleons groaning with the load.
Philosophers maintained on cast-off convent meals
now gaze unblinking at the empty scene.
The distant hum of trade on wharves and wheels
cannot distract them from their empty dream.
Ignoring all, they blankly ruminate—
with war already knocking at their gate.    70
    Wretched Castile, supreme once, now forlorn,
wrapping herself in tatters, closes her mind in scorn.
    The sun is far down the sky. Through the quiet air
the music of distant bells reaches my ear—
time for old women in black to go to prayers.
Two pretty weasels slip out of rocky lairs,
catch sight of me and flee, then peer again
from farther off—so curious . . . Daylight grows dimmer.
Across a white strip of road the inn casts a glimmer
toward darkened fields and stony wastes in the plain.    80

## 26   *El Dios ibero*

Igual que el ballestero
tahúr de la cantiga,
tuviera una saeta el hombre ibero
para el Señor que apedreó la espiga
y malogró los frutos otoñales,
y un "gloria a ti" para el Señor que grana
centenos y trigales
que el pan bendito le darán mañana.

   "Señor de la ruina,
adoro porque aguardo y porque temo:                               10
con mi oración se inclina
hacia la tierra un corazón blasfemo.

   ¡Señor, por quien arranco el pan con pena,
sé tu poder, conozco mi cadena!
¡Oh dueño de la nube del estío
que la campiña arrasa,
del seco otoño, del helar tardío,
y del bochorno que la mies abrasa!

   ¡Señor del iris, sobre el campo verde
donde la oveja pace,                                              20
Señor del fruto que el gusano muerde
y de la choza que el turbión deshace,

   tu soplo el fuego del hogar aviva,
tu lumbre da sazón al rubio grano,
y cuaja el hueso de la verde oliva,
la noche de San Juan, tu santa mano!

   ¡Oh dueño de fortuna y de pobreza,
ventura y malandanza,
que al rico das favores y pereza
y al pobre su fatiga y su esperanza!                              30

   ¡Señor, Señor, en la voltaria rueda
del año he visto mi simiente echada,
corriendo igual albur que la moneda
del jugador en el azar sembrada!

   ¡Señor, hoy paternal, ayer cruento,
con doble faz de amor y de venganza,
a ti, en un dado de tahúr al viento
va mi oración, blasfemia y alabanza!"
   Este que insulta a Dios en los altares,

## 26 *The Iberian God*

Just like the gambling
crossbowman in the song,
the man of Iberia would gladly loose a dart
at the Lord who stoned his wheat
and spoiled his autumn crops,
and chant "Thy name be praised" to him
who packs the wheat ears and the rye
with grain for tomorrow's blessed bread.
"Lord of ruination,
I worship to get my due and still my fears.                    10
A blasphemous heart bows to earth
when I say my prayers.
Lord, by whose will I slave for my daily bread,
I know your might, I recognize my fetters.
Oh, sender of the summer cloud
that devastates the land,
of autumn drought, of frosts that come untimely,
and torrid spells that scorch the grain.
Lord of the rainbow arching the green field
where sheep are grazing,                                        20
Lord of worm-eaten fruit,
of the hut the whirlwind pulls apart,
   your breath blows up the fire in the hearth,
your warming rays toast grain to ripeness,
your sacred hand puts hardness in the stone
of olives green on St. John's Eve!
Oh, arbiter of plenty and of want,
of good times and of bad,
whose favors are kept for the lazy rich,
while the poor are left to toil and hope!                       30
Lord, Lord, the seasons' turning wheel
carries my broadcast seed
to more uncertainty than any gambler's coin
given over to chance.
Lord, kind today but brutal yesterday,
Lord of two faces—vengefulness and love—
I toss you, just like dice tossed in the wind,
my prayer of blasphemy and praise!"
This curser-out of God at his very altar,

no más atento al ceño del destino,                          40
también soñó caminos en los mares
y dijo: es Dios sobre la mar camino.
    ¿No es él quien puso a Dios sobre la guerra,
más allá de la suerte,
más allá de la tierra,
más allá de la mar y de la muerte?
    ¿No dio la encina ibera
para el fuego de Dios la buena rama,
que fue en la santa hoguera
de amor una con Dios en pura llama?          50
    Mas hoy ... ¡Qué importa un día!
Para los nuevos lares
estepas hay en la floresta umbría,
leña verde en los viejos encinares.
    Aún larga patria espera
abrir al corvo arado sus besanas;
para el grano de Dios hay sementera
bajo cardos y abrojos y bardanas.
    ¡Qué importa un día! Está el ayer alerto
al mañana, mañana al infinito,          60
hombres de España, ni el pasado ha muerto,
ni está el mañana—ni el ayer—escrito.
    ¿Quién ha visto la faz al Dios hispano?
Mi corazón aguarda
al hombre ibero de la recia mano,
que tallará en el roble castellano
el Dios adusto de la tierra parda.

## 27 *Orillas del Duero*

    ¡Primavera soriana, primavera
humilde, como el sueño de un bendito,
de un pobre caminante que durmiera
de cansancio en un páramo infinito!
    ¡Campillo amarillento,
como tosco sayal de campesina,

keeping a wary eye for destiny's scowl,                    40
is the same who dreamed of pathways on the oceans
and said that God is a path over the seas.
    Was it not he who fought in the name of the Lord,
past the bounds of fate,
past the ends of the earth,
past ocean and past death?
    Did not the Iberian oak
furnish sound branches for the blaze of God,
limbs that were one with God in purest flame
on the sacred bonfire of love?                             50
    But today . . . what does one day matter!
For men's new homes to rise
there are open stretches in the shady wood,
green timber in ancient stands of oak.
    A long expanse of fatherland still waits
to bare its furrows to the curving plow.
There is fertile ground for sowing God's ripe grain
where thistles, briars, and burdocks now abound.
    What does one day matter! Yesterday stands poised
to face tomorrow, tomorrow faces the infinite:            60
men of Spain, the past has never died
nor is tomorrow—nor yesterday—yet written.
    Who has looked on the face of the Spanish God?
My heart awaits
the man of Iberia with the mighty hand
who shall carve from Castilian oak
the stern God of the drab-brown land.


## 27  *Along the Duero*

    Humble spring of Soria settling in
like the sleep of some blameless man,
some hapless traveler dropping off exhausted
on an endless stretch of plain.
    A yellow roughness in the land
like the raw weave of country clothes,

pradera de velludo polvoriento
donde pace la escuálida merina!
¡Aquellos diminutos pegujales
de tierra dura y fría,                                    10
donde apuntan centenos y trigales
que el pan moreno nos darán un día!
Y otra vez roca y roca, pedregales
desnudos y pelados serrijones,
la tierra de las águilas caudales,
malezas y jarales,
hierbas monteses, zarzas y cambrones.
¡Oh tierra ingrata y fuerte, tierra mía!
¡Castilla, tus decrépitas ciudades!
¡La agria melancolía                                     20
que puebla tus sombrías soledades!
¡Castilla varonil, adusta tierra,
Castilla del desdén contra la suerte,
Castilla del dolor y de la guerra,
tierra inmortal, Castilla de la muerte!
Era una tarde, cuando el campo huía
del sol, y en el asombro del planeta,
como un globo morado aparecía
la hermosa luna, amada del poeta.
En el cárdeno cielo violeta                              30
alguna clara estrella fulguraba.
El aire ensombrecido
oreaba mis sienes, y acercaba
el murmullo del agua hasta mi oído.
Entre cerros de plomo y de ceniza
manchados de roídos encinares,
y entre calvas roquedas de caliza,
iba a embestir los ocho tajamares
del puente el padre río,
que surca de Castilla el yermo frío.                     40
¡Oh Duero, tu agua corre
y correrá mientras las nieves blancas
de enero el sol de mayo
haga fluir por hoces y barrancas,
mientras tengan las sierras su turbante
de nieve y de tormenta
y brille el olifante
del sol, tras de la nube cenicienta! . . .

meadows dusted with new grass
where scrawny sheep are browsing.
   Those tiny plots of ground
still hard and cold                                    10
with shoots of wheat and barley showing through,
our good dark bread in days to come.
   Then rocks and still more rocks,
stone barrens, craggy spurs—
the haunt of lordly eagles—
rock rose and bramble,
upcountry herbs and briarbush and buckthorn.
   Strong and thankless land, my land, Castile,
those crumbling towns of yours,
that acrid melancholy                                  20
that settles on the brooding emptiness.
   Virile, forbidding, this Castilian land
turning its back so haughtily on fate,
this place of woe, this seat of war,
a land undying and a land of death.
   A day was ending. The broad land
fell back, retreating from the sun.
Startling the earth, a beautiful moon appeared,
the kind of violet disk a poet loves.
   Against the deepening purple of the sky             30
a few star-points began to glow.
The shadowy air, brushing my face,
brought sounds of running water to my ears.
   Down through its hills of ash and lead
mottled with mouldering stands of oak,
past naked stretches strewn with chalky stones,
the Duero flowed, the lifestream of Castile,
cutting its way across cold barren plains
to thrust its current at the eight-piered bridge.
   Duero, your flowing waters still shall flow         40
as long as suns of May
melt winter snows and set them loose
through canyons and ravines,
as long as peaks stay capped
in snows and storms
and the sun's bugle flashes
through ashen cloud . . .

¿Y el viejo romancero
fue el sueño de un juglar junto a tu orilla?                    50
¿Acaso como tú y por siempre, Duero,
irá corriendo hacia la mar Castilla?

## 28

¿Eres tú, Guadarrama, viejo amigo,
la sierra gris y blanca,
la sierra de mis tardes madrileñas
que yo veía en el azul pintada?
Por tus barrancos hondos
y por tus cumbres agrias,
mil Guadarramas y mil soles vienen,
cabalgando conmigo, a tus entrañas.

*Camino de Balsaín, 1911.*

## 29 *Campos de Soria*

### I

Es la tierra de Soria árida y fría.
Por las colinas y las sierras calvas,
verdes pradillos, cerros cenicientos,
la primavera pasa
dejando entre las hierbas olorosas
sus diminutas margaritas blancas.
La tierra no revive, el campo sueña.
Al empezar abril está nevada
la espalda del Moncayo;
el caminante lleva en su bufanda                              10
envueltos cuello y boca, y los pastores
pasan cubiertos con sus luengas capas.

### II

Las tierras labrantías,
como retazos de estameñas pardas,
el huertecillo, el abejar, los trozos

And the old *romancero,*
was it dreamed up by a minstrel on your banks?
Like you, then, River Duero, and forever,                    50
shall Castile run downward to the sea?


# 28

Guadarrama, is it you, old friend,
mountains white and gray
that I used to see painted against the blue
those afternoons of the old days in Madrid?
Up your deep ravines
and past your bristling peaks
a thousand Guadarramas and a thousand suns
come riding with me, riding to your heart.

*Balsaín Road, 1911.*


## 29 *The Soria Country*

### I

Round Soria the land is dry and cold.
Over the hills, the barren ranges,
through green bits of meadow,
up the cindery peaks
the spring advances, leaving its small white daisies
scattered in the fragrant grasses.
The earth is not reborn: the country dreams.
When April starts snow still remains
on the back of the Moncayo.
Walking, one needs a muffler                                 10
for mouth and throat. The shepherds pass,
wrapped in their trailing capes.


### II

Worked fields
like patches of brown serge,
small garden plots and beehives,

de verde obscuro en que el merino pasta,
entre plomizos peñascales, siembran
el sueño alegre de infantil Arcadia.
En los chopos lejanos del camino,
parecen humear las yertas ramas                              20
como un glauco vapor—las nuevas hojas—
y en las quiebras de valles y barrancas
blanquean los zarzales florecidos,
y brotan las violetas perfumadas.


                              III
Es el campo undulado, y los caminos
ya ocultan los viajeros que cabalgan
en pardos borriquillos,
ya al fondo de la tarde arrebolada
elevan las plebeyas figurillas,
que el lienzo de oro del ocaso manchan.                      30
Mas si trepáis a un cerro y veis el campo
desde los picos donde habita el águila,
son tornasoles de carmín y acero,
llanos plomizos, lomas plateadas,
circuidos por montes de violeta,
con las cumbres de nieve sonrosada.


                              IV
¡Las figuras del campo sobre el cielo!
Dos lentos bueyes aran
en un alcor, cuando el otoño empieza,
y entre las negras testas doblegadas                         40
bajo el pesado yugo,
pende un cesto de juncos y retama,
que es la cuna de un niño;
y tras la yunta marcha
un hombre que se inclina hacia la tierra,
y una mujer que en las abiertas zanjas
arroja la semilla.
Bajo una nube de carmín y llama,
en el oro fluido y verdinoso
del poniente, las sombras se agigantan.                      50

dark green strips where the merino grazes
under leaden crags
implant a child's bright dream of Arcady.
On distant roadside poplars
stiff branches seem to steam—                                20
a blue-green mist of leaves beginning—
and in the clefts of valleys and ravines
white bloom appears on brambles
and fragrant violets open.


III

This is rolling country. The roads dip,
take travelers from sight
astride their small gray donkeys,
then lift them up
against a flush of evening skies,
small peasant silhouettes                                   30
spotting the gold backdrop of the west.
But if you climb a hill and view the scene
from heights where eagles live,
skies shimmer steel and crimson,
plains are gunmetal gray, hills silver,
with a ring of violet mountains
capped by rose-tinted snow.


IV

Those figures on the land against the sky!
Out on an open slope
a pair of oxen slowly plow                                   40
as autumn starts,
their dark heads bent beneath the heavy yoke.
A basket of furze and rushes hangs between,
the cradle for a child.
A man and woman walk behind,
he bending toward the earth, she casting seed
into the open furrows.
Beneath a flaming crimson cloud,
in the streaming gold and copper green of sunset,
the looming shadows lengthen.                                50

V

La nieve. En el mesón al campo abierto
se ve el hogar donde la leña humea
y la olla al hervir borbollonea.
El cierzo corre por el campo yerto,
alborotando en blancos torbellinos
la nieve silenciosa.
La nieve sobre el campo y los caminos,
cayendo está como sobre una fosa.
Un viejo acurrucado tiembla y tose
cerca del fuego; su mechón de lana                    60
la vieja hila, y una niña cose
verde ribete a su estameña grana.
Padres los viejos son de un arriero
que caminó sobre la blanca tierra,
y una noche perdió ruta y sendero,
y se enterró en las nieves de la sierra.
En torno al fuego hay un lugar vacío,
y en la frente del viejo, de hosco ceño,
como un tachón sombrío
—tal el golpe de un hacha sobre un leño—.              70
La vieja mira al campo, cual si oyera
pasos sobre la nieve. Nadie pasa.
Desierta la vecina carretera,
desierto el campo en torno de la casa.
La niña piensa que en los verdes prados
ha de correr con otras doncellitas
en los días azules y dorados,
cuando crecen las blancas margaritas.

VI

¡Soria fría, *Soria pura,*
*cabeza de Extremadura,*                                80
con su castillo guerrero
arruinado, sobre el Duero;
con sus murallas roídas
y sus casas denegridas!
    ¡Muerta ciudad de señores
soldados o cazadores;
de portales con escudos
de cien linajes hidalgos,
y de famélicos galgos,
de galgos flacos y agudos,                             90
que pululan

V

Snow. The inn looks out across the fields;
you see the hearth within, the smoking logs,
the stewpot bubbling up and boiling.
The north wind sweeps the prostrate land,
lifting the snow in silent swirls.
The falling flakes settle in fields and roads
as if in new-dug graves.
Huddled beside the fire an old man
shudders and coughs. His old wife
spins her twist of wool, a young girl sews                    60
green edgings on her scarlet serge.
The son of these old people drove his mules,
traveling the white land,
but one night lost his way without a trace
and vanished in the mountain snows.
Beside the fire is one empty place;
across the old man's somber brow
a cleft runs deep—
like the gash an ax might leave in wood.
The woman looks outdoors, thinking she hears          70
footsteps in the snow. No one appears,
no one comes down the highway past the door,
nothing but emptiness surrounds the house.
The child is thinking of green meadow grass
where she will romp with other little girls
when days turn gold and blue
and daisies fill the fields.


VI

Soria, cold *pure town,*
*Soria, Extremadura's crown,*
with a castle's ruined flanks                                       80
overhanging the Duero's banks,
town walls eaten by time
houses black with grime.
   Dead city of lords
devoted to hunting and wars,
of doorways bearing signs
of a hundred hidalgo lines,
of scrawny, famished hounds

por las sórdidas callejas,
y a la media noche ululan,
cuando graznan las cornejas!
¡Soria fría! La campana
de la Audiencia da la una.
Soria, ciudad castellana
¡tan bella! bajo la luna.

### VII

¡Colinas plateadas,
grises alcores, cárdenas roquedas                    100
por donde traza el Duero
su curva de ballesta
en torno a Soria, obscuros encinares,
ariscos pedregales, calvas sierras,
caminos blancos y álamos del río,
tardes de Soria, mística y guerrera,
hoy siento por vosotros, en el fondo
del corazón, tristeza,
tristeza que es amor! ¡Campos de Soria
donde parece que las rocas sueñan,                   110
conmigo vais! ¡Colinas plateadas,
grises alcores, cárdenas roquedas! . . .

### VIII

He vuelto a ver los álamos dorados,
álamos del camino en la ribera
del Duero, entre San Polo y San Saturio,
tras las murallas viejas
de Soria—barbacana
hacia Aragón, en castellana tierra.
Estos chopos del río, que acompañan
con el sonido de sus hojas secas                     120
el son del agua, cuando el viento sopla,
tienen en sus cortezas
grabadas iniciales que son nombres
de enamorados, cifras que son fechas.
¡Alamos del amor que ayer tuvisteis
de ruiseñores vuestras ramas llenas;
álamos que seréis mañana liras
del viento perfumado en primavera;

that swarm the dirty streets
and raise their nightly howls                                    90
when the jackdaws' cawing sounds.
    Cold Soria. The courthouse chime
telling the hour strikes a single time.
Castilian Soria—lovely sight
beneath the moon tonight.


                VII

    Silver hills, gray heights,
dark clots of rock
through which the Duero bends
round Soria like a crossbow,
dim stands of oak,                                              100
stone-strewn barrens, naked mountains,
white roads, poplars by the river,
evenings of Soria, mystic and warlike town,
today my heart goes out to you in sadness,
sadness that speaks of love. Landscapes of Soria
where the very rocks appear to dream,
I have brought you along! Silver hills,
gray heights, dark clots of rock . . .


                VIII

    I've seen again the poplars showing gold
that line the river road beside the Duero                       110
between San Polo and San Saturio
beyond the old town walls of Soria—
Soria, lookout post toward Aragon,
inside Castile.
    These poplars by the river
that blend the rustling of their withered leaves
with the water's sound when the wind comes up
have lovers' names carved in their bark,
lovers' initials, numbers
that tell the year.                                             120
Poplars, lovers' trees whose branches
were filled with nightingales just recently,
poplars, trees that soon again shall sound
like lyres in the scented April wind,

álamos del amor cerca del agua
que corre y pasa y sueña,                                    130
álamos de las márgenes del Duero,
conmigo vais, mi corazón os lleva!


IX

¡Oh!, sí, conmigo vais, campos de Soria,
tardes tranquilas, montes de violeta,
alamedas del río, verde sueño
del suelo gris y de la parda tierra,
agria melancolía
de la ciudad decrépita,
me habéis llegado al alma,
¿o acaso estabais en el fondo de ella?          140
¡Gentes del alto llano numantino
que a Dios guardáis como cristianas viejas,
que el sol de España os llene
de alegría, de luz y de riqueza!


# 30

En estos campos de la tierra mía,
y extranjero en los campos de mi tierra
—yo tuve patria donde corre el Duero
por entre grises peñas,
y fantasmas de viejos encinares,
allá en Castilla, mística y guerrera,
Castilla la gentil, humilde y brava,
Castilla del desdén y de la fuerza—,
en estos campos de mi Andalucía,
¡oh, tierra en que nací!, cantar quisiera.          10
Tengo recuerdos de mi infancia, tengo
imágenes de luz y de palmeras,
y en una gloria de oro,
de lueñes campanarios con cigüeñas,
de ciudades con calles sin mujeres
bajo un cielo de añil, plazas desiertas
donde crecen naranjos encendidos
con sus frutas redondas y bermejas;

poplars, lovers' trees beside the water
that flows and slips away and dreams,
poplars on the River Duero's banks,
I have brought you along, I bear you in my heart.

IX

Yes, I have brought you along, landscapes of Soria,
still evenings, lavender hills,                                    130
poplar lanes by the river, green dreaming
of gray soil and drab-brown earth,
aching melancholy of a town's decay,
you have found your way to my heart—
or were you already there?
People of the high Numantian plain
who keep your faith in God like old believers,
may the Spanish sun reward you
with joy and light and plenty!

# 30

Back in the landscape of my native soil,
feeling a stranger to these native scenes—
I had a homeland where the Duero flows
between gray cliffs
and ghosts of ancient stands of oak
up in Castile, mystic and warlike land,
"Castile the noble," the humble, the untamed,
Castile the land of haughtiness and might—
here in these Andalusian scenes of mine,
this soil where I was born, I long to sing.                        10
My childhood memories are here, images of palm trees
        and of light,
and, against golden sunbursts,
of bell towers in the distance with their storks,
cities on whose streets no women walk,
under their indigo skies, deserted squares
planted in orange trees aglow
with round vermilion fruit;

y en un huerto sombrío, el limonero
de ramas polvorientas                                  20
y pálidos limones amarillos,
que el agua clara de la fuente espeja,
un aroma de nardos y claveles
y un fuerte olor de albahaca y hierbabuena;
imágenes de grises olivares
bajo un tórrido sol que aturde y ciega,
y azules y dispersas serranías
con arreboles de una tarde inmensa;
mas falta el hilo que el recuerdo anuda
al corazón, el ancla en su ribera,                     30
o estas memorias no son alma. Tienen,
en sus abigarradas vestimentas,
señal de ser despojos del recuerdo,
la carga bruta que el recuerdo lleva.
Un día tornarán, con luz del fondo ungidos,
los cuerpos virginales a la orilla vieja.

                                    *Lora del Río, 4 abril 1913.*

## 31 *A José María Palacio*

   Palacio, buen amigo,
¿está la primavera
vistiendo ya las ramas de los chopos
del río y los caminos? En la estepa
del alto Duero, Primavera tarda,
¡pero es tan bella y dulce cuando llega! . . .
¿Tienen los viejos olmos
algunas hojas nuevas?
Aún las acacias estarán desnudas
y nevados los montes de las sierras.                   10
¡Oh, mole del Moncayo blanca y rosa,
allá, en el cielo de Aragón, tan bella!
¿Hay zarzas florecidas
entre las grises peñas,
y blancas margaritas
entre la fina hierba?

a shady garden where the dusty limbs
of a lemon tree                                              20
hold out pale yellow lemons
to the clear mirror of the fountain,
scents of clove pink and of spikenard,
the pungent smell of basil and of mint;
images of misty olive groves
beneath a torrid sun that blinds and stuns,
blue mountain ranges spread out under skies
flushed and vast with evening;
but the thread that binds the memory to the heart
is missing, the anchor on its brink,                        30
or else these memories are soulless things.
In their motley dress they have the air
of remnants of remembrance, castoff things
that memory drags along.
One day, fresh risen out of depths of light,
the pristine shapes will find their ancient shore.

*Lora del Río, 4 April 1913.*


## 31 *To José María Palacio*

Palacio, good friend,
are there signs of spring
in the poplars by the river
and on the roadsides? Spring is late
in the high Duero country,
but so soft and lovely when it comes!
Are a few new leaves appearing
on the old elms?
The acacias must be bare still,
the sierra peaks still snowy.                                10
Oh, the massed beauty of Moncayo rising
pink and white in the sky of Aragon!
Are there brambles blooming
among the gray rocks,
white daisies showing
in the new tufts of grass?

Por esos campanarios
ya habrán ido llegando las cigüeñas.
Habrá trigales verdes,
y mulas pardas en las sementeras,  20
y labriegos que siembran los tardíos
con las lluvias de abril. Ya las abejas
libarán del tomillo y el romero.
¿Hay ciruelos en flor? ¿Quedan violetas?
Furtivos cazadores, los reclamos
de la perdiz bajo las capas luengas,
no faltarán. Palacio, buen amigo,
¿tienen ya ruiseñores las riberas?
Con los primeros lirios
y las primeras rosas de las huertas,  30
en una tarde azul, sube al Espino,
al alto Espino donde está su tierra . . .

       *Baeza, 29 de abril 1913.*


# 32 *Poema de un día*

Meditaciones rurales

 Heme aquí ya, profesor
de lenguas vivas (ayer
maestro de gay-saber,
aprendiz de ruiseñor)
en un pueblo húmedo y frío,
destartalado y sombrío,
entre andaluz y manchego.
Invierno. Cerca del fuego.
Fuera llueve un agua fina,
que ora se trueca en neblina,  10
ora se torna aguanieve.
Fantástico labrador,
pienso en los campos. ¡Señor,
qué bien haces! Llueve, llueve
tu agua constante y menuda
sobre alcaceles y habares,

Storks will be turning up now
on all the belfries.
The wheat must be showing green,
the brown mules working in the planted fields,                    20
the country people sowing their late wheat
with the April rains. There'll be bees now
visiting the rosemary and thyme.
Are the plum trees out? Are there violets still?
Stealthy hunters must be about,
sheltering tame partridges in their capes
to lure the wild ones. Palacio, good friend,
are there nightingales on the riverbanks?
When the first lilies open,
and the first garden roses,                                       30
some blue afternoon mount Hawthorn Hill,
high Hawthorn Hill where her plot is . . .

*Baeza, 29 April 1913.*


## 32 *One Day's Poem*

Rural Reflections

    So here I am,
a modern language teacher
(lately master in *gai-saber*,
apprentice to a nightingale)
in a cold, damp town,
sprawling and somber,
part Andalusian, part in La Mancha.
Winter. A fire going.
Outside drizzle falling,
thinning sometimes into mist,                                     10
sometimes turning to sleet.
Picturing myself a farmer,
I think of the planted fields.
Lord, how right of you
to keep your steady sprinkle falling
on crops of bean and barley,

tu agua muda,
en viñedos y olivares.
Te bendecirán conmigo
los sembradores del trigo;                          20
los que viven de coger
la aceituna;
los que esperan la fortuna
de comer;
los que hogaño,
como antaño,
tienen toda su moneda
en la rueda,
traidora rueda del año.
¡Llueve, llueve; tu neblina                         30
que se torne en aguanieve,
y otra vez en agua fina!
¡Llueve, Señor, llueve, llueve!
En mi estancia, iluminada
por esta luz invernal,
—la tarde gris tamizada
por la lluvia y el cristal—,
sueño y medito.
                    Clarea
el reloj arrinconado,
y su tic-tac, olvidado                              40
por repetido, golpea.
Tic-tic, tic-tic . . . Ya te he oído.
Tic-tic, tic-tic . . . Siempre igual,
monótono y aburrido.
Tic-tic, tic-tic, el latido
de un corazón de metal.
En estos pueblos, ¿se escucha
el latir del tiempo? No.
En estos pueblos se lucha
sin tregua con el reló,                             50
con esa monotonía,
que mide un tiempo vacío.
Pero ¿tu hora es la mía?
¿Tu tiempo, reloj, el mío?
(Tic-tic, tic-tic) . . . Era un día
(tic-tic, tic-tic) que pasó,

dropping soundlessly
on olive groves and vineyards.
Many of us will bless you—
those with wheat fresh sown,                    20
those whose livelihood
is olive-picking,
whose one hope in life
is food enough;
those who now, as always,
stake a claim
in fortune's name
on her wheel,
her treacherous year-round wheel.
Keep on raining, let your mist           30
turn to sleet
and back to drizzle.
Keep it falling, falling, Lord.
   In my room, suffused
with this winter light—
gray afternoon that seeps
through rain and window glass—
I meditate and dream.
                  The clock
gleams in its corner,
ticking steadily away,                  40
on and on, till one forgets it.
Tick, tock, tick, tock . . . Yes, I hear you.
Tick, tock, tick, tock . . . Always just the same,
boring and monotonous.
Tick, tock, tick, tock, pulsings
of a metal heart.
Does one hear the pulse of time
in these towns? One does not.
In these towns one's always locked
in a struggle with the clock,           50
with monotony
that measures time as emptiness.
But do you tell my time?
Clock, is your time mine?
(Tick, tock, tick, tock) . . . On a day
(tick, tock, tick, tock) that now is past

y lo que yo más quería
la muerte se lo llevó.
  Lejos suena un clamoreo
de campanas . . .                                            60
Arrecia el repiqueteo
de la lluvia en las ventanas.
Fantástico labrador,
vuelvo a mis campos. ¡Señor,
cuánto te bendecirán
los sembradores del pan!
Señor, ¿no es tu lluvia ley,
en los campos que ara el buey,
y en los palacios del rey?
¡Oh, agua buena, deja vida                                   70
en tu huida!
¡Oh, tú, que vas gota a gota,
fuente a fuente y río a río,
como este tiempo de hastío
corriendo a la mar remota,
con cuanto quiere nacer,
cuanto espera
florecer
al sol de la primavera,
sé piadosa,                                                  80
que mañana
serás espiga temprana,
prado verde, carne rosa,
y más: razón y locura
y amargura
de querer y no poder
creer, creer y creer!
  Anochece;
el hilo de la bombilla
se enrojece,                                                 90
luego brilla,
resplandece,
poco más que una cerilla.
Dios sabe dónde andarán
mis gafas . . . entre librotes,
revistas y papelotes,
¿quién las encuentra? . . . Aquí están.

death took away
the dearest thing I had.
Some bells in the distance
set up a clamor.                                    60
The rain drums harder
on the windowpanes.
Picturing myself a farmer,
I go back to my fields.
How those who sow the wheat
will bless you, Lord!
Is your rain not supreme
in land that oxen plow
and in the halls of kings?
Rainwater, working good,                            70
spreading life as you go,
flow onward, drop by drop,
flow downstream, flow downriver—
like this depressing weather—
on to the far-off sea,
and as you go be kind
to all that seeks a start
in life, that looks ahead
to bloom and blossom
and a warm spring sun,                              80
remember that tomorrow
you'll be ears of early grain,
rosy flesh, green of meadow—
and that's not all: reason, madness,
and the bitter taste
of wanting and of failing
to believe, believe, believe!
    It grows dark.
In the light bulb
the filament shows red,                             90
brightens up,
starts to glow
scarcely brighter than a match.
The Lord knows where my glasses
can have gone . . . In this welter
of books, reviews, old papers,
who'd ever find them? . . . Here they are.

Libros nuevos. Abro uno
de Unamuno.
¡Oh, el dilecto,                                              100
predilecto
de esta España que se agita,
porque nace o resucita!
Siempre te ha sido, ¡oh Rector
de Salamanca!, leal
este humilde profesor
de un instituto rural.
Esa tu filosofía
que llamas diletantesca,
voltaria y funambulesca,                                      110
gran Don Miguel, es la mía.
Agua del buen manantial,
siempre viva,
fugitiva;
poesía, cosa cordial.
¿Constructora?
—No hay cimiento
ni en el alma ni el viento—.
Bogadora,
marinera,                                                    120
hacia la mar sin ribera.
Enrique Bergson: *Los datos*
*inmediatos*
*de la conciencia.* ¿Esto es
otro embeleco francés?
Este Bergson es un tuno;
¿verdad, maestro Unamuno?
Bergson no da como aquel
Immanuel
el volatín inmortal;                                         130
este endiablado judío
ha hallado el libre albedrío
dentro de su mechinal.
No está mal:
cada sabio, su problema,
y cada loco, su tema.
Algo importa
que en la vida mala y corta
que llevamos
libres o siervos seamos;                                     140

New books. I open one
by Unamuno—
the light                                          100
and the delight
of this Spain now astir,
being born or reborn.
This modest teacher
in a country school
has always kept your faith,
Chancellor of Salamanca.
That philosophy of yours
which you call dilettantish,
inconstant, walking tightropes,                    110
is mine as well, Don Miguel.
Water from true springs
welling clear,
flowing on;
poetry, sprung from the heart.
Something to build on?
There is no solid ground
in the spirit or the wind.
Only oar and sail
drifting on,                                        120
down to the shoreless sea.
Henri Bergson: *The Immediate*
*Data of Consciousness.* Could this be
another of those French snares?
This Bergson is a rascal,
wouldn't you say, Master Unamuno?
He can't perform
like that Immanuel,
the immortal handspring on the tightrope.
This devilish Jew has found                         130
the freedom of the will
inside his own four walls.
Not bad at all:
each thinker with his pet idea,
each madman pumping his.
In this life of ours,
troublesome and short,

mas, si vamos
a la mar,
lo mismo nos han de dar.
¡Oh, estos pueblos! Reflexiones,
lecturas y acotaciones
pronto dan en lo que son:
bostezos de Salomón.
¿Todo es
soledad de soledades,
vanidad de vanidades,                              150
que dijo el Eclesiastés?
Mi paraguas, mi sombrero,
mi gabán . . .  El aguacero
amaina . . .  Vámonos, pues.
  Es de noche. Se platica
al fondo de una botica.
—Yo no sé,
Don José,
cómo son los liberales
tan perros, tan inmorales.                         160
—¡Oh, tranquilícese usté!
Pasados los carnavales,
vendrán los conservadores,
buenos administradores
de su casa.
Todo llega y todo pasa.
Nada eterno:
ni gobierno
que perdure,
ni mal que cien años dure.                         170
—Tras estos tiempos, vendrán
otros tiempos y otros y otros,
y lo mismo que nosotros
otros se jorobarán.
Así es la vida, Don Juan.
—Es verdad, así es la vida.
—La cebada está crecida.
—Con estas lluvias . . .
                        Y van
las habas que es un primor.

it matters some
whether we're slave or free.
Yet if we're bound for the sea,                    140
it's no different in the end.
Oh these country towns! Reflections,
readings, jottings
soon show up for what they are:
yawns of Solomon.
Will everything
be solitude of solitudes,
vanity of vanities,
as Ecclesiastes claims?
Here—my hat, umbrella,                              150
overcoat . . . The shower
is letting up . . . Let's be off.
    It's night. People talking
at the back of a drugstore.
"I just don't know,
Don José,
what makes the liberals that way—
so beastly and immoral."
"Oh, never fear,
when the carnival is over,                          160
the conservatives will be here.
They'll know how to keep
the house in order.
Just wait long enough.
Nothing's eternal—
no government
goes on and on,
no trouble lasts forever."
"When these times are over,
there'll be others still, and others,              170
and exactly like ourselves,
others will fume and sputter.
That's how it goes, Don Juan."
"Quite right. That's how it goes."
"The barley's getting tall."
"With all this rain . . ."
                          "And the beans—
lovely the way they're growing."

—Cierto; para marzo, en flor.                              180
Pero la escarcha, los hielos . . .
—Y además, los olivares
están pidiendo a los cielos
agua a torrentes.
        —A mares.
¡Las fatigas, los sudores
que pasan los labradores!
En otro tiempo . . .
        —Llovía
también cuando Dios quería.
—Hasta mañana, señores.
    Tic-tic, tic-tic . . .  Ya pasó           190
un día como otro día,
dice la monotonía
del reló.
  Sobre mi mesa *Los datos*
*de la conciencia,* inmediatos.
No está mal
este yo fundamental,
contingente y libre, a ratos,
creativo, original;
este yo que vive y siente                                  200
dentro la carne mortal
¡ay! por saltar impaciente
las bardas de su corral.

              *Baeza, 1913.*


## 33  *Los olivos*

I

  ¡Viejos olivos sedientos
bajo el claro sol del día,
olivares polvorientos
del campo de Andalucía!
¡El campo andaluz, peinado

"True. By March they'll be in bloom,
barring rime and frosts . . ."
"And besides, the olive groves                                                   180
are begging heaven for a soaking."
                              "For a deluge.
What farmers have to go through—
all the toil and sweat!
In the old days . . ."
                    "It rained
in its own good time, just as now."
"See you tomorrow, gentlemen."
    Tick, tock, tick, tock. Another day
gone by, like all the rest:
so speaks monotony
out of the clock.                                                                190
    On my desk *The Immediate
Data of Consciousness.*
Pretty good
this basic self,
sometimes dependent, sometimes free,
original, creative,
this self alive and feeling
inside the mortal flesh
and so anxious to escape
the confines of its pen!                                                         200

                         *Baeza, 1913.*

## 33 *The Olive Trees*

                    I

    Parched old olive trees
standing full in the sun,
powdery with dust
from the Andalusian earth.
Land of Andalusia combed
by hot midsummer suns,

por el sol canicular,
de loma en loma rayado
de olivar y de olivar!
Son las tierras
soleadas,                                           10
anchas lomas, lueñes sierras
de olivares recamadas!
Mil senderos. Con sus machos,
abrumados de capachos,
van gañanes y arrieros.
De la venta del camino
a la puerta, soplan vino
trabucaires bandoleros!
Olivares y olivares
de loma en loma prendidos                           20
cual bordados alamares!
Olivares coloridos
de una tarde anaranjada;
olivares rebruñidos
bajo la luna argentada!
Olivares centellados
en las tardes cenicientas,
bajo los cielos preñados
de tormentas! . . .
Olivares, Dios os dé                                30
los eneros
de aguaceros,
los agostos de agua al pie,
los vientos primaverales
vuestras flores racimadas;
y las lluvias otoñales,
vuestras olivas moradas.
Olivar, por cien caminos,
tus olivitas irán
caminando a cien molinos.                           40
Ya darán
trabajo en las alquerías
a gañanes y braceros,
¡oh buenas frentes sombrías
bajo los anchos sombreros! . . .

ruled into lines of olives
stretching from hill to hill.
They bask in the sun,
these lands,                                            10
broad hills and far-off ranges
fretted with olive groves.
A thousand trails. The farmhands
and teamsters drive their mules
under bulging baskets.
Before the roadside inns
knots of bandits cluster,
downing their wine and swaggering.
And still the groves of olives
lie draped across the land                              20
and looped about the hills!
Groves tinted orange
in the evening light.
Groves glinting silver
when the moon is bright.
Groves striking sparks
on ashen afternoons
when lowering skies rumble
with thunderstorms . . .
Olive groves,                                           30
may God bestow
January showers
to make you grow
and in August groundwater below;
winds in spring
for your clustered bloom
and autumn rains
for your purple fruit.
Olive groves,
your fruit will move                                    40
down a hundred roads
to a hundred mills,
bringing chores to do
on every farm
to workers and hands—
oh, good faces shadowed
by spreading hats.

¡Olivar y olivareros,
bosque y raza,
campo y plaza
de los fieles al terruño
y al arado y al molino,                                    50
de los que muestran el puño
al destino,
los benditos labradores,
los bandidos caballeros,
los señores
devotos y matuteros! . . .
Ciudades y caseríos
en la margen de los ríos,
en los pliegues de la sierra! . . .
Venga Dios a los hogares                                   60
y a las almas de esta tierra
de olivares y olivares!

II

A dos leguas de Ubeda, la Torre
de Pero Gil, bajo este sol de fuego,
triste burgo de España. El coche rueda
entre grises olivos polvorientos.
Allá, el castillo heroico.
En la plaza, mendigos y chicuelos:
una orgía de harapos . . .
Pasamos frente al atrio del convento                       70
de la Misericordia.
¡Los blancos muros, los cipreses negros!
¡Agria melancolía
como asperón de hierro
que raspa el corazón! ¡Amurallada
piedad, erguida en este basurero! . . .
Esta casa de Dios, decid, hermanos,
esta casa de Dios, ¿qué guarda dentro?
Y ese pálido joven,
asombrado y atento,                                        80
que parece mirarnos con la boca,
será el loco del pueblo,
de quien se dice: es Lucas,
Blas o Ginés, el tonto que tenemos.

Olive groves and olive workers,
trees and race,
country and town,                                              50
of those true to the soil,
to oil mill and plow,
holding fists clenched tight
in the teeth of fate,
trusty peasants,
lordly bandits,
God-fearing squires
with a taste for smuggling . . .
Cities and hamlets
on the banks of rivers,                                        60
in the folds of hills . . .
God bless the homes,
God bless the souls
of this land of olive groves!


                   II

   Two leagues from Ubeda
in this blazing sun, Pero Gil's Tower
(name of a dismal Spanish town). The coach
jogs on past olives gray and dusty.
Over there, the staunch old castle.
Beggars and urchins in the square,                             70
a swarm of rags and tatters.
On we go past the portal
of Mercy Convent.
White walls, dark cypress trees,
melancholy that smarts
like an iron grindstone
rasping the heart. Piety walled up
to tower over this refuse heap.
Now brothers, this house of God, you tell me:
what does this house of God contain?                           80
And that pale youth
watching us astonished,
taking us in with his mouth, you'd say,
he'll be the local idiot,
of whom they simply say: that's Luke,
Blas or Ginés—town fool, you know.

Seguimos. Olivares. Los olivos
están en flor. El carricoche lento,
al paso de dos pencos matalones,
camina hacia Peal. Campos ubérrimos.
La tierra da lo suyo; el sol trabaja;
el hombre es para el suelo:                              90
genera, siembra y labra
y su fatiga unce la tierra al cielo.
Nosotros enturbiamos
la fuente de la vida, el sol primero,
con nuestros ojos tristes,
con nuestro amargo rezo,
con nuestra mano ociosa,
con nuestro pensamiento,
—se engendra en el pecado,
se vive en el dolor. ¡Dios está lejos!—                 100
Esta piedad erguida
sobre este burgo sórdido, sobre este basurero,
esta casa de Dios, decid ¡oh santos
cañones de von Kluck! ¿qué guarda dentro?


# 34 *Proverbios y cantares*

### I

¿Para qué llamar caminos
a los surcos del azar? . . .
Todo el que camina anda,
como Jesús, sobre el mar.

### II

Cantad conmigo en coro: Saber, nada sabemos,
de arcano mar vinimos, a ignota mar iremos . . .
Y entre los dos misterios está el enigma grave;
tres arcas cierra una desconocida llave.
La luz nada ilumina y el sabio nada enseña.
¿Qué dice la palabra? ¿Qué el agua de la peña?

On we go. Olive groves. The trees
are flowering. Our two beasts,
rundown, scraggly, slowly pull us
toward Peal. So rich this countryside.                    90
Earth does its share; the sun toils too.
The land is where man belongs:
he procreates, he sows, he tills,
and by his toil yokes earth to heaven.
We cloud the springs of life,
the pristine sun,
with our unhappy eyes,
our bitter prayers,
our idle hands,
our thinking.                                            100
In sin we are conceived,
in pain we live. God stays away!
This piety that towers
over this sordid village, over this refuse heap,
this house of God—you tell us, blessed
cannons of Von Kluck: What does it contain?

## 34 *Proverbs and Song-Verse*

### I

Why give the name of roads
to the furrows of chance? . . .
Anyone journeying walks
like Jesus on the sea.

### II

Sing along with me: what we know is nothing;
we've come from an arcane sea, to an unknown sea we're
        bound . . .
And these two mysteries hold a deep enigma between,
three chests locked with an unknown key.
Light illumines nothing, the wise have nothing to teach.
What has the word to say? Or the water in the rocks?

III

¡Teresa, alma de fuego,
Juan de la Cruz, espíritu de llama,
por aquí hay mucho frío, padres, nuestros
corazoncitos de Jesús se apagan!

IV

Ayer soñé que veía
a Dios y que a Dios hablaba;
y soñé que Dios me oía . . .
Después soñé que soñaba.

V

Todo hombre tiene dos
batallas que pelear:
en sueños lucha con Dios;
y despierto, con el mar.

VI

Caminante, son tus huellas
el camino, y nada más;
caminante, no hay camino,
se hace camino al andar.
Al andar se hace camino,
y al volver la vista atrás
se ve la senda que nunca
se ha de volver a pisar.
Caminante, no hay camino,
sino estelas en la mar.                          10

VII

¡Oh fe del meditabundo!
¡Oh fe después del pensar!
Sólo si viene un corazón al mundo
rebosa el vaso humano y se hincha el mar.

VIII

Hay dos modos de conciencia:
una es luz, y otra, paciencia.
Una estriba en alumbrar
un poquito el hondo mar;

III

Teresa, fiery soul!
John of the Cross, flaming spirit!
It's very cold hereabouts, good saints;
our sacred little hearts of Jesus need lighting.

IV

Last night I dreamed I saw
God, and was talking to God;
and I dreamed that God was listening . . .
And then I dreamed I was dreaming.

V

Every man has two
battles to wage:
in dreams he wrestles with God;
awake, with the sea.

VI

Wayfarer, the only way
is your footsteps, there is no other.
Wayfarer, there is no way,
you make the way as you go.
As you go, you make the way
and stopping to look behind,
you see the path that your feet
will never travel again.
Wayfarer, there is no way—
only foam trails in the sea.                                    10

VII

Oh, faith born of meditation!
Oh, faith succeeding thought!
If one heart comes into the world,
man's glass brims over and swells the sea.

VIII

Two forms consciousness takes:
one is light, the other is patience.
One means shining a beam
a certain way down in the sea;

otra, en hacer penitencia
con caña o red, y esperar
el pez, como pescador.
Dime tú: ¿Cuál es mejor?
¿Conciencia de visionario
que mira en el hondo acuario      10
peces vivos,
fugitivos,
que no se pueden pescar,
o esa maldita faena
de ir arrojando a la arena,
muertos, los peces del mar?

### IX

Todo pasa y todo queda,
pero lo nuestro es pasar,
pasar haciendo caminos,
caminos sobre la mar.

### X

Ya hay un español que quiere
vivir y a vivir empieza,
entre una España que muere
y otra España que bosteza.
Españolito que vienes
al mundo, te guarde Dios.
Una de las dos Españas
ha de helarte el corazón.

## 35 *Parábolas*

### I

Era un niño que soñaba
un caballo de cartón.
Abrió los ojos el niño
y el caballito no vio.
Con un caballito blanco
el niño volvió a soñar;
y por la crin lo cogía . . .

the other is holding out
with a pole or a line in the hope
of a fish, as fishermen do.
Tell me now: which one is better?
The consciousness of the seer,
watching in the aquarian deep                          10
live fish flashing by,
fish he can never haul out,
or this accursed chore
of throwing up on the sand,
dead, the fish of the sea?

IX

All passes and all remains;
but our lot is to pass,
to pass making roads,
making roads in the sea.

X

Think of it: a Spaniard
wanting to live, starting in
with a Spain on one side of him dying
and a Spain all yawns on the other.
Young Spaniard entering the world,
may God preserve you.
One of these two Spains
will make your blood run cold.

## 35 *Parables*

I

There was a child who dreamed
of a little cardboard horse.
When he opened up his eyes,
the horse was not to be seen.
The child had another dream,
of a little white horse this time.
He grabbed it by the mane . . .

¡Ahora no te escaparás!
Apenas lo hubo cogido,
el niño se despertó.                                    10
Tenía el puño cerrado.
¡El caballito voló!
Quedóse el niño muy serio
pensando que no es verdad
un caballito soñado.
Y ya no volvió a soñar.
Pero el niño se hizo mozo
y el mozo tuvo un amor,
y a su amada le decía:
¿Tú eres de verdad o no?                               20
Cuando el mozo se hizo viejo
pensaba: todo es soñar,
el caballito soñado
y el caballo de verdad.
Y cuando vino la muerte,
el viejo a su corazón
preguntaba: ¿Tú eres sueño?
¡Quién sabe si despertó!

## II

*A D. Vicente Ciurana.*

Sobre la limpia arena, en el tartesio llano
por donde acaba España y sigue el mar,
hay dos hombres que apoyan la cabeza en la mano;
uno duerme, y el otro parece meditar.
El uno, en la mañana de tibia primavera,
junto a la mar tranquila,
ha puesto entre sus ojos y el mar que reverbera,
los párpados, que borran el mar en la pupila.
Y se ha dormido, y sueña con el pastor Proteo,
que sabe los rebaños del marino guardar;              10
y sueña que le llaman las hijas de Nereo,
y ha oído a los caballos de Poseidón hablar.
El otro mira al agua. Su pensamiento flota;
hijo del mar, navega—o se pone a volar.
Su pensamiento tiene un vuelo de gaviota,
que ha visto un pez de plata en el agua saltar.

Now you won't get away!
No sooner was it caught
than the child woke up again.                                    10
His fist was clenched tight shut
but the horse had disappeared!
This was no laughing matter:
he thought there is no truth
in a horse you only dream of—
and he never dreamed again.
But the child became a youth
and the youth soon fell in love.
He used to ask his sweetheart:
Are you really so or not?                                        20
And when the youth grew old,
he thought: it's all a dream—
the little horse you dream of
and the horse that's really there.
And when it came time to die
the old man spoke to his heart:
Are you a dream? he asked.
Perhaps he woke up—who knows!

                    II
*To Don Vicente Ciurana.*
    On the plain of Tarshish, the clean white sand
where Spain comes to an end and the sea goes on,
two men are sitting, head resting in hand;
one is asleep, the other lost in thought.
Beside the quiet sea in the mild spring morning
the first has let his eyelids fall
between the water's glitter and his eyes,
shutting from sight the sparkling sea.
Falling asleep, he dreams of an ocean herdsman,
of Proteus, keeper of the sea-god's flocks.                      10
He dreams he hears the Nereids' voices calling
and knows the words Poseidon's horses speak.
The other watches the water, his thoughts adrift.
Born of the sea they sail or soar aloft.
They plummet like the plunging gull
that sees a fish's silver flash below.

Y piensa: "Es esta vida una ilusión marina
de un pescador que un día ya no puede pescar."
El soñador ha visto que el mar se le ilumina,
y sueña que es la muerte una ilusión del mar.                20

### III

Erase de un marinero
que hizo un jardín junto al mar,
y se metió a jardinero.
Estaba el jardín en flor,
y el jardinero se fue
por esos mares de Dios.

### IV   *Consejos*

Sabe esperar, aguarda que la marea fluya,
—así en la costa un barco— sin que el partir te inquiete.
Todo el que aguarda sabe que la victoria es suya;
porque la vida es larga y el arte es un juguete.
Y si la vida es corta
y no llega la mar a tu galera,
aguarda sin partir y siempre espera,
que el arte es largo y, además, no importa.

### V   *Profesión de fe*

Dios no es el mar, está en el mar; riela
como luna en el agua, o aparece
como una blanca vela;
en el mar se despierta o se adormece.
Creó la mar, y nace
de la mar cual la nube y la tormenta;
es el Criador y la criatura lo hace;
su aliento es alma, y por el alma alienta.
Yo he de hacerte, mi Dios, cual tú me hiciste,
y para darte el alma que me diste                10
en mí te he de crear. Que el puro río
de caridad que fluye eternamente,
fluya en mi corazón. ¡Seca, Dios mío,
de una fe sin amor la turbia fuente!

Life, he thinks, is no more real than the ocean
to a fisherman when his fishing days are done.
But the dreamer sees a brightness sweep the ocean
and dreams that death is no more real than the sea.          20


                    III

Once there was a sailor
made a garden by the sea
and went in for gardening.
The garden was blooming away,
and off the gardener went
sailing God's ocean blue.


        IV   *Advice*

Be content to wait, watch for the turning tide
as a beached boat waits, in no rush to float away.
Whoever waits can be sure he'll win in the end
since life is long and art only a toy.
And if life is short
and the sea never reaches your skiff,
still wait and don't depart, go right on hoping,
for art is long, and besides it doesn't matter.


        V   *Profession of Faith*

God is not the sea. He is of the sea,
he glitters like moon on water, or comes in sight
like a white sail appearing;
the sea is where he wakes up and falls asleep.
He created the sea and is born of the sea,
like clouds and storms:
the Creator he, and his creature makes him;
his breath is spirit and by the spirit he breathes.
You will I make, my God, as you made me,
and that I may give you the soul you've given me,          10
I will create you within me. May the pure stream
of loving-kindness that flows forever
flow in my heart. Oh, Lord, seal up
the clouded springs of unloving faith.

VI

El Dios que todos llevamos,
el Dios que todos hacemos,
el Dios que todos buscamos
y que nunca encontraremos.
Tres dioses o tres personas
del solo Dios verdadero.

VII

Dice la razón: Busquemos
la verdad.
Y el corazón: Vanidad.
La verdad ya la tenemos.
La razón: ¡Ay, quién alcanza
la verdad!
El corazón: Vanidad.
La verdad es la esperanza.
Dice la razón: Tú mientes.
Y contesta el corazón:                    10
Quien miente eres tú, razón,
que dices lo que no sientes.
La razón: Jamás podremos
entendernos, corazón.
El corazón: Lo veremos.

VIII

Cabeza meditadora,
¡qué lejos se oye el zumbido
de la abeja libadora!
Echaste un velo de sombra
sobre el bello mundo, y vas
creyendo ver, porque mides
la sombra con un compás.
Mientras la abeja fabrica,
melifica,
con jugo de campo y sol,                  10
yo voy echando verdades
que nada son, vanidades
al fondo de mi crisol.
De la mar al percepto,

VI

The God we all carry within,
the God we all make,
the God we all seek
and can never hope to find.
Three Gods or just three persons
of the one and only God.

VII

Reason says:
Let's seek the truth.
The heart replies: What's the use?
We already have the truth.
Reason: Ah, to have truth
in one's grasp!
The heart: What's the use?
Truth is in hoping.
Says reason: You lie.
Comes the heart's reply:                                    10
It's you that are lying, reason,
saying things you don't believe.
Reason: Between you and me
there can be no understanding, heart.
The heart: As to that, we'll see.

VIII

Head lost in thought,
you hear so very far off
the hum of the sipping bee!
You've drawn a veil of shadow
over the lovely world. About you go,
supposing you see, when all you do
is stake out shadows with a compass.
While the bee does his distilling,
making honey
from the sap of sun and fields,                             10
I go on dropping truths
with nothing to them, futile things,
into my melting pot.
From the sea to the percept,

del percepto al concepto,
del concepto a la idea
—¡oh, la linda tarea!—,
de la idea a la mar.
¡Y otra vez a empezar!

## 36   *A don Francisco Giner de los Ríos*

Como se fue el maestro,
la luz de esta mañana
me dijo: Van tres días
que mi hermano Francisco no trabaja.
¿Murió? ... Sólo sabemos
que se nos fue por una senda clara,
diciéndonos: Hacedme
un duelo de labores y esperanzas.
Sed buenos y no más, sed lo que he sido
entre vosotros: alma.                                    10
Vivid, la vida sigue,
los muertos mueren y las sombras pasan;
lleva quien deja y vive el que ha vivido.
¡Yunques, sonad; enmudeced, campanas!
   Y hacia otra luz más pura
partió el hermano de la luz del alba,
del sol de los talleres,
el viejo alegre de la vida santa.
... Oh, sí, llevad, amigos,
su cuerpo a la montaña,                                  20
a los azules montes
del ancho Guadarrama.
Allí hay barrancos hondos
de pinos verdes donde el viento canta.
Su corazón repose
bajo una encina casta,
en tierra de tomillos, donde juegan
mariposas doradas ...
Allí el maestro un día
soñaba un nuevo florecer de España.                      30

*Baeza, 21 febrero 1915.*

from the percept to the concept,
from the concept to the idea—
what a delightful game!—
from the idea to the sea.
And off we go again!


## 36   To Don Francisco Giner de los Ríos

    As the master had gone away,
this morning's light said this to me:
It's now three days
that my brother Francis hasn't come to work.
Has he died? We can only say
that the path he left us by was bright
and he told us: Mourn me
with your efforts, with your hopes.
Try simply to be good, to be
what I have been among you: spirit.          10
Live, life doesn't stop,
the dead will die, the shadows pass;
a man takes what he leaves,
and one who has lived, lives on.
Anvils, resound; cease tolling, bells!
    And toward another, purer light
he went, this brother of the dawn,
of sunlight in the workshops,
this man of joy and holy ways.
. . . Oh yes, friends, bear his body off     20
to the mountain country, the blue mountains
of the broad Guadarrama.
Deep ravines are there, where the wind
sings through green pines.
Let his heart be at rest there
in an oak's pure shade,
where the wild thyme draws
the flitting yellow butterflies . . .
Up there the master dreamed one day
that Spain would flower again.          30

*Baeza, 21 February 1915.*

## 37 *Apuntes*

### I

Desde mi ventana,
¡campo de Baeza,
a la luna clara!
¡Montes de Cazorla,
Aznaitín y Mágina!
¡De luna y de piedra
también los cachorros
de Sierra Morena!

### II

Sobre el olivar,
se vio a la lechuza                                    10
volar y volar.
    Campo, campo, campo.
Entre los olivos,
los cortijos blancos.
    Y la encina negra,
a medio camino
de Ubeda a Baeza.

### III

Por un ventanal
entró la lechuza
en la catedral.                                         20
    San Cristobalón
la quiso espantar,
al ver que bebía
del velón de aceite
de Santa María.
    La Virgen habló:
Déjala que beba,
San Cristobalón.

### IV

Sobre el olivar,
se vio a la lechuza                                    30
volar y volar.

# 37 Jottings

### I

Outside my window
the Baeza country
bright in the moon.
Mountains of Cazorla,
Aznaitín and Mágina!
Even the cub hills
of Sierra Morena
all moon and stone!

### II

Over the olive grove
the owl could be seen                    10
flying and flying.
Country, open country.
Among the olives,
the whitewashed farms.
The black oak, too,
halfway down the road
from Ubeda to Baeza.

### III

Through a tall window
the owl found a way
into the cathedral.                      20
Big old St. Chris,
seeing it at the lamp—
the Blessed Virgin's lamp—
drinking up the oil,
tried to scare it off.
Up spoke the Virgin:
Now just let it drink,
Christopher, old thing.

### IV

Over the olive grove
the owl could be seen                    30
flying and flying.

A Santa María
un ramito verde
volando traía.
¡Campo de Baeza,
soñaré contigo
cuando no te vea!

V

Dondequiera vaya,
José de Mairena
lleva su guitarra.                                    40
  Su guitarra lleva,
cuando va a caballo,
a la bandolera.
  Y lleva el caballo
con la rienda corta,
la cerviz en alto.

VI

¡Pardos borriquillos
de ramón cargados,
entre los olivos!

VII

¡Tus sendas de cabras                                 50
y tus madroñeras,
Córdoba serrana!

VIII

¡La del Romancero,
Córdoba la llana! . . .
Guadalquivir hace vega,
el campo relincha y brama.

IX

Los olivos grises,
los caminos blancos.
El sol ha sorbido
la color del campo;                                   60

In its beak it brought
a sprig of green
for Holy Mary.
Country round Baeza,
I'll be dreaming of you
when I cannot see you!

V

Wherever he goes
José de Mairena
takes his guitar.                              40
His guitar goes with him,
slung from his shoulder
as he rides along.
His horse he keeps
tightly reined in,
neck held high.

VI

Little earth-brown burros
carrying loads of brush
among the olive trees!

VII

Your goat-worn paths,                          50
your groves of madrone trees,
Cordova uplands!

VIII

Cordova of the ballads
down on the valley floor . . .
Guadalquivir forms a plain,
the land neighs and bellows.

IX

Olive trees gray,
white of the roads.
The sun has drawn
all color from the land.                        60

y hasta tu recuerdo
me lo va secando
este alma de polvo
de los días malos.

## 38  *Galerías*

### I

En el azul la banda
de unos pájaros negros
que chillan, aletean y se posan
en el álamo yerto.
. . . En el desnudo álamo,
las graves chovas quietas y en silencio,
cual negras, frías notas
escritas en la pauta de febrero.

### II

El monte azul, el río, las erectas
varas cobrizas de los finos álamos,                    10
y el blanco del almendro en la colina,
¡oh nieve en flor y mariposa en árbol!
Con el aroma del habar, el viento
corre en la alegre soledad del campo.

### III

Una centella blanca
en la nube de plomo culebrea.
¡Los asombrados ojos
del niño, y juntas cejas
—está el salón obscuro— de la madre! . . .
¡Oh cerrado balcón a la tormenta!                      20
El viento aborrascado y el granizo
en el limpio cristal repiquetean.

### IV

El iris y el balcón.
                    Las siete cuerdas
de la lira del sol vibran en sueños.

Even your image
has begun to wither
in the dusty mood
of dispirited days.

## 38  *Passageways*

I

Against the blue, black string
of flying birds.
Shrieking and flapping wings,
they settle on the stiff poplar.
. . . On the naked poplar
the solemn choughs without a stir or sound,
like cold black notes
set down on February's staff.

II

Blue mountain, river, upward sweep
of coppery wands on slender poplars.                    10
White of almond trees on the hill—
oh, bloom of snow and butterfly of tree!
Spreading the fragrance of the bean field,
the wind roams gaily through the empty land.

III

A white flash
slithers through leaden clouds.
Astonished eyes of the child,
the mother's frowning look,
in the darkness of the room.
Balcony panes shut tight against the storm!          20
Gusts of wind and hailstones
clatter against the clean-washed glass.

IV

Rainbow and balcony.
                    The seven strings
of the sun's lyre pulsate across a dream.

Un tímpano infantil da siete golpes
—agua y cristal—.
            Acacias con jilgueros.
Cigüeñas en las torres.
                En la plaza,
lavó la lluvia el mirto polvoriento.
En el amplio rectángulo ¿quién puso
ese grupo de vírgenes risueño,                          30
y arriba ¡hosanna! entre la rota nube,
la palma de oro y el azul sereno?


                        V

Entre montes de almagre y peñas grises,
el tren devora su raíl de acero.
La hilera de brillantes ventanillas
lleva un doble perfil de camafeo,
tras el cristal de plata, repetido . . .
¿Quién ha punzado el corazón del tiempo?


                        VI

    ¿Quién puso, entre las rocas de ceniza,
para la miel del sueño,                                 40
esas retamas de oro
y esas azules flores del romero?
La sierra de violeta
y, en el poniente, el azafrán del cielo,
¿quién ha pintado? ¡El abejar, la ermita,
el tajo sobre el río, el sempiterno
rodar del agua entre las hondas peñas,
y el rubio verde de los campos nuevos,
y todo, hasta la tierra blanca y rosa
al pie de los almendros!                                50


                        VII

    En el silencio sigue
la lira pitagórica vibrando,
el iris en la luz, la luz que llena
mi estereoscopio vano.

Toy chimes strike seven times—
raindrops and windowpane.
                    Linnets in the acacias.
Storks on the belfries.
                In the square
the rain has washed the dusty myrtle clean.
Who placed that group of laughing girls
in the spacious quadrangle,                              30
and overhead, hosannah! in the breaking cloud,
the golden palm frond, the pure patch of blue?


                    V

    Past gray crags and red chalk mountains
the train advances, swallowing steel rail.
The row of shiny windows
carries a double imprint, cameolike,
seen through the silver pane, repeated.
Who has pierced the heart of time?


                    VI

    Who set that golden broom,
those blue rosemary blossoms,                            40
among the cindery rocks
to yield dream-honey?
Who painted the mountains lavender,
who thought of saffron for the sunset sky?
The hermitage, the hives,
the gash where the river runs
with ceaseless sound of water deep in rock,
the greenish-yellow of new fields,
and everything—the pink and white of the very ground
under the almond trees!                                  50


                    VII

    In the silence,
Pythagoras' lyre goes on vibrating,
the rainbow in the light,
the light that floods my empty stereoscope.

Han cegado mis ojos las cenizas
del fuego heraclitano.
El mundo es, un momento,
transparente, vacío, ciego, alalo.

## 39 *Canciones de tierras altas*

### I

Por la sierra blanca . . .
La nieve menuda
y el viento de cara.
Por entre los pinos . . .
con la blanca nieve
se borra el camino.
Recio viento sopla
de Urbión a Moncayo.
¡Páramos de Soria!

### II

Ya habrá cigüeñas al sol,                    10
mirando la tarde roja,
entre Moncayo y Urbión.

### III

Se abrió la puerta que tiene
gonces en mi corazón,
y otra vez la galería
de mi historia apareció.
Otra vez la plazoleta
de las acacias en flor,
y otra vez la fuente clara
cuenta un romance de amor.                    20

### IV

Es la parda encina
y el yermo de piedra.

My eyes are blinded by the ash
of Heraclitean fire.
Just now the world is
empty, transparent, voiceless, blind.

## 39  Highland Songs

### I

In the white hills . . .
Snow very fine
and wind in the face.
  Between the pines . . .
the road is blurred out
by white snow.
  A high gale is blowing
from Urbión to Moncayo.
Highlands of Soria!

### II

Storks will be out in the sun                    10
watching the evening redden
between Moncayo and Urbión.

### III

The hinged door in my heart
swung open. Once again
the view cleared down the passageway
of my past story.
  Once more the little square
with acacia trees in bloom,
the clear fountain again
singing ballads of love.                          20

### IV

The gray of oaks
and the stony barrens.

Cuando el sol tramonta,
el río despierta.
¡Oh montes lejanos
de malva y violeta!
En el aire en sombra
sólo el río suena.
¡Luna amoratada
de una tarde vieja,                                    30
en un campo frío,
más luna que tierra!

V

Soria de montes azules
y de yermos de violeta,
¡cuántas veces te he soñado
en esta florida vega
por donde se va,
entre naranjos de oro,
Guadalquivir a la mar!

VI

¡Cuántas veces me borraste,                            40
tierra de ceniza,
estos limonares verdes
con sombras de tus encinas!
¡Oh campos de Dios,
entre Urbión el de Castilla
y Moncayo el de Aragón!

VII

En Córdoba, la serrana,
en Sevilla, marinera
y labradora, que tiene
hinchada, hacia el mar, la vela;                       50
y en el ancho llano
por donde la arena sorbe
la baba del mar amargo,
hacia la fuente del Duero
mi corazón ¡Soria pura!

When the sun goes down
the river wakens.
  Oh, distant mountains
violet and mauve!
In the dark of the air
only the river is heard.
  Lavender moon
of an age-old evening,                                    30
in the cold country,
more moon than earth!

                    V

  Blue mountains of Soria,
lavender barrens—
in my dreams so often
on this flowering plain
where Guadalquivir's waters
flow past gold orange trees
on their way to the sea!

                    VI

  How often, ashy land,                                   40
have you blurred my view
of these green lemon groves
with your oak trees' shadows!
  Oh, uplands of God
between Urbión in Castile
and Moncayo in Aragon!

                    VII

  Upcountry in Cordova,
seaward in Seville—
market town straining sails
in the wind from the sea—                                 50
on the broad plain, too,
where the spongy sand
sucks the salt sea's dribble,
my heart kept returning
toward the Duero's source,

se tornaba . . . ¡Oh, fronteriza
entre la tierra y la luna!
  ¡Alta paramera
donde corre el Duero niño,
tierra donde está su tierra!                    60

### VIII

  El río despierta.
En el aire obscuro,
sólo el río suena.
  ¡Oh, canción amarga
del agua en la piedra!
. . . Hacia el alto Espino,
bajo las estrellas.
  Sólo suena el río
al fondo del valle,
bajo el alto Espino.                            70

### IX

  En medio del campo,
tiene la ventana abierta
la ermita sin ermitaño.
  Un tejadillo verdoso.
Cuatro muros blancos.
  Lejos relumbra la piedra
del áspero Guadarrama.
Agua que brilla y no suena.
  En el aire claro,
¡los alamillos del soto,                         80
sin hojas, liras de marzo!

### x    *Iris de la noche*

*A D. Ramón del Valle-Inclán.*
  Hacia Madrid, una noche,
va el tren por el Guadarrama.
En el cielo, el arco iris
que hacen la luna y el agua.
¡Oh luna de abril, serena,
que empuja las nubes blancas!

pure Soria . . . Oh, borderland
between earth and moon!
  High tablelands
where the infant Duero runs,
lands that enclose her earth!                    60

          VIII

  The river awakens.
In the dark of the air
only the river is heard.
  Oh, the bitter song
of water over rocks.
  . . . By Hawthorn Hill,
in starlight.
  Only the river is heard
deep in the valley
under Hawthorn Hill.                             70

          IX

  Out on the land,
the hermitless hermitage
has its window open.
  Spot of greenish tiled roof.
Four white walls.
  Far off glints the rock
of the harsh Guadarrama.
Water glistening but mute.
  In the limpid air,
young poplars in their grove,                    80
leafless, lyres for March.

      X   Rainbow at Night

*To Don Ramón del Valle-Inclán.*
  One night in the Guadarrama
the train is bound for Madrid.
Up in the sky a rainbow
formed of water and moonlight.
  Oh, April moon, so serene,
urging the white clouds along!

La madre lleva a su niño,
dormido, sobre la falda.
Duerme el niño y, todavía,                    90
ve el campo verde que pasa,
y arbolillos soleados,
y mariposas doradas.
   La madre, ceño sombrío
entre un ayer y un mañana,
ve unas ascuas mortecinas
y una hornilla con arañas.
   Hay un trágico viajero,
que debe ver cosas raras,
y habla solo y, cuando mira,                  100
nos borra con la mirada.
   Yo pienso en campos de nieve
y en pinos de otras montañas.
   Y tú, Señor, por quien todos
vemos y que ves las almas,
dinos si todos, un día,
hemos de verte la cara.


# 40  *Canciones*

### I

Junto a la sierra florida,
bulle el ancho mar.
El panal de mis abejas
tiene granitos de sal.

### II

Junto al agua negra.
Olor de mar y jazmines.
Noche malagueña.

### III

La primavera ha venido.
Nadie sabe cómo ha sido.

The mother holds her child
fast asleep in her lap.
The child in his sleep                                90
still sees green fields go by,
with little sunlit trees
and yellow butterflies.
    The mother, her dark frown set
between yesterday and tomorrow,
sees embers dying
and spiders in the oven.
    A tragic passenger is along,
who must be seeing sights.
He talks to himself, glances up,                     100
and looks right through us.
    I think of fields of snow
and pines of other mountains.
    And you, Lord, seer of souls,
by whom all of us see,
tell us if a day will come
when all of us see your face.


# 40 *Songs*

### I

By flowering hills
the broad sea is seething.
In my bees' honeycomb
are tiny grains of salt.

### II

Beside the black water.
Smell of sea and jasmine.
Málaga night.

### III

Spring is here.
But how did it appear?

### IV

La primavera ha venido.                    10
¡Aleluyas blancas
de los zarzales floridos!

### V

¡Luna llena, luna llena,
tan oronda, tan redonda
en esta noche serena
de marzo, panal de luz
que labran blancas abejas!

### VI

Noche castellana;
la canción se dice,
o, mejor, se calla.                        20
Cuando duerman todos,
saldré a la ventana.

### VII

Canta, canta en claro rimo,
el almendro en verde rama
y el doble sauce del río.
Canta de las parda encina
la rama que el hacha corta,
y la flor que nadie mira.
De los perales del huerto
la blanca flor, la rosada                   30
flor del melocotonero.
Y este olor
que arranca el viento mojado
a los habares en flor.

### VIII

La fuente y las cuatro
acacias en flor
de la plazoleta.
Ya no quema el sol.

IV

Spring is here.                                    10
White cries of hallelujah
from the flowering brambles!


V

Full moon, full moon,
so puffed up and round
this cloudless March night—
luminous honeycomb
worked by white bees.


VI

Castilian night;
a song is spoken,
or, rather, unsaid.                                20
When everyone's asleep
I'll come to the window.


VII

Sing, sing, in a clear rhythm,
the green-limbed almond tree
and the double river willow.
   Sing of the gray oak's branch
struck off by the ax,
of its flower that no one sees.
   Sing of the orchard trees,
white-blooming pear,                               30
pink-blooming peach.
   And this scent
that the damp wind skims
from the blossoming bean rows.


VIII

The fountain with the four
acacia trees in bloom
in the little square.
The sun no longer burning.

¡Tardecita alegre!
Canta, ruiseñor.                                          40
Es la misma hora
de mi corazón.


IX

¡Blanca hospedería,
celda de viajero,
con la sombra mía!


X

El acueducto romano
—canta una voz de mi tierra—
y el querer que nos tenemos,
chiquilla, ¡vaya firmeza!


XI

A las palabras de amor                                   50
les sienta bien su poquito
de exageración.


XII

En Santo Domingo,
la misa mayor.
Aunque me decían
hereje y masón,
rezando contigo,
¡cuánta devoción!


XIII

Hay fiesta en el prado verde
—pífano y tambor—.                                       60
Con su cayado florido
y abarcas de oro vino un pastor.
    Del monte bajé,
sólo por bailar con ella;
al monte me tornaré.

Cheery late afternoon!
Sing, nightingale.                                    40
The hour is in tune
with my heart, too.


IX

White hostelry,
traveler's cubicle,
my shadow in it!


X

The Roman aqueduct
(a local voice sings)
and our love for each other—
there's steadiness, girl!


XI

The language of love                                 50
was never the worse
for some overstatement.


XII

At high mass
in Santo Domingo.
They used to call me
a heretic and Mason.
Praying with you, though,
how pious I was!


XIII

A fiesta is on in the meadow,
with fife and drum.                                  60
A shepherd came in gold sandals,
and a flowering crook.
    I've come down from the hills
just to dance with her;
I'll go back to the hills.

En los árboles del huerto
hay un ruiseñor;
canta de noche y de día,
canta a la luna y al sol.
Ronco de cantar:                                    70
al huerto vendrá la niña
y una rosa cortará.
    Entre las negras encinas,
hay una fuente de piedra,
y un cantarillo de barro
que nunca se llena.
    Por el encinar,
con la blanca luna,
ella volverá.

XIV

    Contigo en Valonsadero,                         80
fiesta de San Juan,
mañana en la Pampa,
del otro lado del mar.
Guárdame la fe,
que yo volveré.
    Mañana seré pampero,
y se me irá el corazón
a orillas del alto Duero.

XV

    Mientras danzáis en corro,
niñas, cantad:                                      90
Ya están los prados verdes,
ya vino abril galán.
    A la orilla del río,
por el negro encinar,
sus abarcas de plata
hemos visto brillar.
Ya están los prados verdes,
ya vino abril galán.

Out in the garden
a nightingale sings
night and day in the treetops,
in moonlight, in sunlight.
He sings himself out:                                              70
the girl will come to the garden
and pick a rose.
  Among the dark oaks
there's a stone spring
and a little earthen jug
that never fills up.
  Through the oak grove
she will return
by white moonlight.

      XIV

With you in Valonsadero                                           80
on St. John's Eve;
on the pampas tomorrow
across the seas.
Keep faith with me,
I'll be back.
  Tomorrow at work on the pampas,
my heart will slip away
to where the Duero rises.

      XV

  Sing, maidens,
and dance your rounds.                                            90
Sing meadows green again
and April back a-courting.
  In the dark oak grove
by the riverbank,
we've caught the gleam
of his silver sandals.
Sing meadows green again,
and April back a-courting.

# 41 *Proverbios y cantares*

*A José Ortega y Gasset.*

I

El ojo que ves no es
ojo porque tú lo veas;
es ojo porque te ve.

II

Para dialogar,
preguntad, primero;
después . . . escuchad.

III

Todo narcisismo
es un vicio feo,
y ya viejo vicio.

IV

Mas busca en tu espejo al otro,
al otro que va contigo.

V

Entre el vivir y el soñar
hay una tercera cosa.
Adivínala.

VI

Ese tu Narciso
ya no se ve en el espejo
porque es el espejo mismo.

VII

¿Siglo nuevo? ¿Todavía
llamea la misma fragua?
¿Corre todavía el agua
por el cauce que tenía?

VIII

Hoy es siempre todavía.

# 41  *Proverbs and Song-verse*

*To José Ortega y Gasset.*

### I

The eye you see is an eye
not because you see it;
it's an eye because it sees you.

### II

For dialogue,
first ask,
then . . . listen.

### III

Any narcissism
is an ugly vice—
and an old one by now.

### IV

But seek out the other in your mirror,
the other who keeps you company.

### V

In between living and dreaming
comes something else.
Guess what it is.

### VI

That Narcissus of yours
can't see himself in the mirror now
because he *is* the mirror.

### VII

A new era?
Does the same forge still flare?
Does the water still run
in the same old channels?

### VIII

Today always is still.

### IX

Sol en Aries. Mi ventana
está abierta al aire frío.
—¡Oh rumor de agua lejana!—
La tarde despierta al río.

### X

En el viejo caserío
—¡oh anchas torres con cigüeñas!—
enmudece el son gregario,
y en el campo solitario
suena el agua entre las peñas.

### XI

Como otra vez, mi atención
está del agua cautiva;
pero del agua en la viva
roca de mi corazón.

### XII

¿Sabes, cuando el agua suena,
si es agua de cumbre o valle,
de plaza, jardín o huerta?

### XIII

Encuentro lo que no busco:
las hojas del toronjil
huelen a limón maduro.

### XIV

Nunca traces tu frontera,
ni cuides de tu perfil;
todo eso es cosa de fuera.

### XV

Busca a tu complementario,
que marcha siempre contigo,
y suele ser tu contrario.

IX

Sun in the Ram. My window
is open to the cold air.—
Oh sound of distant water!—
Evening awakens the river.

X

In the old town—
oh sturdy towers with storks!—
the bells cease their pealing
and from the empty land
come sounds of water in rocks.

XI

Once again my attention
is bound by water—
but water in the live
rock of my heart.

XII

From the sound of water, can you tell
if it's water of peak or valley,
town fountain, garden or grove?

XIII

How unexpected:
I find rose-balm leaves
with a smell of ripe lemon.

XIV

Never set down your limits
or fuss with your profile;
they're only externals.

XV

Look for your counterpart
who's always alongside you
and is usually your opposite.

### XVI

Si vino la primavera,
volad a las flores;
no chupéis cera.

### XVII

En mi soledad
he visto cosas muy claras,
que no son verdad.

### XVIII

Buena es el agua y la sed;
buena es la sombra y el sol;
la miel de flor de romero,
la miel de campo sin flor.

### XIX

A la vera del camino
hay una fuente de piedra,
y un cantarillo de barro
—glu-glu—que nadie se lleva.

### XX

Adivina adivinanza,
qué quieren decir la fuente,
el cantarillo y el agua.

### XXI

... Pero yo he visto beber
hasta en los charcos del suelo.
Caprichos tiene la sed ...

### XXII

Sólo quede un símbolo:
*quod elixum est ne assato.*
No aséis lo que está cocido.

XVI

Now that spring's here,
fly off to the flowers;
don't chew on the wax.


XVII

In my solitude
I've seen very clearly
things that aren't so.


XVIII

Good are water and thirst,
good are shadow and sun,
rosemary-blossom honey,
honey from flowerless fields.


XIX

At the roadside
there's a stone spring
and a small earthen jug—gurgle, gurgle—
that no one removes.


XX

Riddle me this:
what's meant by the spring,
the jug, and the water?


XXI

. . . Still I've seen people drink
from mud puddles even.
Thirst has its whims . . .


XXII

Let this symbol suffice:
*quod elixum est ne assato.*
Don't roast what's been boiled.

XXIII

Canta, canta, canta,
junto a su tomate,
el grillo en su jaula.

XXIV

Despacito y buena letra:
el hacer las cosas bien
importa más que el hacerlas.

XXV

Sin embargo . . .
                    ¡Ah!, sin embargo,
importa avivar los remos,
dijo el caracol al galgo.

XXVI

¡Ya hay hombres activos!
Soñaba la charca
con sus mosquitos.

XXVII

¡Oh calavera vacía!
¡Y pensar que todo era
dentro de ti, calavera!,
otro Pandolfo decía.

XXVIII

Cantores, dejad
palmas y jaleo
para los demás.

XXIX

Despertad, cantores:
acaben los ecos,
empiecen las voces.

XXIII

Singing and singing away
beside his tomato—
the cricket in his cage.

XXIV

Slowly now, nice neat letters:
the point is to do things well,
not just to do them.

XXV

Just the same . . .
                    Ah yes, just the same,
better keep those flanks moving,
said the snail to the greyhound.

XXVI

At last some active men!
There the puddle was,
dreaming of its mosquitoes.

XXVII

Oh empty skull!
To think that it all
went on inside you!
a second Pandolfo was saying.

XXVIII

Singers, the clapping
and cheers should be left
to the others.

XXIX

Singers, wake up.
Time for echoes to end
and voices to start.

XXX

Mas no busquéis disonancias;
porque, al fin, nada disuena,
siempre al son que tocan bailan.

XXXI

Luchador superfluo,
ayer lo más noble,
mañana lo más plebeyo.

XXXII

Camorrista, boxeador,
zúrratelas con el viento.

XXXIII

—Sin embargo . . .
                                    ¡Oh!, sin embargo,
queda un fetiche que aguarda
ofrenda de puñetazos.

XXXIV

*O rinnovarsi o perire* . . .
No me suena bien.
*Navigare è necessario* . . .
Mejor: ¡vivir para ver!

XXXV

Ya maduró un nuevo cero,
que tendrá su devoción:
un ente de acción tan huero
como un ente de razón.

XXXVI

No es el yo fundamental
eso que busca el poeta,
sino el tú esencial.

XXX

But don't hunt for dissonance:
There is no such thing;
people dance to all tunes.

XXXI

An unneeded champion:
all so noble yesterday,
tomorrow all so cheap.

XXXII

Fight-picker, boxer,
take it out on the wind.

XXXIII

Just the same . . .
                    Oh, just the same,
there's a fetish awaiting
its quota of punches.

XXXIV

*O rinnovarsi o perire . . .*
That doesn't sound right.
*Navigare è necessario . . .*
Better: living is seeing.

XXXV

A new cipher has blossomed
and will have its cult:
a being of action, just as useless
as a rational being.

XXXVI

It's not the basic I
that the poet is after
but the essential you.

### XXXVII

Viejo como el mundo es
—dijo un doctor—, olvidado,
por sabido, y enterrado
cual la momia de Ramsés.

### XXXVIII

Mas el doctor no sabía
que hoy es siempre todavía.

### XXXIX

Busca en tu prójimo espejo;
pero no para afeitarte,
ni para teñirte el pelo.

### XL

Los ojos por que suspiras,
sábelo bien,
los ojos en que te miras
son ojos porque te ven.

### XLI

—Ya se oyen palabras viejas.
—Pues, aguzad las orejas.

### XLII

Enseña el Cristo: a tu prójimo
amarás como a ti mismo,
mas nunca olvides que es otro.

### XLIII

Dijo otra verdad:
busca el tú que nunca es tuyo
ni puede serlo jamás.

### XLIV

No desdeñéis la palabra;
el mundo es ruidoso y mudo,
poetas, sólo Dios habla.

XXXVII

As old as the world,
a learned man said, means: forgotten
as obvious, dead and buried
like Rameses' mummy.

XXXVIII

But the learned man forgot
that today always is still.

XXXIX

Find a mirror in your fellow man,
but not one for shaving
or dyeing your hair.

XL

Those eyes you long for,
make no mistake,
eyes you see yourself in—
are eyes because they see you.

XLI

"Old words are being spoken."
"Prick up your ears, then."

XLII

Christ teaches love your neighbor
as yourself. But never forget
he is someone else.

XLIII

He spoke another truth:
find the you that is never yours
and can never be.

XLIV

Don't look down on words.
The world is noisy and mute,
poets; God alone speaks.

### XLV

¿Todo para los demás?
Mancebo, llena tu jarro,
que ya te lo beberán.

### XLVI

Se miente más de la cuenta
por falta de fantasía:
también la verdad se inventa.

### XLVII

Autores, la escena acaba
con un dogma de teatro:
En el principio era la máscara.

### XLVIII

Será el peor de los malos
bribón que olvide
su vocación de diablo.

### IL

¿Dijiste media verdad?
Dirán que mientes dos veces
si dices la otra mitad.

### L

Con el tú de mi canción
no te aludo, compañero;
ese tú soy yo.

### LI

Demos tiempo al tiempo:
para que el vaso rebose
hay que llenarlo primero.

### LII

Hora de mi corazón:
la hora de una esperanza
y una desesperación.

XLV

Everything for others?
Fill your jug, young man,
they'll drink it up, never fear.

XLVI

So much lying goes on
for lack of imagination:
truth, too, can be invented.

XLVII

Authors, to end a scene,
here's a rule of the theater:
in the beginning was the mask.

XLVIII

Doubtless the worst of the wicked
is the rogue who forgets
his devil's vocation.

XLIX

Did you speak a half-truth?
They'll call you liar twice over
if you speak the other half.

L

That you in my song
doesn't go for you, friend.
That you is me.

LI

Don't try to rush things:
for the cup to run over,
it must first be filled.

LII

Telling time by my heart:
time for a hope
and time for despair.

### LIII

Tras el vivir y el soñar,
está lo que más importa:
despertar.

### LIV

Le tiembla al cantar la voz.
Ya no le silban sus coplas:
que silban su corazón.

### LV

Ya hubo quien pensó:
*cogito ergo non sum.*
¡Qué exageración!

### LVI

Conversación de gitanos:
—¿Cómo vamos, compadrito?
—Dando vueltas al atajo.

### LVII

Algunos desesperados
sólo se curan con soga;
otros, con siete palabras:
la fe se ha puesto de moda.

### LVIII

Creí mi hogar apagado,
y revolví la ceniza . . .
Me quemé la mano.

### LIX

¡Reventó de risa!
¡Un hombre tan serio!
. . . Nadie lo diría.

### LX

Que se divida el trabajo:
los malos unten la flecha;
los buenos tiendan el arco.

LIII

After living and dreaming
comes what matters most:
waking up.

LIV

His voice quivers when he sings.
It's not his lyrics they hiss at—
it's his heart.

LV

Now they've thought of this:
*Cogito ergo non sum.*
What an overstatement!

LVI

Gypsy conversation:
"Pal, how're we doing?"
"Taking a stroll on the shortcut."

LVII

Some who give up
end it all with a rope;
others with four little words:
faith's back in style.

LVIII

I thought my fireplace cold
and stirred up the ashes;
my fingers got burnt.

LIX

He laughed till he burst!
Such a serious man . . .
Who would have thought it?

LX

Let the job be split up:
bad people dipping the arrows,
good ones flexing the bow.

LXI

Como don San Tob,
se tiñe las canas,
y con más razón.

LXII

Por dar al viento trabajo,
cosía con hilo doble
las hojas secas del árbol.

LXIII

Sentía los cuatro vientos,
en la encrucijada
de su pensamiento.

LXIV

¿Conoces los invisibles
hiladores de los sueños?
Son dos: la verde esperanza
y el torvo miedo.
Apuesta tienen de quién
hile más y más ligero,
ella, su copo dorado;
él, su copo negro.
Con el hilo que nos dan
tejemos, cuando tejemos.                    10

LXV

Siembra la malva:
pero no la comas,
dijo Pitágoras.
Responde al hachazo
—ha dicho el Buda ¡y el Cristo!—
con tu aroma, como el sándalo.
Bueno es recordar
las palabras viejas
que han de volver a sonar.

LXI

Like Don Sem Tob,
he dyes his white hair—
and with much more reason.

LXII

To keep the wind working,
he used reinforced thread
on the dead leaves of trees.

LXIII

He could feel the four winds
at the crossroads
of his thought.

LXIV

Do you know the invisible
spinners of dreams?
They are two: fresh hope
and shifty-eyed fear.
   They've a wager as to who
will spin fastest and most—
its gold ball, hope;
its black one, fear.
   We weave with the thread we are given,
when we weave.                                    10

LXV

Sow mallow
but don't eat it,
Pythagoras said.
   Greet a slash of the ax,
said the Buddha—and said Christ!—
with your scent, like the sandalwood.
   It's good to recall
the old sayings.
Their time's not up yet.

LXVI

Poned atención:
un corazón solitario
no es un corazón.

LXVII

Abejas, cantores,
no a la miel, sino a las flores.

LXVIII

Todo necio
confunde valor y precio.

LXIX

Lo ha visto pasar en sueños . . .
Buen cazador de sí mismo,
siempre en acecho.

LXX

Cazó a su hombre malo,
el de los días azules,
siempre cabizbajo.

LXXI

Da doble luz a tu verso,
para leído de frente
y al sesgo.

LXXII

Mas no te importe si rueda
y pasa de mano en mano:
del oro se hace moneda.

LXXIII

De un "Arte de Bien Comer,"
primera lección:
No has de coger la cuchara
con el tenedor.

LXVI

Pay attention to this:
a lone heart
is no heart at all.

LXVII

Bees, singers, it's not honey
you're after—it's blossoms.

LXVIII

Every simpleton
mixes up value and price.

LXIX

He saw him go by in a dream.
Good at tracking himself,
always lying in wait.

LXX

He tracked down his evil genius,
the one who on bright blue days
was always hanging his head.

LXXI

Give double lighting to your verse
for reading straight on
and sideways.

LXXII

But don't worry if it goes the rounds,
slipping from hand to hand:
coins, too, are made out of gold.

LXXIII

In a "Guide to Table Manners"
the first lesson is this:
never pick up the spoon
with the fork.

LXXIV

Señor San Jerónimo,
suelte usted la piedra
con que se machaca.
Me pegó con ella.

LXXV

Conversación de gitanos:
—Para rodear,
toma la calle de en medio;
nunca llegarás.

LXXVI

El tono lo da la lengua,
ni más alto ni más bajo;
sólo acompáñate de ella.

LXXVII

¡Tartarín en Koenigsberg!
Con el puño en la mejilla,
todo lo llegó a saber.

LXXVIII

Crisolad oro en copela,
y burilad lira y arco
no en joya, sino en moneda.

LXXIX

Del romance castellano
no busques la sal castiza;
mejor que romance viejo,
poeta, cantar de niñas.
Déjale lo que no puedes
quitarle: su melodía
de cantar que canta y cuenta
un ayer que es todavía.

LXXIV

Good St. Jerome,
let go of that stone
you're pounding yourself with.
So he hit me with it.

LXXV

Gypsy conversation:
"For the long way round,
take the middle road;
you'll never get there."

LXXVI

The tongue gives you your tone,
not too high, not too low.
Only see you stay with it.

LXXVII

Tartarin in Koenigsberg!
Propping cheek on fist,
he learned all there was to know.

LXXVIII

Melt gold down in a smelter,
engrave lyre and bow
on a coin, not a jewel.

LXXIX

Though old ballads give you
the pure salt of Castilian,
poet, little girls' songs
give you more than old ballads.
    They give you one thing
that can't be removed:
song-tunes singing and telling
of yesterdays that still are.

LXXX

Concepto mondo y lirondo
suele ser cáscara hueca;
puede ser caldera al rojo.

LXXXI

Si vivir es bueno
es mejor soñar,
y mejor que todo,
madre, despertar.

LXXXII

No el sol, sino la campana,
cuando te despierta, es
lo mejor de la mañana.

LXXXIII

¡Qué gracia! En la Hesperia triste,
promontorio occidental,
en este cansino rabo
de Europa, por desollar,
y en una ciudad antigua,
chiquita como un dedal,
¡el hombrecillo que fuma
y piensa, y ríe al pensar:
cayeron las altas torres;
en un basurero están                                    10
la corona de Guillermo,
la testa de Nicolás!

                                    *Baeza, 1919.*

LXXXIV

Entre las brevas soy blando;
entre las rocas, de piedra.
¡Malo!

LXXXV

¿Tu verdad? No, la Verdad,
y ven conmigo a buscarla.
La tuya, guardatela.

LXXX

A concept that's chemically pure
is generally an empty husk;
it can be a red-hot cauldron.

LXXXI

If it's good to live,
it's better to dream,
and the best thing of all
is waking up.

LXXXII

Not the sun but the bell,
when it wakes you up,
is the best part of morning.

LXXXIII

What a joke! In gloomy Hesperia,
this westernmost promontory,
this tail end of Europe
that's really the limit,
and in an ancient city
about the size of a thimble,
a little old man thinking away,
smoking and chuckling as he thinks:
how the lofty towers are fallen,
into the trash can they've gone:                10
the crown of the Kaiser,
the noddle of the Czar!

                        *Baeza, 1919.*

LXXXIV

Among figs I am soft;
among rocks, stony-hard.
No good!

LXXXV

Your truth? No, Truth;
come seek it with me.
As for yours, you can keep it.

LXXXVI

Tengo a mis amigos
en mi soledad;
cuando estoy con ellos
¡qué lejos están!

LXXXVII

¡Oh Guadalquivir!
Te vi en Cazorla nacer;
hoy, en Sanlúcar morir.
Un borbollón de agua clara,
debajo de un pino verde,
eras tú, ¡qué bien sonabas!
Como yo, cerca del mar,
río de barro salobre,
¿sueñas con tu manantial?

LXXXVIII

El pensamiento barroco
pinta virutas de fuego,
hincha y complica el decoro.

LXXXIX

Sin embargo ...
                   —Oh, sin embargo,
hay siempre un ascua de veras
en su incendio de teatro.

XC

¿Ya de su olor se avergüenzan
las hojas de la albahaca,
salvias y alhucemas?

XCI

Siempre en alto, siempre en alto.
¿Renovación? Desde arriba.
Dijo la cucaña al árbol.

LXXXVI

In my solitude
I have my friends with me;
when I'm with them,
they're so far away!

LXXXVII

Oh Guadalquivir!
I saw you born in Cazorla,
and dying today in Sanlúcar!
You were clear water bubbling
beneath a green pine.
What a fine sound you made!
Like me, as you near the sea,
river of brackish mud,
do you dream of your springs?

LXXXVIII

Baroque thought
paints shavings in flaming spirals,
swells and swarms with adornment.

LXXXIX

Just the same . . .
               —Oh, just the same,
there's always one real live coal
beneath its theatrical blaze.

XC

So now leaves of sweet basil,
lavender, and sage
are ashamed to be fragrant?

XCI

Onward and upward, onward and upward.
Renewal? From above.
So spoke the greased pole to the tree.

XCII

Dijo el árbol: teme al hacha,
palo clavado en el suelo:
contigo la poda es tala.

XCIII

¿Cuál es la verdad? ¿El río
que fluye y pasa
donde el barco y el barquero
son también ondas del agua?
¿O este soñar del marino
siempre con ribera y ancla?

XCIV

Doy consejo, a fuer de viejo:
nunca sigas mi consejo.

XCV

Pero tampoco es razón
desdeñar
consejo que es confesión.

XCVI

¿Ya sientes la savia nueva?
Cuida, arbolillo,
que nadie lo sepa.

XCVII

Cuida de que no se entere
la cucaña seca
de tus ojos verdes.

XCVIII

Tu profecía, poeta.
—Mañana hablarán los mudos:
el corazón y la piedra.

XCII

Answered the tree: be wary of axes,
oh pole stuck in the ground:
pruning is felling for you.

XCIII

Which is the truth?
The river flowing by,
carrying boat and boatman—
so many more waves in the water?
Or this dreaming the sailor does,
of banks and anchors always?

XCIV

Take an old man's word:
never follow my advice.

XCV

And yet it's not wise
to spurn the advice
that's in fact a confession.

XCVI

Do you feel new sap rising?
Take care, my fine sapling,
that no one finds out.

XCVII

Be sure the dry pole
doesn't get word
of your green eyes.

XCVIII

Poet, your prophecy.
"Tomorrow the dumb shall speak:
hearts and stones."

XCIX

—¿Mas el arte? . . .

—Es puro juego,
que es igual a pura vida,
que es igual a puro fuego.
Veréis el ascua encendida.

## 42 *Los ojos*

*Al gigante ibérico, Miguel de Unamuno,*
*por quien la España actual alcanza*
*proceridad en el mundo.*

I

Cuando murió su amada
pensó en hacerse viejo
en la mansión cerrada,
solo, con su memoria y el espejo
donde ella se miraba un claro día.
Como el oro en el arca del avaro,
pensó que guardaría
todo un ayer en el espejo claro.
Ya el tiempo para él no correría.

II

Mas pasado el primer aniversario,                        10
¿cómo eran—preguntó—, pardos o negros,
sus ojos? ¿Glaucos? . . . ¿Grises?
¿Cómo eran, ¡Santo Dios!, que no recuerdo? . . .

III

Salió a la calle un día
de primavera, y paseó en silencio
su doble luto, el corazón cerrado . . .

XCIX

"But art? . . ."
              "Simply play,
which is to say, simply life,
and that is to say, simply fire.
You'll see the glowing coal."

## 42 *The Eyes*

*For the giant of Iberia, Miguel de Unamuno,*
*thanks to whom present-day Spain is achieving*
*eminence in the world.*

I

When his beloved died
he thought he'd just grow old,
shutting himself in the house
alone, with memories and the mirror
that she had looked in one bright day.
Like gold in the miser's chest,
he thought he'd keep all yesterday
in the clear mirror intact.
For him time's flow would cease.

II

But after a year had passed,                    10
he began to wonder about her eyes:
"Were they brown or black? Or green? . . . Or grey?
What were they like? Good God! I can't recall . . ."

III

One day in spring he left the house
and took his double mourning down the street
in silence, his heart tight shut . . .

De una ventana en el sombrío hueco
vio unos ojos brillar. Bajó los suyos
y siguió su camino . . . ¡Como ésos!


**43**  *Esto soñé*

Que el caminante es suma del camino,
y en el jardín, junto del mar sereno,
le acompaña el aroma montesino,
ardor de seco henil en campo ameno;
que de luenga jornada peregrino
ponía al corazón un duro freno,
para aguardar el verso adamantino
que maduraba el alma en su hondo seno.
Esto soñé. Y del tiempo, el homicida,
que nos lleva a la muerte o fluye en vano,                    10
que era un sueño no más del adanida.
Y un hombre vi que en la desnuda mano
mostraba al mundo el ascua de la vida,
sin cenizas el fuego heraclitano.


**44**  *Al escultor Emiliano Barral*

. . .Y tu cincel me esculpía
en una piedra rosada,
que lleva una aurora fría
eternamente encantada.
Y la agria melancolía
de una soñada grandeza,
que es lo español (fantasía
con que adobar la pereza),
fue surgiendo de esa roca,
que es mi espejo,                                            10
línea a línea, plano a plano,

In the dim hollow of a window
he caught a flash of eyes. He lowered his
and walked right on . . . Like those!

## 43 *This Was My Dream*

The traveler is the aggregate of the road.
In gardens by the quiet sea's shore
the scent of sunburnt hay is with him still,
brought down from highland meadows hours before.
Wayfarer of a long day's journeying,
he drew the reins in tight around his heart
and let hard lines of verse take shape within,
molded by depths of spirit into art.
This was my dream. And that the slayer, time,
that leads us off to die or flows in vain,                    10
was just a dream within a mortal mind.
And then I saw a man hold up to view
in naked hands the glowing coal of life,
ashless the fire that Heraclitus knew.

## 44 *To the Sculptor Emiliano Barral*

. . . And your chisel picked me out,
out of rose-colored rock
that holds a chilly dawnlight
forever spellbound.
And the aching melancholy
of grandeur dreamt about—
that very Spanish thing, a gloss
of fancy over indolence—
came slowly forth from that rock
that is my mirror,                                             10
came line by line, plane by plane:

y mi boca de sed poca,
y, so el arco de mi cejo,
dos ojos de un ver lejano,
que yo quisiera tener
como están en tu escultura:
cavados en piedra dura,
en piedra, para no ver.

## 45   *Los sueños dialogados*

I

¡Cómo en el alto llano tu figura
se me aparece! . . . Mi palabra evoca
el prado verde y la árida llanura,
la zarza en flor, la cenicienta roca.
Y al recuerdo obediente, negra encina
brota en el cerro, baja el chopo al río;
el pastor va subiendo a la colina;
brilla un balcón de la ciudad: el mío,
el nuestro. ¿Ves? Hacia Aragón, lejana,
la sierra de Moncayo, blanca y rosa . . .                    10
Mira el incendio de esa nube grana,
y aquella estrella en el azul, esposa.
Tras el Duero, la loma de Santana
se amorata en la tarde silenciosa.

II

¿Por qué, decísme, hacia los altos llanos,
huye mi corazón de esta ribera,
y en tierra labradora y marinera
suspiro por los yermos castellanos?
Nadie elige su amor. Llevóme un día
mi destino a los grises calvijares
donde ahuyenta al caer la nieve fría
las sombras de los muertos encinares.

my mouth with its want of thirst
and two eyes with a far-off look
beneath the arch of the brow,
eyes I wish could be mine
just as they look in your bust:
eyes scooped out of hard rock,
out of rock, so as not to see.

## 45  Dreams in Dialogue

### I

Your figure in the highlands rises up
so sharp before me . . . My words evoke
green meadows, dry plateaus,
brambles in flower, rocks cinder-gray.
  Summoned by memory, things fall into place:
oaks on the hill, poplars by the stream,
the shepherd moving slowly up the slope,
a lighted balcony in town—my own,
    our own. See, off there toward Aragon,
the pink and white Moncayo range.                    10
Look how the fire smoulders in that cloud.
  Beloved, one star is shining in the blue.
Beyond the Duero, in the evening calm,
Santana Hill is turning lavender.

### II

You wonder why my heart rejects this coast
and strains toward the high plateaus,
why amid fertile fields, seagoing folk,
I yearn for the bare high country of Castile.
  One does not love by choice. Destiny chose
to lead me to the gray and barren spaces
where falling snow among the eerie shapes
of oaks long dead obliterates their shadows.

De aquel trozo de España, alto y roquero,
hoy traigo a ti, Guadalquivir florido,                          10
una mata del áspero romero.
Mi corazón está donde ha nacido,
no a la vida, al amor, cerca del Duero . . .
. . . ¡El muro blanco y el ciprés erguido!

### III

Las ascuas de un crepúsculo, señora,
rota la parda nube de tormenta,
han pintado en la roca cenicienta
de lueñe cerro un resplandor de aurora.
Una aurora cuajada en roca fría
que es asombro y pavor del caminante
más que fiero león en claro día,
o en garganta de monte osa gigante.
Con el incendio de un amor, prendido
al turbio sueño de esperanza y miedo,                          10
yo voy hacia la mar, hacia el olvido
—y no como a la noche ese roquedo,
al girar del planeta ensombrecido—.
No me llaméis, porque tornar no puedo.

### IV

¡Oh soledad, mi sola compañía,
oh musa del portento, que el vocablo
diste a mi voz que nunca te pedía!,
responde a mi pregunta: ¿con quién hablo?
Ausente de ruidosa mascarada,
divierto mi tristeza sin amigo,
contigo, dueña de la faz velada,
siempre velada al dialogar conmigo.
Hoy pienso: este que soy será quien sea;
no es ya mi grave enigma este semblante                        10
que en el íntimo espejo se recrea,
sino el misterio de tu voz amante.
Descúbreme tu rostro, que yo vea
fijos en mí tus ojos de diamante.

I bring you today, flowering Guadalquivir,
out of that high and rocky spur of Spain                    10
a sprig of rosemary, bristly and wild.
    My heart I leave where . . . not its life,
its love began, beside the Duero . . .
the pointed cypress and the whitewashed wall.

### III

Lady, the drab storm cloud comes apart
at the sky's west edge. Embers of a dusk
stain rocky cinders of some distant hill
with glimmers as of dawn.
    As of a dawn congealing on cold rock
that strikes the traveler with such awe and dread
as never mountain lion at high noon
or bear uprearing in a mountain gorge.
    Dreaming turbid dreams of hope and fear
lit up by flames of love,                                   10
I move on toward the sea, toward mindlessness.
    Unlike that rock mass moving into night,
shored by the turning motion of the world,
for me there's no return—don't try to call.

### IV

Oh solitude, sole sharer of my life,
wonder-working muse that gave my voice
the word I never asked for, tell me this:
with whom have I been speaking?
    My sadness shuns the noisy masquerade
and knows no friend to seek it out.
You ease it, lady, when we two converse,
although I never see your face unveiled.
    Today I think: it is not this self of mine
that puzzles me—the face that glances back         10
when I search my inner mirror.
    No, it's the lover's mystery in your voice.
So come, remove the veil and let me see
those diamond eyes of yours fastened on me.

# 46 *De mi cartera*

### I

Ni mármol duro y eterno,
ni música ni pintura,
sino palabra en el tiempo.

### II

Canto y cuento es la poesía.
Se canta una viva historia,
contando su melodía.

### III

Crea el alma sus riberas;
montes de ceniza y plomo,
sotillos de primavera.

### IV

Toda la imaginería          10
que no ha brotado del río,
barata bisutería.

### V

Prefiere la rima pobre,
la asonancia indefinida.
Cuando nada cuenta el canto,
acaso huelga la rima.

### VI

Verso libre, verso libre . . .
Líbrate, mejor, del verso
cuando te esclavice.

### VII

La rima verbal y pobre,          20
y temporal, es la rica.
El adjetivo y el nombre
remansos del agua limpia,

# 46  *From My Portfolio*

### I

Neither hard and timeless marble,
nor painting, nor music,
but the word in time.

### II

Poetry is song and telling.
A live story is sung
when the melody is told.

### III

The spirit casts up its banks,
mountains of ash and lead,
spring garden groves.

### IV

All of the imagery                                          10
that has not sprung from the river—
call it poor trinketry.

### V

Prefer the weak rhyme,
the uncertain assonance.
When the song has nothing to tell,
there may be no need for rhyme.

### VI

Free verse, free verse . . .
Free yourself from verse, instead,
if you find it enslaving . . .

### VII

Weak rhymes that fall on verbs                              20
and time-words, these are the strong ones.
Noun and adjective
are backwaters in the clear stream,

son accidentes del verbo
en la gramática lírica,
del Hoy que será Mañana,
del Ayer que es Todavía.
                                    *1924.*

# 47 *Sonetos*

### I

Tuvo mi corazón, encrucijada
de cien caminos, todos pasajeros,
un gentío sin cita ni posada,
como en andén ruidoso de viajeros.
  Hizo a los cuatro vientos su jornada,
disperso el corazón por cien senderos
de llana tierra o piedra aborrascada,
y a la suerte, en el mar, de cien veleros.
  Hoy, enjambre que torna a su colmena
cuando el bando de cuervos enronquece          10
en busca de su peña denegrida,
  vuelve mi corazón a su faena,
con néctares del campo que florece
y el luto de la tarde desabrida.

### II

Verás la maravilla del camino,
camino de soñada Compostela
—¡oh monte lila y flavo!—, peregrino,
en un llano, entre chopos de candela.
  Otoño con dos ríos ha dorado
el cerco del gigante centinela
de piedra y luz, prodigio torreado
que en el azul sin mancha se modela.
  Verás en la llanura una jauría
de agudos galgos y un señor de caza,          10
cabalgando a lejana serranía,
  vano fantasma de una vieja raza.
Debes entrar cuando en la tarde fría
brille un balcón de la desierta plaza.

incidental to the verb
in the lyric grammar
of Today on the way to Tomorrow,
of Yesterday that is Still.

*1924.*

# 47 *Sonnets*

### I

My heart was where a hundred roads
converged and then moved on.
Always crowds of travelers hurrying through,
as in a bustle of departing trains.
      It struck out to the four ends of the earth,
scattered itself along a hundred paths,
rugged terrain and smooth it took in stride,
and staked its chances on a hundred ships.
      Today, like a swarm returning to the hive
at the hour when crows go hoarse,                          10
flapping back to roost on beetling crags,
      my heart takes up its task again
with nectar drawn from flowering fields
and the drab mournfulness of evening.

### II

Pilgrim, a wonder awaits you on the road,
the road to the Compostela of a dream:
a flax and lilac mountain in a plain
seen through a screen of incandescent poplars.
      Following two rivers, autumn has traced in gold
a ring around the giant sentinel
all stone and light, superbly turreted,
that lifts its mass against the spotless blue.
      On the plain you'll see a pack of eager hounds
and a country squire heading for the hunt—          10
the hollow remnant of an ancient race
      riding away toward a line of distant hills.
Plan to arrive when the evening chill sets in
and a balcony slants its beam to the empty square.

### III

¿Empañé tu memoria? ¡Cuántas veces!
La vida baja como un ancho río,
y cuando lleva al mar alto navío
va con cieno verdoso y turbias heces.
Y más si hubo tormenta en sus orillas,
y él arrastra el botín de la tormenta,
si en su cielo la nube cenicienta
se incendió de centellas amarillas.
Pero aunque fluya hacia la mar ignota,
es la vida también agua de fuente                    10
que de claro venero, gota a gota,
    o ruidoso penacho de torrente,
bajo el azul, sobre la piedra brota.
Y allí suena tu nombre ¡eternamente!

### IV

Esta luz de Sevilla . . . Es el palacio
donde nací, con su rumor de fuente.
Mi padre, en su despacho. —La alta frente,
la breve mosca, y el bigote lacio—.
Mi padre, aún joven. Lee, escribe, hojea
sus libros y medita. Se levanta;
va hacia la puerta del jardín. Pasea.
A veces habla solo, a veces canta.
Sus grandes ojos de mirar inquieto
ahora vagar parecen, sin objeto                       10
donde puedan posar, en el vacío.
Ya escapan de su ayer a su mañana;
ya miran en el tiempo, ¡padre mío!
piadosamente mi cabeza cana.

## 48 *Viejas canciones*

### I

A la hora del rocío,
de la niebla salen
sierra blanca y prado verde
¡El sol en los encinares!

III

Have I soiled your memory? Countless times.
Like a broad river, life flows to the sea
and when it carries some tall vessel down
the slimy depths are churned, the dregs are stirred.
All the more if storms have raged along the banks,
swelling the stream with jetsam and debris,
if overhead an ashen cloud
has cracked and burst in flames.
Yet flow as it will down to the unknown sea,
life is nonetheless spring water,                                 10
releasing its clear trickle drop by drop
    or spurting up from rock beneath the blue
in a burst of noisy spray.
And there your name resounds, and always will.

IV

This light of Seville . . . The great house once again
where I was born, filled with fountain sounds.
My father in his study. High forehead,
touch of beard, the moustache drooping.
    My father, young still. He reads and writes,
leafs through his books and muses. He gets up,
goes toward the garden door and walks about.
Sometimes he talks out loud, sometimes he sings.
    And then his large eyes with the restless look
seem to be wandering in a void,                                  10
unable to settle anywhere.
    They slip off from his yesterday to look through time
to his tomorrow and, Father, there they light
so pityingly on my gray head.

# 48 *Old Songs*

I

With the morning dew,
stand forth from the mists
white peaks, green meadows.
The sun on the oak groves!

Hasta borrarse en el cielo,
suben las alondras.
¿Quién puso plumas al campo?
¿Quién hizo alas de tierra loca?
Al viento, sobre la sierra,
tiene el águila dorada                          10
las anchas alas abiertas.
Sobre la picota
donde nace el río
sobre el lago de turquesa
y los barrancos de verdes pinos;
sobre veinte aldeas,
sobre cien caminos . . .
Por los senderos del aire,
señora águila,
¿dónde vais a todo vuelo tan de mañana?          20

      II

Ya había un albor de luna
en el cielo azul.
¡La luna en los espartales,
cerca de Alicún!
Redonda sobre el alcor,
y rota en las turbias aguas
del Guadiana menor.
Entre Ubeda y Baeza
—loma de las dos hermanas:
Baeza, pobre y señora,                           10
Ubeda, reina y gitana—.
Y en el encinar,
¡luna redonda y beata,
siempre conmigo a la par!

      III

Cerca de Ubeda la grande,
cuyos cerros nadie verá,
me iba siguiendo la luna
sobre el olivar.
Una luna jadeante,
siempre conmigo a la par.

The larks climb so far
they melt into sky.
Who feathered the fields?
Who made wings of wild earth?
    Above the tall ranges,
on broad sunlit wings                                    10
the eagle rides the wind.
    Above the sharp peak
where the river rises,
the turquoise lake,
the ravines deep in pines,
above twenty hamlets
and a hundred roads . . .
    Mistress eagle, where bound
so early in the morning,
so steadily flapping down highways of air?              20


                    II

    A white moon showed
in a sky still blue.
The feather grass near Alicún
lit up by the moon!
Moon round over the hill
and shattered on dull water
in the Lesser Guadiana.
    Between Ubeda and Baeza—
hill of the two sisters:
Baeza, poor and a lady;                                 10
Ubeda, gypsy and queen.
And through the oak grove,
the moon smug and round,
keeping right up with me.


                    III

    Near the great town of Ubeda,
whose hills will never be seen,
the moon was on my trail
above the olive grove.
    A moon breathing hard,
keeping right up with me.

Yo pensaba: ¡bandoleros
de mi tierra!, al caminar
en mi caballo ligero.
¡Alguno conmigo irá!                                      10
Que esta luna me conoce
y, con el miedo, me da
el orgullo de haber sido
alguna vez capitán.


                    IV

En la sierra de Quesada
hay un águila gigante,
verdosa, negra y dorada,
siempre las alas abiertas.
Es de piedra y no se cansa.
Pasado Puerto Lorente,
entre las nubes galopa
el caballo de los montes.
Nunca se cansa: es de roca.
En el hondón del barranco                                 10
se ve al jinete caído,
que alza los brazos al cielo.
Los brazos son de granito.
Y allá donde nadie sube
hay una virgen risueña
con un río azul en brazos.
Es la Virgen de la Sierra.


## 49  *Rosa de fuego*

Tejidos sois de primavera, amantes,
de tierra y agua y viento y sol tejidos.
La sierra en vuestros pechos jadeantes,
en los ojos los campos florecidos,
    pasead vuestra mutua primavera,
y aún bebed sin temor la dulce leche
que os brinda hoy la lúbrica pantera,
antes que, torva, en el camino aceche.

Riding along
on my nimble horse,
I thought: my hometown bandits!
One must be riding with me.                    10
    This moon knows who I am.
It scares me—and yet
makes me proud to have been
a bandit chief once.


IV

In the Quesada mountains
is a giant eagle,
greenish, black, and gold,
wings always outstretched.
It's stone; it never tires.
    Beyond the Lorente Pass,
on the gallop in the clouds
is a mountain horse.
It never gets tired; it is rock.
    At the bottom of the ravine              10
the fallen horseman can be seen
raising his arms to heaven.
They are granite arms.
    And up where no one climbs
there's a virgin smiling
and cradling a blue river.
She's the Virgin of the Mountains.


## 49 *The Flaming Rose*

    Lovers, the stuff you're woven of is spring,
is wind and water, earth and sun.
You've hills in your heaving chests,
blossoming fields in your eyes:
    go forth with the spring you share
and freely drink of the sweet milk
the wanton panther offers you today—
soon enough she'll stalk you foully in your path.

Caminad, cuando el eje del planeta
se vence hacia el solsticio de verano,                                    10
verde el almendro y mustia la violeta,
   cerca la sed y el hontanar cercano,
hacia la tarde del amor, completa,
con la rosa de fuego en vuestra mano.

## 50  *Al gran Cero*

Cuando el *Ser que se es* hizo la nada
y reposó, que bien lo merecía,
ya tuvo el día noche, y compañía
tuvo el hombre en la ausencia de la amada.
   *Fiat umbra!* Brotó el pensar humano.
Y el huevo universal alzó, vacío,
ya sin color, desubstanciado y frío,
lleno de niebla ingrávida, en su mano.
   Toma el cero integral, la hueca esfera,
que has de mirar, si lo has de ver, erguido.                              10
Hoy que es espalda el lomo de tu fiera,
   y es el milagro del no ser cumplido,
brinda, poeta, un canto de frontera
a la muerte, al silencio y al olvido.

## 51  *Ultimas lamentaciones de Abel Martín*

Hoy, con la primavera,
soñé que un fino cuerpo me seguía
cual dócil sombra. Era
mi cuerpo juvenil, el que subía
de tres en tres peldaños la escalera.
   —Hola, galgo de ayer. (Su luz de acuario
trocaba el hondo espejo
por agria luz sobre un rincón de osario.)
   —¿Tú conmigo, rapaz?
                                   —Contigo, viejo.

Walk on when the tilt of the globe
points toward the summer solstice,
with the almond fully leaved, the violet withered,
    thirst close at hand, springs to slake it near—
on toward the fullness of love's afternoon,
holding in your hands the flaming rose.

## 50 *To the Great Nought*

When the *Being that is* made nothingness
and settled back, as well it might,
there was night for day and company
for man in woman's absence.
    *Fiat umbra.* Human thought appeared
and held up in its hand
the empty, colorless, weightless, cold,
matterless, mist-filled universal egg.
    Take the integral nought, the empty sphere—
if you want to see it at all you must stand erect.          10
Today, as a two-footed, not a four-footed beast,
    with the miracle of non-being carried out,
poet, propose a song, a borderline song
to death, to silence, to forgetting.

## 51 *Last Lamentations of Abel Martín*

Today with spring in the air,
I dreamt a slight figure dogged my steps,
meek as a shadow—
my little boy self, the one
that used to take the stairs three at a time.
    "Hey there, onetime loper." (In the mirror's depths
the water-slanted light became
the harsh light on a bone heap.)
    "You here with me, young fellow?"
                    "Right here, old friend."

Soñé la galería                                    10
al huerto de ciprés y limonero;
tibias palomas en la piedra fría,
en el cielo de añil rojo pandero,
y en la mágica angustia de la infancia
la vigilia del ángel más austero.
     La ausencia y la distancia
volví a soñar con túnicas de aurora;
firme en el arco tenso la saeta
del mañana, la vista aterradora
de la llama prendida en la espoleta            20
de su granada.
               ¡Oh Tiempo, oh Todavía
preñado de inminencias!
tú me acompañas en la senda fría,
tejedor de esperanzas e impaciencias.

     ¡El tiempo y sus banderas desplegadas!
(¿Yo, capitán? Mas yo no voy contigo.)
¡Hacia lejanas torres soleadas
el perdurable asalto por castigo!

     Hoy, como un día, en la ancha mar violeta
hunde el sueño su pétrea escalinata,          30
y hace camino la infantil goleta,
y le salta el delfín de bronce y plata.
     La hazaña y la aventura
cercando un corazón entelerido . . .
Montes de piedra dura
—eco y eco— mi voz han repetido.
     ¡Oh, descansar en el azul del día
como descansa el águila en el viento,
sobre la sierra fría,
segura de sus alas y su aliento!                40
     La augusta confianza
a ti, Naturaleza, y paz te pido,
mi tregua de temor y de esperanza,
un grano de alegría, un mar de olvido . . .

I dreamed of the passageway                                    10
to the cypress and lemon garden;
doves warm against cold stone,
red kite on indigo sky,
and childhood's troubled magic
watched over by the sternest angel.
   Absence and distance I dreamed back,
costumed in dawn,
the arrow set to fly in the taut bow
of tomorrow, the terrifying sight
of fire creeping down the fuse                                 20
of its grenade.
                Oh Time, oh Still and Now,
pregnant with things impending.
You travel the cold path with me,
arousing restlessness and hope.

   Time with banners flying!
(What, captain, *I*? But I am not going with you.)
To pay the price of endless pushing on
toward sunlit towers far away!

   Today, as long ago, dream steps lead down
from the stone rim of broad violet seas                        30
and the child's schooner slips along
with a bronze and silver dolphin leaping near.
   Great deeds and great adventures
pressing in on a timid heart . . .
Hard stone mountains
have echoed back my voice.
   To sink back on the blue of sky
as the eagle settles on the wind
above cold mountain ranges,
trusting to wings and breath!                                  40
   Nature, give me lofty confidence
and give me peace,
surcease of fear and hope,
one grain of joy, an ocean of forgetting . . .

## 52 *Siesta*

En memoria de Abel Martín

Mientras traza su curva el pez de fuego,
junto al ciprés, bajo el supremo añil,
y vuela en blanca piedra el niño ciego,
y en el olmo la copla de marfil
de la verde cigarra late y suena,
honremos al Señor
—la negra estampa de su mano buena—
que ha dictado el silencio en el clamor.
Al Dios de la distancia y de la ausencia,
del áncora en el mar, la plena mar . . .                    10
El nos libra del mundo—omnipresencia—,
nos abre senda para caminar.
Con la copa de sombra bien colmada,
con este nunca lleno corazón,
honremos al Señor que hizo la Nada
y ha esculpido en la fe nuestra razón.

## 53 *Recuerdos de sueño, fiebre y duermivela*

I

Esta maldita fiebre
que todo me lo enreda,
siempre diciendo: ¡claro!
Dormido estás: despierta.
¡Masón, masón!
                Las torres
bailando están en rueda.
Los gorriones pían
bajo la lluvia fresca.
¡Oh, claro, claro, claro!
Dormir es cosa vieja,                                         10
y el toro de la noche
bufando está a la puerta.

## 52 Siesta

In Memory of Abel Martín

While the goldfish traces flashing coils
beside the cypress, under the vaulting blue,
and blind Cupid flutters wings of stone;
while the ivory jingle of the green cicada
comes dilating from the elm,
let us praise the Lord—
the dark impression of his goodly hand—
the Lord who summoned silence out of clamor.
The God of distance and of absence,
of the anchor in the sea, the open sea . . .                    10
He frees us from the world in its omnipresence,
and opens up a way where we can walk . . .
By this glass filled with darkness to the brim
and this heart that's never full,
let us praise the Lord, maker of Nothingness,
who carved our reason out of faith.

## 53 Memories of Dreaming, Fever, and Dozing

I

This wretched fever,
always tangling things up,
telling me: "Of course!
You're asleep: wake up.
You damned Mason!"
                              The turrets
are dancing in circles.
The sparrows chirp
in the cooling rain.
Oh, yes, yes, of course!
Anyone can sleep,                                              10
and just outside the door
the bull of night is snorting.

A tu ventana llego
con una rosa nueva,
con una estrella roja
y la garganta seca.
¡Oh, claro, claro, claro!
¿Velones? En Lucena.
¿Cuál de las tres? Son una
Lucía, Inés, Carmela;                         20
y el limonero baila
con la encinilla negra.
¡Oh, claro, claro, claro!
Dormido estás. Alerta.
Mili, mili, en el viento;
glu-glu, glu-glu, en la arena.
Los tímpanos del alba,
¡qué bien repiquetean!
¡Oh, claro, claro, claro!

### II

En la desnuda tierra . . .                     30

### III

Era la tierra desnuda,
y un frío viento, de cara,
con nieve menuda.
Me eché a caminar
por un encinar de sombra:
la sombra de un encinar.
El sol las nubes rompía
con sus trompetas de plata.
La nieve ya no caía.
La vi un momento asomar                        40
en las torres del olvido.
Quise y no pude gritar.

### IV

¡Oh, claro, claro, claro!
Ya están los centinelas
alertos. ¡Y esta fiebre
que todo me lo enreda! . . .

I've come to your window
with a rose fresh open,
with a red star
and a dry throat.
Oh, yes, yes, of course!
Lanterns? In Lucena.
Which girl of the three? They're all
the same: Lucy, Inez, Carmela;                    20
and the lemon tree is dancing
with that dark little oak.
Oh, yes, yes, of course!
You're asleep. Come to.
Click, click in the wind;
trickle, trickle in the sand.
The wind chimes of dawn—
just listen to them tinkle!
Oh, yes, yes, of course!

II

On the bare earth . . .                           30

III

The earth was bare,
a cold wind blowing
fine snow in the face.
    I started to walk
through a shadowy oak grove:
the shade of an oak grove.
    The sun pierced the clouds
with silver trumpets.
The snow had stopped falling.
    For a moment she came in sight              40
on towers of time forgotten.
I tried to shout—I couldn't.

IV

    Oh, yes, yes, of course!
The sentinels by now
are on the alert. And this fever,
tangling everything up . . .

Pero a un hidalgo no
se ahorca; se degüella,
seor verdugo. ¿Duermes?
Masón, masón, despierta.                                    50
Nudillos infantiles
y voces de muñecas.

  ¡Tan-tan! ¿Quién llama, di?
—¿Se ahorca a un inocente
en esta casa?
          —Aquí
se ahorca, simplemente.

  ¡Qué vozarrón! Remacha
el clavo en la madera.
Con esta fiebre . . .  ¡Chito!
Ya hay público a la puerta.                                60
La solución más linda
del último problema.
Vayan pasando, pasen;
que nadie quede fuera.

  —¡Sambenitado, a un lado!
—¿Eso será por mí?
¿Soy yo el sambenitado,
señor verdugo?
          —Sí.

  ¡Oh, claro, claro, claro!
Se da trato de cuerda,                                     70
que es lo infantil, y el trompo
de música resuena.
Pero la guillotina,
una mañana fresca . . .
Mejor el palo seco,
y su corbata hecha.
¿Guitarras? No se estilan.
Fagotes y cornetas,
y el gallo de la aurora,
si quiere. ¿La reventa                                     80
la hacen los curas? ¡Claro!
¡¡¡Sambenitón, despierta!!!

But hidalgos are never
hanged, they're beheaded,
Mr. Executioner. Are you asleep?
Wake up, you damned Mason!                    50
Children's knuckles
and their little doll's voices.

   Rap, rap! Who's knocking? Who?
"Is this where they're hanging
an innocent man?"
         "Here
a hanging's in progress, that's all."

   What a rough voice! Ramming
the nail right through the wood.
With this fever . . . Shh!
We've customers outside.                      60
The neatest solution
to the ultimate problem.
Come right in, do;
no one's to stay outside.

   "You there, condemned man, one side!"
"You couldn't mean me?
Am I the condemned man,
Mr. Executioner?"
         "You're it."

   Oh, yes, yes, of course!
They wind you up by the throat—              70
child's play, you could call it—
and the top unwinds its music.
But the guillotine
some cool morning . . .
Give me the plain old gallows
with its neckpiece all ready.
Guitars? It's not done.
Bassoons and hunting horns
and the cock at daybreak,
if it will. Do the priests take a cut          80
on the tickets? Of course!
Condemned man, *wake up.*

V

Con esta bendita fiebre
la luna empieza a tocar
su pandereta; y danzar
quiere, a la luna, la liebre.
De encinar en encinar
saltan la alondra y el día.
En la mañana serena
hay un latir de jauría,                    90
que por los montes resuena.
Duerme. ¡Alegría! ¡Alegría!

VI

Junto al agua fría,
en la senda clara,
sombra dará algún día
ese arbolillo en que nadie repara.
Un fuste blanco y cuatro verdes hojas
que, por abril, le cuelga primavera,
y arrastra el viento de noviembre, rojas.
Su fruto, sólo un niño lo mordiera.        100
Su flor, nadie la vio. ¿Cuándo florece?
Ese arbolillo crece
no más que para el ave de una cita,
que es alma —canto y plumas— de un instante,
un pajarillo azul y petulante
que a la hora de la tarde lo visita.

VII

¡Qué fácil es volar, qué fácil es!
Todo consiste en no dejar que el suelo
se acerque a nuestros pies.
Valiente hazaña, ¡el vuelo!, ¡el vuelo!, ¡el vuelo!   110

VIII

¡Volar sin alas donde todo es cielo!
Anota este jocundo
pensamiento: Parar, parar el mundo
entre las puntas de los pies,

V

With this delightful fever,
the moon starts tapping
its tambourine, with the hare
itching to dance to the moon.
Skipping along the oak groves
go the lark and the light of day.
In the clear morning air
the yelp of hunting dogs                                    90
echoing through the hills.
Sleep on. Hark, hark, for joy!

VI

That sapling no one sees
will one day cast a shadow
across the bright path
beside the cold water.
Just a white stalk. The few green leaves
that spring hangs on its twigs—
November shakes them loose, after they're red.
Its fruit only a boy would sample.                         100
Its bloom is never seen. Does it ever bloom?
That sapling has grown there
just so a bird may pay its call
and light up a moment with song and feathers,
a blue and saucy little bird
that visits it toward evening.

VII

There's nothing to flying, nothing at all!
Just see you keep the ground
from coming too near your feet.
Brave work, indeed, to fly, to fly, to fly!                110

VIII

To be flying wingless where everything is sky!
Jot down this cheery thought:
Catch the world and hold it
between the tips of your toes,

y luego darle cuerda del revés,
para verlo girar en el vacío,
coloradito y frío,
y callado —no hay música sin viento—.
¡Claro, claro! ¡Poeta y cornetín
son de tan corto aliento! ...                    120
Sólo el silencio y Dios cantan sin fin.


IX

Pero caer de cabeza,
en esta noche sin luna,
en medio de esta maleza,
junto a la negra laguna ...


—¿Tú eres Caronte, el fúnebre barquero?
Esa barba limosa ...
                    —¿Y tú, bergante?
—Un fúnebre aspirante
de tu negra barcaza a pasajero,
que al lago irrebogable se aproxima.            130
¿Razón?
        —La ignoro. Ahorcóme un peluquero.
—(Todos pierden memoria en este clima).
—¿Delito?
        —No recuerdo.
                    —¿Ida, no más?
—¿Hay vuelta?
            —Sí.
                —Pues ida y vuelta, ¡claro!
—Sí, claro ... y no tan claro: eso es muy caro.
Aguarda un momentín, y embarcarás.


X

¡Bajar a los infiernos como el Dante!
¡Llevar por compañero
a un poeta con nombre de lucero!
¡Y este fulgor violeta en el diamante!           140
*Dejad toda esperanza* ...   Usted, primero.
¡Oh, nunca, nunca, nunca! Usted delante.

then wind it up counterclockwise
and watch it twirl in space,
flushed and cold
and quiet—there's no music without wind.
Of course, of course. The poet and the horn player
are forever getting winded . . .                               120
Only silence and God sing forever.


IX

But to plunge headfirst
this moonless night
into all this underbrush
beside the black lagoon.

"You're Charon, the doleful boatman?
With that slimy beard . . ."
                        "And you, you joker?"
"A doleful candidate for a passenger's place
in your dark barge,
who now draws near the lake of no return."          130
"What grounds?"
                  "I've no idea. A barber strung me up."
("Once they reach here, their memory goes.")
"Offense?"
             "I can't recall."
                      "A one-way trip?"
"Do you give returns?"
              "Yes."
                     "Well then, round trip of
                     course!"
"Of course . . .! What do you mean 'of course'? It costs a lot.
But wait a bit, then you can come aboard."


X

To go down to hell as Dante did!
To travel with a poet
with a light-bearing name!
And that purple glow from the diamond?                  140
*Abandon all hope* . . . After you, please.
Oh never, never, no. Please, you go first.

Palacios de mármol, jardín con cipreses,
naranjos redondos y palmas esbeltas.
Vueltas y revueltas,
eses y más eses.
"Calle del Recuerdo." Ya otra vez pasamos
por ella. "Glorieta de la Blanca Sor."
"Puerta de la Luna." Por aquí ya entramos.
"Calle del Olvido." Pero ¿adónde vamos            150
por estas malditas andurrias, señor?
—Pronto te cansas, poeta.
—"Travesía del Amor" . . .
¡y otra vez la "Plazoleta
del Desengaño Mayor!" . . .


XI

—Es ella . . . Triste y severa.
—Di, más bien, indiferente
como figura de cera.

—Es ella . . . Mira y no mira.
—Pon el oído en su pecho                          160
y, luego, dile: respira.

—No alcanzo hasta el mirador.
—Háblale.
            —Si tú quisieras . . .
—Más alto.
            —darme esa flor.
¿No me respondes, bien mío?
¡Nada, nada!
Cuajadita con el frío
se quedó en la madrugada.


XII

¡Oh, claro, claro, claro!
Amor siempre se hiela.                            170
¡Y en esa "Calle Larga"
con reja, reja y reja,
cien veces, platicando
con cien galanes, ella!

Marble mansions, cypress gardens,
round orange trees, and graceful palms.
Twists and turns
and endless S-curves.
"Memory Street." We came this way before.
"Circle of the White-robed Sister."
"Moon Gate." We came through here.
"Street of Forgetting." But where are we bound, sir,          150
on these wretched highways and byways?
    "Poet, you tire quickly . . ."
"Crosswalk of Love" . . .
and back we come to the "Square
of the Greatest Disillusion!"

### XI

"It's she . . . grim and sad."
"You mean indifferent, don't you,
like a figure of wax?"

"It's she . . . She looks without looking."
"Put your ear to her chest,          160
then tell her to breathe."

"The balcony's too high for me."
"Speak to her."
                "If you would agree . . ."
"Louder."
        "to give me that flower.
Won't you answer, my treasure?"
Not a word, not a word.
Poor little thing—frozen stiff
in the cold of dawn.

### XII

Oh, yes, yes, of course!
Love always gets frozen.          170
And down that "Long Street"
at those grated windows
she'll be talking time after time
with one suitor after another.

¡Oh, claro, claro, claro!
Amor es calle entera,
con celos, celosías,
canciones a las puertas ...
Yo traigo un do de pecho
guardado en la cartera.                               180
¿Qué te parece?
                    —Guarda.
Hoy cantan las estrellas,
y nada más.
                    —¿Nos vamos?
—Tira por esa calleja.
—Pero ¿otra vez empezamos?
"Plaza Donde Hila la Vieja."
Tiene esta plaza un relente ...
¿Seguimos?
                    —Aguarda un poco.
Aquí vive un cura loco
por un lindo adolescente.                             190
Y aquí pena arrepentido,
oyendo siempre tronar,
y viendo serpentear
el rayo que lo ha fundido.
"Calle de la Triste Alcuza."
—Un barrio feo. Gentuza.
¡Alto! ... "Pretil del Valiente."
—Pregunta en el tres.
                    —¿Manola?
—Aquí. Pero duerme sola:
está de cuerpo presente.                              200
¡Claro, claro! Y siempre clara,
le da la luna en la cara.
—¿Rezamos?
                    —No.Vamonós ...
Sí la madeja enredamos
con esta fiebre, ¡por Dios!,
ya nunca la devanamos.
... Sí, cuatro igual dos y dos.

Oh, yes, yes, of course!
Love is a whole street long
with jalousies for the jealous
and singing at the doors . . .
I've got a good low C
stowed away in my briefcase.                    180
How about it?
                    "Leave it there.
The stars are singing today,
nothing else."
                    "Shall we be going?"
"Take that alleyway there."
"What, not all over again!
'Square of the Old Woman Spinning.'
There's a dampness about this square . . .
Shall we go on?"
                    "Wait a moment.
Here lives a priest who's gone mad
for love of a handsome youth.                    190
Now he knows the price, he's sorry:
he hears thunder forever crashing
and watches the zigzags flashing
from the bolt that laid him low.
'Street of the Dreary Cruet.' "
"Bad neighborhood. Scum.
Stop! . . . 'The Brave Man's Walk.' "
"Inquire at Number Three."
                    "Manola?"
"This is it. But she sleeps alone:
she's laid out on display.                    200
Of course! Fair enough! And always fair,
the moonlight striking her face."
"Shall we pray?"
                    "No, let's leave.
If we get this skein tangled up,
with this fever, heavens alive,
we'll never be able to wind it.
. . . Yes, four equals two plus two."

## 54 Canciones a Guiomar

### I

No sabía
si era un limón amarillo
lo que tu mano tenía,
o el hilo de un claro día,
Guiomar, en dorado ovillo.
Tu boca me sonreía.
Yo pregunté: ¿Qué me ofreces?
¿Tiempo en fruto, que tu mano
eligió entre madureces
de tu huerta?                                    10
    ¿Tiempo vano
de una bella tarde yerta?
¿Dorada ausencia encantada?
¿Copia en el agua domida?
¿De monte en monte encendida,
la alborada
verdadera?
¿Rompe en sus turbios espejos
amor la devanadera
de sus crepúsculos viejos?                        20

### II

En un jardín te he soñado,
alto, Guiomar, sobre el río,
jardín de un tiempo cerrado
con verjas de hierro frío.
Un ave insólita canta
en el almez, dulcemente,
junto al agua viva y santa,
toda sed y toda fuente.
En ese jardín, Guiomar,
el mutuo jardín que inventan                      30
dos corazones al par,
se funden y complementan
nuestras horas. Los racimos
de un sueño —juntos estamos—
en limpia copa exprimimos,
y el doble cuento olvidamos.

# 54  *Songs for Guiomar*

### I

I could not tell
if what I saw in your hand
was a yellow lemon, Guiomar,
or the thread of a cloudless day—
a gold thread wound in a ball.
On your lips was a smile.
    I asked, what is this gift,
time come into fruit
and culled by your hand
from the ripeness of your grove?                    10
    Unfulfilled time
of some fair evening stilled?
A likeness asleep in a pool?
Absence spellbound and gold?
The one true dawning aflame
over hills for miles around?
Does love in its cloudy mirrors
shatter the spool
on which old twilights are wound?


### II

I dreamed you into a garden,                    20
Guiomar, up over the river,
a garden of time shut away
behind a cold iron grating.
    A rare bird is singing sweetly
in a branch of the lotus tree
by the sacred running water
that rouses and soothes all thirst.
    This garden, Guiomar,
is the garden two hearts contrive
where each fulfills the other,                    30
where our hours run together.
There the two of us press
the clustered grapes of a dream
in a pure glass and forget
that a story must have two sides.

(Uno: Mujer y varón,
aunque gacela y león,
llegan juntos a beber.
El otro: No puede ser                                    40
amor de tanta fortuna:
dos soledades en una,
ni aun de varón y mujer.)


Por ti la mar ensaya olas y espumas,
y el iris, sobre el monte, otros colores,
y el faisán de la aurora canto y plumas,
y el búho de Minerva ojos mayores.
Por ti, ¡oh, Guiomar! . . .


III
                              Tu poeta
piensa en ti. La lejanía
es de limón y violeta,                                   50
verde el campo todavía.
Conmigo vienes, Guiomar;
nos sorbe la serranía.
De encinar en encinar
se va fatigando el día.
El tren devora y devora
día y riel. La retama
pasa en sombra; se desdora
el oro de Guadarrama.
Porque una diosa y su amante                             60
huyen juntos, jadeante,
los sigue la luna llena.
El tren se esconde y resuena
dentro de un monte gigante.
Campos yermos, cielo alto.
Tras los montes de granito
y otros montes de basalto,
ya es la mar y el infinito.
Juntos vamos; libres somos.                              70
Aunque el Dios, como en el cuento

(One: that a woman and man,
though they be lion and gazelle,
will drink at a single well.
The other: two solitudes
will not be made into one,                                      40
even those of woman and man.
Such luck love does not bring.)


For you the sea tries out new waves and foam,
the rainbow tries new colors on the hill,
the pheasant sports at dawn new plumes and music,
the eyes of Minerva's owl grow wider still.
All for you, Guiomar! . . .


      III

Your poet's thoughts
turn to you. The distance
is lemon-yellow and violet,                                     50
green the landscape still.
You are along with me, Guiomar,
the mountains engulf us.
With each passing oak grove
the day's strength dwindles.
The train keeps consuming
daytime and track. Clumps of broom
slip by in shadow; the glitter
of Guadarrama gold fades.
With a goddess and her lover                                    60
in full flight, the full moon
is hot on their trail.
Into a giant mountain
the train ducks and bellows.
Barren fields, sky far above.
Behind the granite mountains
and a further basalt range
lie the sea and the infinite.
We're together, we're free.
Though the god,                                                 70
like fierce kings in old tales,

fiero rey, cabalgue a lomos
del mejor corcel del viento,
aunque nos jure, violento,
su venganza,
aunque ensille el pensamiento,
libre amor, nadie lo alcanza.

  Hoy te escribo en mi celda de viajero,
a la hora de una cita imaginaria.
Rompe el iris al aire el aguacero,
y al monte su tristeza planetaria.                    80
Sol y campanas en la vieja torre.
¡Oh, tarde viva y quieta
que opuso al *panta rhei* su *nada corre*,
tarde niña que amaba tu poeta!
¡Y día adolescente
—ojos claros y músculos morenos—,
cuando pensaste a Amor, junto a la fuente,
besar tus labios y apresar tus senos!
Todo a esta luz de Abril se transparenta;
todo en el hoy de ayer, el Todavía                    90
que en sus maduras horas
el tiempo canta y cuenta,
se funde en una sola melodía,
que es un coro de tardes y de auroras.
A ti, Guiomar, esta nostalgia mía.


## 55 *Otras canciones a Guiomar*

(A la manera de Abel Martín y de Juan de Mairena)

I

  ¡Sólo tu figura,
como una centella blanca,
en mi noche obscura!

  ¡Y en la tersa arena,
cerca de la mar,

comes astride
the wind's swiftest steed,
though he rants and he swears
he'll take his revenge,
though he saddles thought itself,
love is free, none can catch it.

   I write you today from my traveler's cubicle,
at the hour of an imaginary tryst.
The rainbow dispels the shower in the air,           80
the planetary sadness in the mountain.
In the old tower, sunlight and bells.
Oh, afternoon alive and still,
that countered *panta rhei* with *nothing passes,*
child-afternoon your poet loved!
And adolescent day—
bright eyes and sun-tanned muscles—
when your thoughts turned to love beside the fountain,
kissing your lips, cupping your breasts!
In this April light everything grows transparent;     90
everything in yesterday's today, the Still
that time in its hours of ripeness
tells of and sings—
all blends to a single melody,
one chorus of evenings and of dawns.
To you, Guiomar, goes this longing of mine.


# 55 *Other Songs for Guiomar*

(In the manner of Abel Martín and Juan de Mairena)

     I

   Only your figure
like a bright flash
in my dark night!

   And on the dark sand
beside the sea,

tu carne rosa y morena,
súbitamente, Guiomar!

En el gris del muro,
cárcel y aposento,
y en un paisaje futuro                                    10
con sólo tu voz y el viento;

en el nácar frío
de tu zarcillo en mi boca,
Guiomar, y en el calofrío
de una amanecida loca;

asomada al malecón
que bate la mar de un sueño,
y bajo el arco del ceño
de mi vigilia, a traición,
¡siempre tú!
        Guiomar, Guiomar,                                20
mírame en ti castigado:
reo de haberte creado,
ya no te puedo olvidar.


            II

Todo amor es fantasía;
él inventa el año, el día,
la hora y su melodía;
inventa el amante y, más,
la amada. No prueba nada,
contra el amor, que la amada
no haya existido jamás.                                  30


            III

Escribiré en tu abanico:
te quiero para olvidarte,
para quererte te olvido.


            IV

Te abanicarás
con un madrigal que diga:
en amor el olvido pone la sal.

your tanned and rosy flesh
of a sudden, Guiomar!

On the gray of the wall—
my dungeon and lodging—
and in a landscape of tomorrow                    10
only your voice and the wind;

on the pearly chill
of your earring in my mouth,
and in the flush and quiver
of a wild daybreak, Guiomar;

coming in sight on the embankment
where the sea of a dream is breaking,
and under the frowning arch
of my sleeplessness, surreptitiously,
always you!
            Guiomar, Guiomar—                     20
you've turned into my punishment:
for the fault of your creation,
I'm unable to forget you.


    II

Love is imagining, always;
it invents the year, the day,
the hour, the song of the hour;
it invents the lover and even
invents the beloved. Nothing is proved
against love for the beloved's
never having existed.                             30


    III

I'll write on your fan:
I love you so as to forget you,
I forget you so as to love you.


    IV

You'll fan yourself
with a madrigal that says:
in love forgetting adds the spice.

V

Te pintaré solitaria
en la urna imaginaria
de un daguerrotipo viejo,
o en el fondo de un espejo,                                    40
viva y quieta,
olvidando a tu poeta.

VI

Y te enviaré mi canción:
"Se canta lo que se pierde,"
con un papagayo verde
que la diga en tu balcón.

VII

Que apenas si de amor el ascua humea
sabe el poeta que la voz engola
y, barato cantor, se pavonea
con su pesar o enluta su viola;                                50
y que si amor da su destello, sola
la pura estrofa suena,
fuente de monte, anónima y serena.
Bajo el azul olvido, nada canta,
ni tu nombre ni el mío, el agua santa.
Sombra no tiene de su turbia escoria
limpio metal; el verso del poeta
lleva el ansia de amor que lo engendrara
como lleva el diamante sin memoria
—frío diamante— el fuego del planeta               60
trocado en luz, en una joya clara . . .

VIII

Abre el rosal de la carroña horrible
su olvido en flor, y extraña mariposa,
jalde y carmín, de vuelo imprevisible,
salir se ve del fondo de una fosa.
Con el terror de víbora encelada,
junto al lagarto frío,
con el absorto sapo en la azulada
libélula que vuela sobre el río,

V

I'll paint you all alone
on the imaginary urn
of an old daguerrotype
or in a mirror's depths,                                    40
live and still,
forgetting your poet.

VI

And I'll send you my song:
"One sings what one loses,"
plus a green parakeet
to say it on your balcony.

VII

For if the live coal of love so much as smoulder,
the poet knows his voice is being forced
and he's strutting with his pain like some cheap tenor
or hanging crepe on his viola;                              50
if love emits its glow, he knows
that nothing but limpid verse is heard,
like a mountain spring, anonymous and serene.
Beneath the blue of oblivion the sacred water
sings nothing—not your name, not mine.
Not a trace of the turbid slag
is left in shiny metal; the poet's line
bears the unease of love that brought it forth
as the unremembering diamond—
cold diamond now—bears fire of the planet              60
turned into light, the gleam of a bright gem . . .

VIII

Its unremembering of awful carrion
the rose turns into bloom. One sees
strange butterflies, sulphur and scarlet,
dart unpredictably from depths of tombs.
The terror of the viper roused,
of the lizard's coldness,
the toad's fixation with the dragonfly
glinting blue above the river,

con los montes de plomo y de ceniza,                          70
sobre los rubios agros
que el sol de mayo hechiza,
se ha abierto un abanico de milagros
—el ángel del poema lo ha querido—
en la mano creadora del olvido . . .

. . . . . . . . . . . . . . . . . . . . . . . . . .

## 56 *Muerte de Abel Martín*

> *Pensando que no veía*
> *porque Dios no le miraba,*
> *dijo Abel cuando moría:*
> *Se acabó lo que se daba.*
>
>            J. de Mairena: *Epigramas.*

I

Los últimos vencejos revolean
en torno al campanario;
los niños gritan, saltan, se pelean.
En su rincón, Martín el solitario.
¡La tarde, casi noche, polvorienta,
la algazara infantil, y el vocerío,
a la par, de sus doce en sus cincuenta!

¡Oh alma plena y espíritu vacío,
ante la turbia hoguera
con llama restallante de raíces,                              10
fogata de frontera
que ilumina las hondas cicatrices!

Quien se vive se pierde, Abel decía.
¡Oh, distancia, distancia!, que la estrella
que nadie toca, guía.
¿Quién navegó sin ella?
Distancia para el ojo —¡oh lueñe nave!—,
ausencia al corazón empedernido,
y bálsamo suave
con la miel del amor, sagrado olvido.                        20

the mountains of ash and lead                                    70
overhanging bright fields of grain
bewitched by a sun of May: these have flung
the fan of wonderments wide open—
the angel of the poem willed it so—
in forgetting's creative hand . . .

. . . . . . . . . . . . . . . . . .


## 56  *The Death of Abel Martín*

> *Thinking he could not see*
> *because God's eye wasn't on him,*
> *Abel said as he was dying:*
> *whatever it was is over.*
> J. de Mairena: *Epigrams.*

I

Late swifts in wheeling flight
about the belfry,
children shouting, hopping, scuffling.
Martín, the lonely one, off by himself.
Dusty evening, nearly night,
the children's noisiness, and with it,
his own twelve-year-old shouts reaching his fifties.

Oh, empty spirit and full soul
facing the smoky bonfire,
the crackle of flames through roots,                             10
the watchfire on the border
lighting up deep scars!

Living on is losing out, Abel was saying.
Oh, distance, distance guided by the star
that nobody can touch!
Who has ever sailed without it?
Distance for the eye—oh, far-off ship!—
absence for the heart grown hard,
and gentle balm
with honey of love, blessed forgetting.                          20

¡Oh gran saber del cero, del maduro
fruto, sabor que sólo el hombre gusta,
agua de sueño, manantial oscuro,
sombra divina de la mano augusta!
Antes me llegue, si me llega, el Día,
la luz que ve, increada,
ahógame esta mala gritería,
Señor, con las esencias de tu Nada.

### II

El ángel que sabía
su secreto salió a Martín al paso.                                    30
Martín le dio el dinero que tenía.
¿Piedad? Tal vez. ¿Miedo al chantaje? Acaso.
Aquella noche fría
supo Martín de soledad; pensaba
que Dios no le veía,
y en su mudo desierto caminaba.

### III

Y vio la musa esquiva,
de pie junto a su lecho, la enlutada,
la dama de sus calles, fugitiva,
la imposible al amor y siempre amada.                                 40
Díjole Abel: Señora,
por ansia de tu cara descubierta,
he pensado vivir hacia la aurora
hasta sentir mi sangre casi yerta.
Hoy sé que no eres tú quien yo creía;
mas te quiero mirar y agradecerte
lo mucho que me hiciste compañía
con tu frío desdén.
                    Quiso la muerte
sonreír a Martín, y no sabía.

### IV

Viví, dormí, soñé y hasta he creado—                                  50
pensó Martín, ya turbia la pupila—
un hombre que vigila
el sueño, algo mejor que lo soñado.

Oh, deep wisdom of the cipher, savor
of ripe fruit for man alone to taste,
dream-water and dark wellsprings,
God-given shade cast by the mighty hand!
Let my Day arrive, if arrive it must—
the increate light that sees—
only drown out this ugly clamor for me, Lord,
with essences of your Nothing.

II

The angel who knew
what Martín's secret was, confronted him.                    30
Martín gave him all the coin he had.
Piety? Perhaps. Afraid of blackmail? Possibly.
That cold night
Martín discovered loneliness;
he thought he was not seen by God
and walked on his soundless desert.

III

And he saw, standing beside his bed,
the elusive muse, the shrouded one,
the lady always withdrawing down his streets,
the one beyond love's reach and always loved.                40
Abel said to her: Dear lady,
I had thought to live into dawn,
hoping to glimpse your face unveiled,
live till I felt the chill spread in my blood.
Today I know you are not the muse I thought,
yet I want to gaze on you in gratitude
since you have kept me company so long
with the cold of your disdain.
                         Death tried
to smile at Martín and could not manage it.

IV

I lived, I slept, I dreamed, even created—                   50
thought Martín, his eye beginning to cloud—
a man to keep a watch on sleep,
that's better than on things dreamt.

Mas si un igual destino
aguarda al soñador y al vigilante,
a quien trazó caminos,
y a quien siguió caminos, jadeante,
al fin, sólo es creación tu pura nada,
tu sombra de gigante,
el divino cegar de tu mirada.                    60


                    V

  Y sucedió a la angustia la fatiga,
que siente su esperar desesperado,
la sed que el agua clara no mitiga,
la amargura del tiempo envenenado.
¡Esta lira de muerte!
                    Abel palpaba
su cuerpo enflaquecido.
¿El que todo lo ve no le miraba?
¡Y esta pereza, sangre del olvido!
¡Oh, sálvame, Señor!
                    Su vida entera,
su historia irremediable aparecía                    70
escrita en blanda cera.
¿Y ha de borrarte el sol del nuevo día?
Abel tendió su mano
hacia la luz bermeja
de una caliente aurora de verano,
ya en el balcón de su morada vieja.
Ciego, pidió la luz que no veía.
Luego llevó, sereno,
el limpio vaso, hasta su boca fría,
de pura sombra —¡oh, pura sombra!— lleno.                    80


## 57  *Otro clima*

  ¡Oh cámaras del tiempo y galerías
del alma ¡tan desnudas!,
dijo el poeta. De los claros días
pasan las sombras mudas.

But if a single fate
awaits the dreamer and the open-eyed,
the man who has laid out roads
and one who has panted down them,
in the end the sole creation is your Nothingness,
your giant's shadow,
the divine blinding of your glance.                     60

                    V

    But anguish gave way to weariness
born of the hopelessness of hoping,
to the thirst clear water does not slake,
the bitterness of time envenomed.
This lyre of death!
                    Abel ran his hand
over his emaciated body.
Was the one whose eye sees all not watching him?
And this lethargy, the blood of mindlessness!
Oh save me, Lord!
                    His life entire,
the story in final form, rose up before him           70
written in soft wax.
And must you be melted down by the new day's sun?
Abel stretched out his hand
toward the orange-red light
of a hot summer's dawn beginning to show
through the balcony of his old abode.
Blind, he asked for light he could not see,
and then serenely lifted
the clear glass to his cold lips,
the glass filled full of shadow—shadow alone.        80


## 57  Another Climate

    Oh recesses of time and passageways
of spirit, stripped so bare!
the poet said. Mute shadows
of the bright days pass.

Se apaga el canto de las viejas horas
cual rezo de alegrías enclaustradas;
el tiempo lleva un desfilar de auroras
con séquito de estrellas empañadas.
¿Un mundo muere? ¿Nace
un mundo? ¿En la marina                                    10
panza del globo hace
nueva nave su estela diamantina?
¿Quillas al sol la vieja flota yace?
¿Es el mundo nacido en el pecado,
el mundo del trabajo y la fatiga?
¿Un mundo nuevo para ser salvado
otra vez? ¡Otra vez! Que Dios lo diga.
Calló el poeta, el hombre solitario,
porque un aire de cielo aterecido
le amortecía el fino estradivario.                         20
Sangrábale el oído.
Desde la cumbre vio el desierto llano
con sombras de gigantes con escudos,
y en el verde fragor del oceano
torsos de esclavos jadear desnudos.
Y un nihil de fuego escrito
tras de la selva huraña,
en áspero granito,
y el rayo de un camino en la montaña . . .


## 58

   ¿En dónde, sobre piedra aborrascada,
vieja ciudad de pardo caserío
te he visto, y entre montes empinada?
Al fondo de un barranco suena un río.
   ¿Vieja ciudad, la luna amoratada
asoma, enorme, en el azul vacío
sobre tu fortaleza torreada?
¡Oh ruina familiar de un sueño mío!
   Mas esos claros chopos de ribera
—¡cual vence una sonrisa un duro ceño!—                    10

The singing of old hours dies away
like the prayer of cloistered joys;
time brings dawns in procession
and a train of dimmed-out stars.
Is a world dying? A world
being born? Upon the seas,                                          10
paunch of the globe, is a new ship
leaving its wake of diamonds?
Are the old keels beached and overturned?
Is it true the world was born in sin,
the world of toil and weariness?
Shall there be a new world to be saved
again? Again! For God to say.
There the poet, lonely man, stopped speaking;
just then a chilling gust out of the sky
muffled his subtle Stradivarius.                                    20
His ear was bleeding.
From the summit he could see the empty plain
and shadows of giants bearing shields,
and amidst the green din of ocean,
slaves' torsos panting naked.
And a *nihil* in fiery letters
written on harsh granite
beyond the hostile woods,
and the zigzag of a road on the mountainside . . .

# 58

Where have I seen you, heaped
on stormy rock, old town of earth-brown houses
clustered in mountain steeps?
Deep in a ravine a river sounds.
    Is a violet moon ascending
enormous in the empty blue,
old town, above your towered castle?
Oh ruins known so well from a dream of mine!
    But those bright poplars by the river—
like smiles that overcome a scowl—                                 10

me tornan a un jardín de primavera,
   gonces del sueño, al verdear risueño.
¡Rosa carmín y blanca arrebolera
también salís del fondo de mi sueño!

*1907—copiado en 1924.*


## 59 *Otras coplas*

   Otra vez el mundo antiguo,
sin pecado original:
el claro mundo de Homero.
Nausica vuelve a lavar
su ropa; las eleusinas,
hijas de Keleo, van
con ánforas a la fuente.
Dioses, ¡qué hermosas están!
Junto a los pozos partenios
Deméter vuelve a pasar.                        10


## 60 *Apunte de sierra*

   Abrió la ventana.
Sonaba el planeta.
En la piedra el agua.
   Hasta el río llegan
de la sierra fría
las uñas de piedra.
   ¡A la luna clara,
canchos de granito
donde bate el agua!
   ¡A la luna llena!                          10
Guadarrama pule
las uñas de piedra.
   Por aquí fue España.
Llamaban Castilla
a unas tierras altas . . .

on them dream hinges turn to take me back
  to a spring garden, to new smiling green.
Crimson roses and white four-o'clocks—
you too emerge from deep inside my dream.

*1907—copied 1924.*


## 59 *Further Lines*

The ancient world again,
untouched by Adam's sin:
the bright world of Homer.
Nausicaa washing clothes
again; Eleusinian women,
daughters of Celeos, bearing
amphoras to the well.
Oh, you gods, how lovely they look!
Beside the virgin springs
Demeter passes again.                    10


## 60 *Mountain Note*

He opened the window,
heard the planet turning,
water on stone.
  Stone claws of the cold
mountain range
reach into the river.
  In the bright moon,
granite bluffs
where the water swirls.
  In the full moon!                      10
Guadarrama sharpening
its stony claws.
  Spain passed this way
and some highlands were given
the name of Castile . . .

## 61    *Recuerdo infantil (de Juan de Mairena)*

Mientras no suena un paso leve
y oiga una llave rechinar,
el niño malo no se atreve
a rebullir ni a respirar.
El niño Juan, el solitario,
oye la fuga del ratón,
y la carcoma en el armario,
y la polilla en el cartón.
El niño Juan, el hombrecito,
escucha el tiempo en su prisión:                     10
una quejumbre de mosquito
en un zumbido de peón.
El niño está en el cuarto oscuro,
donde su madre lo encerró;
es el poeta, el poeta puro
que canta: ¡el tiempo, el tiempo y yo!

## 62    *El poeta recuerda las tierras de Soria*

¡Ya su perfil zancudo en el regato,
en el azul el vuelo de ballesta,
o, sobre el ancho nido de ginesta,
en torre, torre y torre, el garabato
    de la cigüeña! . . . En la memoria mía
tu recuerdo a traición ha florecido;
y hoy comienza tu campo empedernido
el sueño verde de la tierra fría,
    Soria pura, entre montes de violeta.
Di tú, avión marcial, si el alto Duero                 10
adonde vas recuerda a su poeta,
    al revivir su rojo Romancero;
¿o es, otra vez, Caín, sobre el planeta,
bajo tus alas, moscardón guerrero?

# 61 Childhood Memory (of Juan de Mairena)

Until he hears soft footsteps sound
and a key turn in the lock,
the naughty child does not even dare
to stir or draw a breath.
Little John, the lonely child,
can hear the scurrying of a mouse,
the borer working in the wood,
the moth in the ragpaper box.
Little John, the little man,
listens in his prison to time:                              10
the whining of a mosquito
like the humming of a top.
The child is in the dark room,
his mother has locked him in;
he is the poet, the absolute poet,
and his song is time, time and I!

# 62 The Poet Remembers the Soria Country

Taking its spindly stance in a watercourse,
lifting its crossbow form into the blue
or perching on flat nests of gorse
atop every tower, in pothook pose,
    the stork again . . . Within my mind
your memory has blossomed treacherously.
By now in your flinty countryside
green dreams are showing through the chilly earth,
    pure Soria, where the peaks rise lavender.
Warplane, let me know if the upper Duero,                   10
to which you're bound, recalls its poet still
    amid red ballad sagas reenacted.
Or is it a Cain on the planet's face once more
beneath your wings, hornet droning war?

## 63  *Meditación*

Ya va subiendo la luna
sobre el naranjal.
Luce Venus como una
pajarita de cristal.
Ambar y berilo
tras de la sierra lejana,
el cielo, y de porcelana
morada en el mar tranquilo.
Ya es de noche en el jardín
—¡el agua en sus atanores!—                    10
y sólo huele a jazmín
ruiseñor de los olores.
¡Cómo parece dormida
la guerra, de mar a mar,
mientras Valencia florida
se bebe al Guadalaviar!
Valencia de finas torres
y suaves noches, Valencia,
¡estaré contigo,
cuando mirarte no pueda,                        20
donde crece la arena del campo
y se aleja la mar de violeta!

*Rocafort, mayo de 1937.*


## 64  *El crimen fue en Granada*

A Federico García Lorca

I    *El crimen*

Se le vio, caminando entre fusiles,
por una calle larga,
salir al campo frío,
aún con estrellas, de la madrugada.
Mataron a Federico
cuando la luz asomaba.
El pelotón de verdugos
no osó mirarle la cara.

# 63 Meditation

Above the orange grove
the moon begins to climb.
Venus glistens,
a toy glass bird.
The sky is beryl and amber
beyond the far-off range,
porcelain and purple
over the quiet sea.
Night has come to the garden—
the sound of running water!—                    10
and everything smells of jasmine,
the nightingale of scents.
The war—how asleep it seems
from this to the other sea,
while blossoming Valencia
drinks in the Guadalaviar.
Valencia of the slender towers
and balmy nights, Valencia,
I shall be with you still
long after I cease to see you,                    20
where sand overspreads the land
and the violet sea withdraws.

                          *Rocafort, May 1937.*

# 64 The Crime Was in Granada

To Federico García Lorca

    I    *The Crime*

He was seen, surrounded by rifles,
moving down a long street
and out to the country
in the chill before dawn, with the stars still out.
They killed Federico
at the first glint of daylight.
The band of assassins
shrank from his glance.

Todos cerraron los ojos;
rezaron: ¡ni Dios te salva!                                    10
Muerto cayó Federico
—sangre en la frente y plomo en las entrañas—.
. . . Que fue en Granada el crimen
sabed — ¡pobre Granada! —, en su Granada . . .

  II   *El Poeta y la Muerte*

   Se le vio caminar solo con Ella,
sin miedo a su guadaña.
—Ya el sol en torre y torre; los martillos
en yunque — yunque y yunque de las fraguas.
Hablaba Federico,
requebrando a la muerte. Ella escuchaba.        20
"Porque ayer en mi verso, compañera,
sonaba el golpe de tus secas palmas,
y diste el hielo a mi cantar, y el filo
a mi tragedia de tu hoz de plata,
te cantaré la carne que no tienes,
los ojos que te faltan,
tus cabellos que el viento sacudía,
los rojos labios donde te besaban . . .
Hoy como ayer, gitana, muerte mía,
qué bien contigo a solas,                         30
por estos aires de Granada, ¡mi Granada!"

        III

    Se le vio caminar . . .
                Labrad, amigos,
de piedra y sueño, en el Alhambra,
un túmulo al poeta,
sobre una fuente donde llore el agua,
y  eternamente diga:
el crimen fue en Granada, ¡en su Granada!

They all closed their eyes,
muttering: "See if God helps you now!"                    10
Federico fell,
lead in his stomach, blood on his face.
And Granada was the scene of the crime.
Think of it—poor Granada—, his Granada . . .

    II  *The Poet and Death*
    He was seen with her, walking alone,
unafraid of her scythe.
Sunlight caught tower after tower,
hammers pounded on anvils,
on anvil after anvil in the forges.
Federico was speaking,                                    20
playing up to Death. She was listening.
"The clack of your fleshless palms
was heard in my verse just yesterday, friend;
you put ice in my song, you gave my tragedy
the cutting edge of your silver scythe;
so I'll sing to you now of your missing flesh,
your empty eyes,
your wind-snatched hair,
those red lips of yours that knew kisses once . . .
Now, as always, gypsy, my own death,                      30
how good being alone with you,
in these breezes of Granada, my Granada!"

          III
    He was seen walking . . .
                        Friends, carve a monument
out of dream stone
for the poet in the Alhambra,
over a fountain where the grieving water
shall say forever:
The crime was in Granada, his Granada.

Notes to the Introduction

Notes to the Poems

Key to Poem Numbers

Index of Titles and First Lines

# Abbreviations

Belitt   Antonio Machado, *Juan de Mairena*, translated by Ben Belitt (Berkeley and Los Angeles: University of California Press, 1963).

*Comp.*   Antonio Machado, *Los complementarios*, ed. Domingo Ynduráin (Madrid: Taurus, 1972); vol. I: Facsímil; vol. II, Transcripción.

G-P   *Antonio Machado*, ed. Ricardo Gullón and Allen W. Phillips (Madrid: Taurus, 1973).

*JM*   Antonio Machado, *Juan de Mairena*, ed. J. M. Valverde (Madrid: Castalia, 1971).

*NCCA*   Antonio Machado, *Nuevas canciones y De un cancionero apócrifo*, ed. J. M. Valverde (Madrid: Castalia, 1971).

*OPP*   Antonio Machado, *Obras. Poesía y prosa*, ed. Aurora de Albornoz and Guillermo de Torre (Buenos Aires: Losada, 1964).

*Poesie*   *Poesie di Antonio Machado*, ed. Oreste Macrì. 3d. ed. (Milan: Lerici, 1969); Spanish text with facing Italian translation.

# Notes to the Introduction

1. Salvador de Madariaga, *Spain: A Modern History* (New York: Praeger, 1958), 78–79.

2. The family was by that time in effect a matriarchy, since Machado's father and grandfather had died.

3. Autobiographical notice supplied to Gerardo Diego for his 1931 anthology of contemporary Spanish poetry; reproduced in *OPP*, 51.

4. So Machado recalls himself in "One Day's Poem" (No. 32). A first brief visit to Soria in May 1907, after Machado had been named to the post there, is in all likelihood recorded in the posthumously published sonnet: "Where have I seen you, heaped on stormy rock" (No. 58).

5. Note on *Campos de Castilla* included in *Poesías completas* of 1917 (*OPP*, 47).

6. *OPP*, 904.

7. See *OPP*, 937, remarks in undated letters of the early 1930s to Guiomar; for example, "As for me, now that I see a possible triumph of the Republic as only too imminent, I intend to adhere to the parties furthest from power. That is our mission."

8. Three of these poems are included in this book: "The Crime Was in Granada" (No. 64), an elegy for Lorca following his murder in 1936; "Meditation" (No. 63), written in Rocafort in 1937; and the undated sonnet "The Poet Remembers the Soria Country" (No. 62), in which the sight of a war plane heading for the upper Duero Valley touches off, for the last time and with tragic overtones, a train of memories that in all likelihood date back to the sonnet presumably of 1907 (No. 58); see Note 4.

9. For example, by Nancy A. Newton, from whose "Structures of Cognition: Antonio Machado and the *Via Negativa*," *Modern Language Notes*, 90 (1975), 231, the quoted remark is taken. Likewise by Arthur Terry, *Antonio Machado: Campos de Castilla*. Critical Guides to Spanish Texts (London: Grant and Cutler in association with Tamesis Books, 1973), 17. See also Michael P. Predmore, "The Nostal-

gia for Paradise and the Dilemma of Solipsism in the Early Poetry of Antonio Machado," *Revista hispánica moderna*, 38 (1974–1975), 47.

10. These states of mind have received their most sensitive analysis from Javier Herrero, "El sistema poético de la obra temprana de Machado," *Cuadernos hispanoamericanos*, 304-307 (1975–1976), I: 559-583, a study which considers pieces written through 1907.

11. See, especially, "Portrait" (No. 24) and the last section of "From My Portfolio" (No. 46).

12. "From My Portfolio" (No. 46, I). In the original edition of *Nuevas canciones* (Madrid: Mundo Nuevo, 1924), where "From My Portfolio" first appears, as the closing poem, the phrase "Jottings of 1902" (*Apuntes de 1902*) completes the title. If one may take Machado at his word in this dating—and his dating was sometimes capricious—this series of seven brief reflections on poetry would well antedate his direct exposure to Bergson's thought at the Collège de France in 1911. Two of them (II and VII) were later entered in his notebook (June 1914), *Comp.*, II, 35.

13. *Comp.*, II, 173-174. The quotation immediately following is from *JM*, 80. This, the best edition of *Juan de Mairena*, contains the fifty newspaper articles written by Machado under that name between November 1934 and June 1936. The subsequent series, written during the Civil War, appears in *OPP*, 523-636. Ben Belitt has translated parts of the first series in his *Juan de Mairena*. When I have quoted from passages translated by Belitt, though the translations are always my own, I have referred the reader to Belitt's versions as follows: Belitt, 21 (the present case). The swimming fish as an aesthetic symbol appears much earlier, in 1917; see No. 34, VIII.

14. *OPP*, 46–47.

15. The first quotation is from an undated letter of Machado to Ramón del Valle-Inclán, *OPP*, 930.

16. For example, *OPP*, 50, 565. The lines that follow in the text come from "From My Portfolio" (No. 46, IV). In No. 24 Machado will declare his poetry sprung from clear springs.

17. The poet's grandfather Antonio Machado y Núñez had lost his own chair of Natural Sciences in the University of Seville on the fall of the First Republic. (He had served the Republic as Chancellor of the University and Governor of Seville.) The Madrid appointment to a chair in Natural Sciences was in reality a restoration to the chair of which he had been deprived in Seville.

18. On C.-J. Krause (1781–1832), his philosophy and its importance in Spain, see Juan López-Morillas, *The Krausist Movement and Intellectual Change in Spain, 1854–1874*, translated by Frances López-Morillas (London: Cambridge University Press, 1981).

19. The purely symbolic roads that first appear in the "Proverbs and Song-Verse" of *The Castilian Country* (No. 34), despite the brevity with which they are treated, are among the most subtly suggestive in Machado's entire production: strangely paradoxical (I), em-

bodiments of profound disorientation and distress with biographical roots (VI, 1913), traditional expressions of transience to which he gives an unmistakably personal turn (IX). The reader will easily recognize other, often earlier, handlings of the road motif that follow lines to which I have alluded. On metaphysical nuances of the road symbolism, see Pedro Cerezo, *Palabra en el tiempo. Poesía y filosofía en Antonio Machado* (Madrid: Gredos, 1975), 55-79.

20. "I am a man extraordinarily sensitive to the place in which I live." From a 1938 interview quoted in Manuel Tuñón de Lara, *Antonio Machado, poeta del pueblo* (Barcelona: Nova Terra, 1967), 63.

21. No. 39, IV. The line quoted is from the long narrative poem, "La tierra de Alvargonzález," included in *Campos de Castilla* (*Poesie*, 480).

22. *OPP*, 905.

23. In one of several farewells from afar to Soria, a sonnet of 1919, Machado pinned down the elusive aesthetic-spiritual entity he called *alma* (soul) as, in one sense, a state of sensibility arising from the temporal, spatial, or, in general, the imaginative distancing of an experience: ". . . No me pidáis presencia; / las almas huyen para dar canciones: / alma es distancia y horizonte: ausencia." (. . . Don't require my presence; / souls flee to bring forth songs: / soul is distance and horizon: absence.) (Autograph reproduced in *Comp.*, I, fol. 169r. The date appears to be 1913.)

24. On Bergson and Machado, see Juan López-Morillas, "Antonio Machado's Temporal Interpretation of Poetry," *Journal of Aesthetics and Art Criticism*, 6 (1947), 161-171, and Nigel Glendinning, "The Philosophy of Henri Bergson in the Poetry of Antonio Machado," *Revue de littérature comparée*, 36 (1962), 50-70.

25. *OPP*, 917.

26. See J. L. Aranguren, "Esperanza y desesperanza de Dios en la experiencia de la vida de Antonio Machado," in G-P, 302-307; and Cerezo, *Palabra en el tiempo*, 360-379.

27. A brief, uncollected poem (No. 59) records the delight of rediscovering a pristine Hellenic world. The lyre of Pythagoras mentioned in the next sentence was already being elaborated in personal fashion in the early verse, for example, No. 22 (1907).

28. See, for example, JM, 60; Belitt, 11; *OPP*, 548, 577, 665-671, 814-819.

29. T. S. Eliot, "The Metaphysical Poets," in *Homage to John Dryden: Three Essays on Poetry of the Seventeenth Century* in The Hogarth Essays (New York: Doubleday, Doran, 1938), 218. The essay, written for the *Times Literary Supplement*, first appeared in book form in the *Homage* in 1924. Cerezo explores the fusion of the poetic and the philosophical in Machado at length throughout his *Palabra en el tiempo*.

30. The passage dated 1931 is from *OPP*, 50; that of 1923, from *Comp.*, II, 121. With the latter compare Eliot's observation: "A philo-

sophical theory which has entered into poetry is established, for its truth or falsity in one sense ceases to matter, and its truth in another sense is proved" ("Metaphysical Poets," 221).

31. *OPP*, 714. For the critical notice alluded to in the next sentence, see, respectively, Pedro Laín Entralgo, "Díptico machadiano. I. Intimidad y pueblo en Antonio Machado," *Cuadernos hispanoamericanos*, 304–307 (1975–1976), I: 10, and Helen F. Grant, " 'Angulos de enfoque' en la poesía de Antonio Machado," *La Torre*, 12 (1964), 468. Nelson Orringer reminds me that Max Scheler, of whose thought there are echoes later in *Juan de Mairena*, was already speaking of *Mitgefühl* in 1913 in *Zur Phänomenologie und Theorie der Sympathiegefühle*.

32. Of these poems, my selection includes the sonnets "The Flaming Rose" (No. 49) and "To the Great Nought" (No. 50) from the original "Songbook," and, from a later expansion included in the *Complete Poems* of 1933, "Last Lamentations of Abel Martín" (No. 51) and "Memories of Dreaming, Fever, and Dozing" (No. 53). Also from the 1933 "Songbook" are "Siesta" (No. 52) by Martín's disciple Juan de Mairena (1865–1909), written in memory of his master; the three "Songs for Guiomar" (No. 54), presumably felt to be written in the manner of Abel Martín and Juan de Mairena, as Machado expressly indicates is the case with a subsequent series of such songs (No. 55); and two closely linked compositions with which the expanded "Songbook" ends: "The Death of Abel Martín" (No. 56) and "Another Climate" (No. 57), in which the master's final moments are related.

33. Introduction to *NCCA*, 45–46, 73. See also Xavier Tilliette, "Antonio Machado, poète philosophe," *Revue de littérature comparée*, 36 (1932), 37–43.

34. Valverde in his Introduction to *JM*, 9, 15.

35. Included in this book is one of the interpolated poems, "Childhood Memory (of Juan de Mairena)," No. 61.

36. *OPP*, 935.

37. The words quoted are from *OPP*, 849.

38. *OPP*, 638–639.

39. *JM*, 98; Belitt, 14.

40. *OPP*, 582; compare No. 40, LXIV.

41. See *JM*, 158–159.

42. See *JM*, 108–109.

43. *Confessions*, Book X, beginning of ch. 19, translated by R. S. Pine-Coffin (Harmondsworth: Penguin Books, 1961), 225.

44. Early impressions of the passageways, patio, and garden of the Palacio de las Dueñas, and especially of its lemon trees and fountain, evolve into recurrent symbols in Machado's verse. See Nos. 3; 17; 30; 47, IV; 51.

45. *JM*, 157.

46. For a discussion of this process, see the note to Poem 28.

47. Geoffrey Ribbans reminds me that this reflex of irony is found in "Ars poetica" dating from 1904 (*Poesie*, 964), a poem subsequently eliminated. The last line reads: "¡Oh, para ser ahorcado, hermoso día!" (Oh, what a beautiful day to be hanged!). Michael Predmore, in the article cited in Note 9, 41–44 especially, comments extensively on this "vein of irony and mockery and irreverence" perceptible in Machado's early work.

48. Speaking of successive post-Romantic developments in poetry, Machado writes in 1931 of the late nineteenth century: "This is the literally *profound* stage of the lyric, when the poet goes down into his own hells, giving up all soaring flight" (*OPP*, 849).

49. *Comp.*, II, 69; passage from about 1920.

50. In an undated letter quoted in *OPP*, 934. *Enunciación en serie* (sequential utterance) is Machado's phrase elsewhere (*NCCA*, 217) for what I have called temporal sequentiality.

51. *OPP*, 849 (1931).

52. In an "excerpt" from a "political" speech of Juan de Mairena, Machado sums up in 1935 at least part of this pervasive tendency: "Half of our heart stays in our home region; but the other half cannot be contained within such narrow limits. With it we lovingly invade the whole of our glorious Spain. And if we had a third part at our disposal, we would devote it entire to the love of all humanity." (*JM*, 164).

53. *OPP*, 859.

54. *OPP*, 47–48. "We weave with the thread we are given, / when we weave," he will write more resignedly later on in one of the "Proverbs and Song-Verse" (No. 41, LXIV) of *New Songs*.

55. *JM*, 72 (1934), 80 (1935); Belitt, 18, 21.

56. So Juan de Mairena had pinned down the time in question in 1924–1925 (*NCCA*, 217). But in the same period, in his notebook Machado was already speaking more broadly, less personally, of the temporal dimensions of poetry. Compare the passage quoted earlier, the origin of which is indicated in Note 13.

57. There is a slight difference in the Spanish titles of Nos. 25 and 27, which the English does not reproduce.

58. One sees this in the marked military cast of the topographical metaphors and in the detail of the majestically soaring birds, who are also hunters of carrion and who anticipate at once the bravery and the ruthlessness of the conquistadors—"lions" and "crows"—that appear later. The long dragging lines, with their displaced internal pauses and their maladjustment to the couplet form, "telling" as well as "singing" of the physical strain of the climb, signify the difficulty of reaching and sustaining a genuine vision of the Castilian past and present, whose harsh hues other details of the scene underscore—the pungency of the crushed herbs, the merciless sun.

59. Compare Machado's description of *alma* in Note 23.

60. The best treatment of this development is by José María Val-

verde in *Antonio Machado,* 2nd ed. (Madrid: Siglo Veintiuno, 1975), 115-125.

61. See Rafael Láinez Alcalá, "Recuerdo de Antonio Machado en Baeza: La diligencia de Acribite," in G-P, 95–96.

62. The fourth and fifth parables had already appeared as "Humoradas" (Whims) in 1912 in *The Castilian Country.* They thus antedate the Baeza years.

63. See Geoffrey Ribbans, *Niebla y Soledad: Aspectos de Unamuno y Machado* (Madrid: Gredos, 1971), 300–306, especially a statement of Machado's to Unamuno in 1904 (quoted on 302) which reveals the latter's liberating influence: "I, at least, would be lacking in gratitude if I did not recognize that to you I owe my having leaped the walls of my pen or garden."

64. *OPP,* 922.

65. See Aurora de Albornoz, *La presencia de Miguel de Unamuno en Antonio Machado* (Madrid: Gredos, 1968), p. 240.

66. See Poem No. 34, VIII.

67. There are at least two discernible "learned" influences on the "Proverbs and Song-Verse": Sem Tob and Nietzsche. The term "proverbs" of the title unquestionably owes something to Machado's reading of the *Moral Proverbs* of the mid-fourteenth-century rabbi and physician Sem Tob (Santob). Sem Tob's nearly seven hundred quatrains introduced into Spanish poetry the Hebraic and Moslem strains of pithy moral utterance—aphorisms, anecdotes, and advice—traceable ultimately to Biblical and Talmudic sources. Segundo Serrano Poncela has noted analogies in manner and theme between Sem Tob and Machado in "Machado y Don Sem Tob," *Del romancero a Machado* (Caracas: Universidad Central, 1962), 174–184. See also below, note to No. 41, LXI. As for Nietzsche, Gonzalo Sobejano in *Nietzsche en España* (Madrid: Gredos, 1967) notes Machado's ambivalence toward the German writer: "He detests his anti-Christianity and furious and contagious iconoclasm, reserving his admiration for the moralist, the psychologist, the visionary of the eternal return, and the writer" (420). Sobejano notes Juan de Mairena's recommendation of Nietzsche as "master of the aphorism and the epigram" (*JM,* 256; Belitt, 111) and sees "similarity between the sententious poetry of Machado and that of Nietzsche" (423). A third strain in Machado's proverbs is the semi-learned semi-popular one of the sayings traditionally attributed to Pythagoras.

68. *OPP,* 387; *JM,* 89–90.

69. I have selected for inclusion ten of the fifty-three "Proverbs and Song-Verse" found in the definitive version of *The Castilian Country* incorporated in the *Poesías completas* of 1917. (There had been only twenty-eight in 1912.) I have omitted none of the *New Songs* series, for it is only in the latter that Machado truly hits his stride and it seemed desirable to provide a full sample of this vein in his production. The former series, for its part, contains verse in-

dispensable to any critical consideration of the poet. I refer separately to many of the individual selections from it.

70. Quoted in *NCCA*, 94, from Manuel Tuñón de Lara, "Un texto de Don Antonio Machado," *Bulletin hispanique*, 71 (1969), 315. This hitherto unnoticed answer of Machado to an inquiry concerning his views on the current literary scene appears in *La Internacional*, no. 48 (17 Sept. 1920). In the original (1924) edition of *New Songs*, Machado groups the "Proverbs and Song-Verse" together with certain other compositions in a section entitled "Folklore." Although there is more than *autofolklore* in this section and in *New Songs* as a whole, the term is a felicitous coinage.

71. Tuñón de Lara, "Un texto de Don Antonio Machado," 313.

72. This, we are told at the beginning of the exposition of the apocryphal Abel Martín's philosophy, is the title of one of several works ascribed to him (*NCCA*, 187).

73. *OPP*, 569 (1937). The quotation that follows (*OPP*, 856) is from a draft of an undelivered acceptance speech following Machado's election to the Royal Spanish Academy in 1927. Machado never occupied his chair, and his speech of acceptance was written in 1931.

74. *OPP*, 800. The Shakespearean line is from *King John*, IV.ii.11.

75. See note to Poem No. 30, lines 29–30.

76. See Francis Very, "Antonio Machado and the Oil-drinking Owl," *Modern Language Notes*, 78 (1963), 200–202.

77. Unlike the other poems in the series, the final one had appeared in print before: in 1923, in the review *La Pluma*. It is a poem of "open-ended vision," rather than of vision recalled. It is discussed, along with Poems 42, 44, and 38, in the text following Note 87.

78. "The poem was written by Machado for the music of Father Enrique Villalba of Valladolid" (Macrì in *Poesie*, 1228).

79. This series, first published separately in 1925, was incorporated in 1928 in the *Nuevas canciones* section of the *Poesías completas*, 2nd ed.

80. *JM*, 172; Belitt, 68. (Text of 1935.)

81. *OPP*, 826, "Reflections on the Lyric" (1925).

82. *OPP*, 852.

83. *OPP*, 829 (1925).

84. *OPP*, 849.

85. The expansiveness is conveyed by the simple device of repetition ("flying and flying," "country, open country") even more marked in the original (No. 37, II, lines 3–4; IV, line 3).

86. See No. 56, "The Death of Abel Martín," III.

87. *JM*, 98.

88. *JM*, 98.

89. I have exemplified this composite character of the imagery in "Antonio Machado and the Lyric of Ideas," *Aquila*. Chestnut Hill

Studies in Modern Languages and Literatures, IV (Brookline, Mass.: Boston College; Florence: Licosa, 1979), 193–218.

90. *JM*, 134; Belitt, 47–48.

91. *JM*, 251: "With old Heraclitus we believe that the world is ruled by lightning." Macrì (*Poesie*, 1226) first drew attention to this remark of Machado's, which follows very closely Heraclitus' "Everything is ruled by lightning" (Fragment 64 in *Herakleitos von Ephesos, griechisch und deutsch*, ed. Hermann Diels, 2nd ed. [Berlin, 1909], an edition which Machado very possibly used). The subsequently mentioned notions are found in Fragments 30, 60, 90, 76, and 8. The Heraclitean fire is also present in the last of the "Proverbs and Song-Verse" of *New Songs* (No. 41, XCIX). For fuller detail see Trueblood, "Antonio Machado and the Lyric of Ideas."

92. *NCCA*, 123n.

93. Similar imagery reappears with similar symbolic associations in No. 55, VII, where one also becomes aware of its Greek links.

94. A fifth sonnet has not been translated in this book.

95. Facsimile and transcription in *Comp.*, I, fol. 178v; II, 205–206.

96. In the first section of the *Apocryphal Songbook* (1924–1926); *NCCA*, 185–203.

97. Valverde comments suggestively on the reasons why the "Other Songs for Guiomar," separated by some six years from the first (1929 and 1935), are said to be written "in the manner of Abel Martín and Juan de Mairena." In the draft of Machado's undelivered acceptance speech following election to the Royal Spanish Academy he writes: "The truth is that what has ceased to figure within range of our hopes, if it should by chance appear before us, will not be able to convince us of its truth" (*OPP*, 843). Valverde comments: "However passionately Antonio Machado may have loved 'Guiomar,' he could never quite convince himself of the reality of that love, or of her, because he was less and less convinced of his own reality, and everything he wrote had to be placed in the mouth of his 'apocryphal poets' " (*NCCA*, Introduction, 88).

98. The concept of *olvido* (forgetting) offers problems to the translator. It implies a more active and less involuntary process than in English, a definitive putting out of mind. (Thus, the unlettered Sancho Panza can tell Don Quixote [I, 30] that once he had dictated his master's letter to Dulcinea from memory to a scribe, "I set about forgetting it.") Machado's handling tends to bring out these more dynamic implications of the term. (He calls forgetting a *potencia activa*, an "active capability" [*OPP*, 538].) I have consequently been obliged to resort to different English approximations to convey what seemed the key implication in each instance.

99. *JM*, 76–78; *OPP*, 376–378.

100. *JM*, 77.

101. See notes to this poem, lines 59–61.

102. "The Flaming Rose" is cited in Juan de Mairena's exposition

of Abel Martín's philosophy of love in the "Apocryphal Songbook," *NCCA*, 193–194 (*OPP*, 298).

103. Both included in the "Apocryphal Songbook," *NCCA*, 211, 237–238, respectively; *OPP*, 311, 330. Belitt, 121, has translated "Siesta."

104. *NCCA*, 212; *OPP*, 311. Juan de Mairena will later (1936) remark that his master felt that "God could not be a creator of the world because the world is an aspect of the Godhead itself; that the true creation of God was Nothingness" (*JM*, 251).

105. Newton, "Structures of Cognition," 241; quotations from 236, 241.

106. Newton, 241.

107. All three poems belong to the *Poesías completas*, 3rd ed., 1933.

108. Reproduced in *OPP*, 784–787.

109. Valverde in his Introduction to *NCCA*, 90–91.

110. Five years after writing the poem, in 1936, Machado was saying: "Juan de Mairena would have said of the Surrealists: those waterwheel mules still haven't understood that there's no waterwheel without water" (*JM*, 266).

111. Valverde quotes the passage (not reproduced in *OPP*) in his Introduction to *NCCA*, 26–27.

112. Valverde, Introduction, 90.

113. On Charon, see Valverde, Introduction, 91. Described identically as *el fúnebre barquero* (the doleful boatman), Charon appears in a sonnet of *New Songs* to Valle-Inclán (*Poesie*, 742) in which Macrì (*Poesie*, 1238) sees, among other reminiscences, one of Lucian's dialogue. No reminiscences of Lucian have been pointed out in the present poem, however, so far as I know. See notes to lines 126–136.

114. *JM*, 172.

115. *OPP*, 829.

116. The phrase quoted, from *Macbeth*, I.iii.58, is also cited in this same period in *JM*, 102 (1935).

117. Compare "It is also true that, as the point of view and the points of reference are continually varying, quantitatively and qualitatively, no happening in our past will ever appear to us twice as exactly the same" (*OPP*, 567).

118. *JM*, 174.

119. *JM*, 210.

120. In lines from a poem of 1907 not translated in this book (Poem XIII, *Poesie*, 246), the speaker greets a radiant sunset with the exclamation: "¡Hermosa tarde, nota de la lira inmensa / toda desdén y armonía; / hermosa tarde, tú curas la pobre melancolía / de este rincón vanidoso, oscuro rincón que piensa!" (Lovely evening, note of the immense lyre / all harmony and disdain— / lovely evening, you cure the petty melancholy / of this proud cranny, this dark nook of thought!)

121. *JM,* 104.

122. *OPP,* 810.

123. *OPP,* 555.

124. *NCCA,* 119.

125. *Comp.,* II, 73–75. Compare *OPP,* 875, where Machado echoes the remark of Fray Luis de León that St. Teresa wrote "not in Spanish but in celestial language."

126. *JM,* 192.

127. *JM,* 172. *Cegar* expresses an act, not a state: that of going blind. In its active force it is similar to *olvido.*

128. In a different vein one perhaps sees reappearing here, as well, Machado's differences with his younger contemporaries. He offers, not without a certain irony, his own version of a "creationist" poetics, one not organic or ludic like theirs, but firmly, if obscurely, grounded in philosophical thought, as he felt theirs was not.

129. *OPP,* 564. Misquoted from "Ebauche d'un serpent," where the lines read: "Que l'univers n'est qu'un défaut / dans la pureté du Non-être."

130. *JM,* 71.

131. *JM,* 69; *Poesie,* 1086.

132. In the "Arte poética" of the "Apocryphal Songbook," *NCCA,* 217.

133. *JM,* 72.

134. *OPP,* 563; for subsequent quoted observations of Machado on Heidegger, see 562–564.

135. See text following Note 44.

136. *JM,* 259.

137. Compare No. 55, VII, and note to lines 59–61.

138. Even later than the passage to which the previous note refers is the following: "At bottom, my thought is sad. Nevertheless, I am not a sad man, nor do I think I contribute to making anyone else sad. In other words, the lack of commitment to my own thought frees me from its evil influence; or, alternately, deeper than my own thought is my confidence in its vacuity, the Fountain of Youth in which my heart constantly bathes" (*OPP,* 579).

139. Machado also reaches the limits of his fellow-feeling for Plato. In 1936 he writes: "Man finds it hard to give up anchoring in the river of Heraclitus, to give up believing that what is conceived, defined, immutable, amid everything that seems to change, actually *is.* Against Platonic ideas there is only one argument: . . . *the idea of death,* of death which extinguishes everything: ideas as well as everything else" (*JM,* 262).

140. *OPP,* 566.

141. *OPP,* 531. The lines that conclude this Introduction are from Poem No. 34, VI.

# Notes to the Poems

*Where line numbers in the translations do not correspond to those in the original Spanish, the line number of the Spanish poem is noted first, followed by a slash and the line number of the translation.*

2    The motif of the return to the fountain in the enclosed garden is borrowed from Verlaine. See Paul Ilie, "Verlaine and Machado: the Aesthetic Rôle of Time," *Comparative Literature*, 14 (1962), 261-265.

    9. *parque:* "Garden" is an approximate equivalent, because *parque* may be a private or public enclosure and may comprise trees and lawns as well as flower beds.

    25/26. In its insistence the fountain emblematizes the lure of the probe into the psyche. The dialogue articulates almost too obviously both the "monotonous" presentness of all past experience and its metamorphosis by the current of the inner life.

3    Like Baudelaire a poet of scents and odors, like Mallarmé one of evocative absences, Machado makes the pervasive "scent of absence" evoke a fulfillment lying just out of reach, which finally breaks through, via particular scents, thanks to a coalescence of the moment of recalling and the moment recalled: a moment of early spring before florescence, when herb scents still prevail.

    24/26. *hierbabuena* (mint—literally, the good herb) reinforces the characteristically straightforward stress on goodness already strong in the repeated *bueno.*

4    See in the Introduction, in the paragraph following Note 74 where No. 41, LXXIX, is discussed, the remarks on Machado's predilection for children's songs.

5    The imprecision of the opening—one cannot know whether it is to be one experience or many, whether the roads are real, dreamt of, or recalled—typically encloses a particular phenomenon in others like it. By the fifth line the road has become one only, the occasion a single one. This focus, further sharpened by the song, is relinquished with the numb heart and the brooding land, only to be regained in the sudden final reprise. This characteristically Macha-

dian pattern may be connected with his reading of Bergson. See notes to Poems 28 and 30.

9. The motif of the interpolated *copla*, with its popular ring, reaches Machado via a poem of the nineteenth-century Galician poet Rosalía de Castro: "Unha vez tiven un cravo" (I once had a nail). In her poem the speaker utters a prayer, not a *copla*. See Luis Rosales, "Un antecedente de 'Yo voy soñando caminos,'" *Cuadernos hispanoamericanos*, 304-307 (1975–1976), II: 1029-1041.

7      11. *quimeras rosadas:* Rather than the monstrous chimaeras of myth, the "rose-gowned fantasies" are wispy, wraithlike feminine figures, embodiments of the ideal, in vogue in post-Symbolist poetry and art nouveau at the turn of the century. *Rosadas* in the 1903 *Soledades* had read *sombrías* (somber, shadowy). By 1907 Machado evidently wished to retain no longer this somewhat inconsistent throwback to the darker mood of the opening.

10     In lines published in the periodical *La Lectura* in 1916 and never reprinted by Machado, he writes: "Si hablo, suena / mi propia voz como un eco / y está mi canto tan hueco / que ya ni espanta mi pena" (If I speak, my own voice sounds like an echo and my song is so hollow that my pain is no longer frightening; *Poesie*, 1018). In a 1924 entry in his notebook he writes: "It should not be forgotten . . . that our nature contains materials for the shaping of many personalities, all of them as rich, coherent and complete as that one— whether chosen or assigned—which is called our character. What is commonly understood as personality is only the supposed character that in the long run seems to have the leading role. But is this character always played by the same actor?" (*Comp.*, II, 220).

2. Compare No. 7, line 6.

30. In Poem XXIII (*Poesie*, 264 [1903]), Machado writes: "El salmo verdadero / de tenue voz hoy torna / al corazón" (The true psalm / with the small voice / returns to the heart today). A predilection for this aesthetic sort of religiosity characterizes the intimist mood of much of the poetry of the turn of the century. As Geoffrey Ribbans notes (*Niebla y Soledad*, 149-150), it proceeds from the minor Symbolists, replacing prayer in a milieu needing spiritual uplift but lacking faith. The aesthetic and the sentimental overlap in the expression of such religiosity, as in Poem 8.

11     Title: One still sees around the Mediterranean basin this mechanism of Arabic origin that preceded the pump as a means of drawing up water from a well. The mule plods a circular path, turning a shaft that makes the wheel revolve. The water in the scoops is tripped into a spillway. The mules, which wear blinders or blindfolds, sometimes go blind. Machado in effect makes the depths of darkness from which the water is drawn the recesses of dream. The water communicates its dream quality to the blindfolded mule, transforming its blindness into inner vision and setting its motion in

phase with the water's rhythms and in harmony with the sound of its spilling.

15    There is no doubt that this poem, expressive of aspiration to faith but not of its possession, is nourished on Machado's reading of the Bible and the Spanish mystics. Two significant interpretations have focused on different strains of sources which may in fact be fused in the poem. Fernando Lázaro has seen in the imagery an allusion to the three theological virtues: in the first three stanzas, successively faith, hope, and charity ("Glosa a un poema de Antonio Machado," *Insula*, 119 [1955], 11, 13). For R. A. Molina the successive stages of the mystic process are evoked: the *via purgativa, via illuminativa,* and *via unitiva* (*Variaciones sobre Antonio Machado, el hombre y el lenguaje* [Madrid: Insula, 1973], 29-44). I shall note only the most apposite of the many texts cited by the two critics.

3-8. *fontana* (fountain): Lázaro (11) points to John 14:14: "the water that I shall give him shall be in him a well of water springing up into everlasting life." Molina traces this figure, as well as those of the two succeeding stanzas, to *Las moradas* (The Mansions) of St. Teresa, who says of the works of the soul that enjoys God's grace that they are pure "because they proceed from that fountain of life . . . Be it observed that the fountain is in the center of the soul" (cited by Molina, 34).

11-16. *colmena* (hive): Although Lázaro finds no source in "religious cryptology" for this image, he notes its clear reference to "hope" in Machado's No. 16 (present numbering). Molina (37) cites "comparisons very similar" to Machado's image in St. Teresa: "Humility always toils like the bee in the hive; otherwise it is unavailing. But let us keep in mind that the bee is always flying forth to bring back flowers; so the soul does in self-knowledge." The bee imagery is not uncommon in manuals of devotion. Fray Luis de Granada in his *Book of Prayer and Contemplation,* speaking of ways by which the believer can bring vividly to life the truths or events of the faith, notes the possibility of situating them within one's own heart and adds: "And this commonly greatly helps the soul achieve a contemplative state, busying itself toiling like a bee inside the cork of its honeycomb" (*Biblioteca de Autores Españoles,* VIII [Madrid: Hernando, 1925], 13a ). (Machado has a few class notes on Fray Luis de Granada in *OPP*, 875-876.)

15/14. *las amarguras viejas* (the bitter past): Whereas the emphasis of the mystical writers cited is on the humility and the diligence of the bees, with Machado it is characteristically on the mysterious powers of creative transformation of their honey-making process, powers here seen at their most striking.

19. *ardiente sol* (hot sun): Lázaro cites a sermon of the Blessed John of Avila which speaks of the Holy Sacrament as a fire by which the Christian is first warmed externally and which he then absorbs

within himself so that "he completely becomes an oven of love." Molina (37-38) cites Teresa's observation that "that glowing sun that is in the center of the soul does not lose its glow and beauty, which are always in the soul."

23-24. Lázaro quotes St. John of the Cross on the effect of divine illumination: "An immense light [striking on] weak, impure vision will turn it into complete shadow." The "tears" in the present case may indicate spiritual relief as well.

**16**    2. *Colmenares de mis sueños* (beehives of my dreams): The familiar symbol for the activity of poetic creation.

4. *la noria del pensamiento* (the waterwheel of the mind): For another such symbol, compare No. 11.

**17**    The coherent imagery creates an inner form centered on the fragility and evanescence of the process of involuntary recall: rainbow, lantern glass, windowpanes, soap bubbles—enclosures for bright epiphanies set both in the world recalled and in the experience of recalling. The Bergsonian coalescence of states of feeling here depends on imagery of air and space, not of water.

13. Memory here functions traditionally, more as a well than as a reservoir.

**18**    1-2. *el ángel más hermoso* (the fairest angel): Presumably Lucifer. Compare No. 53, lines 138-139 and note to these.

6. Compare No. 7, line 5.

**19**    13. *garabato* (pothook): The Spanish, like the English, evokes both the literal and extended sense: the pothook-shaped curlicues of children learning to write. The suggestion is constant in Machado. Compare No. 62, line 4.

**20**    "These lines, written many years ago . . . may be given an unequivocal Heideggerian interpretation . . . [The first eight lines are quoted.] *Anguish*, so often alluded to by our Unamuno and earlier by Kierkegaard, appears in these lines—and perhaps in many others—as a radical psychic fact, which one neither can nor would define but does affirm as a persistent human note, as existential uneasiness (*Sorge*) rather than real Heideggerian anguish (*Angst*), though it will be transformed into this" (*OPP*, 564; text dated Valencia, December 1937).

**22**    The subdued pulsation of the traveling wave of this poem exemplifies Machado's quoted retrospective observation that in his earliest work the essential poetic element was "a deep pulsing of spirit."

**24**    This poem first appeared in the Madrid newspaper *El Liberal* on 1 Feb. 1908 (Heliodoro Carpintero, "Precisiones sobre el 'retrato' de Antonio Machado," *Insula*, nos. 344-345 [1975], 10). It was in response to a request of the paper that Machado appear in a "gallery of literary self-portraits."

13-20. Machado sets himself apart from the epigones of *modernismo*, who carried to often affected extremes the stylistic and thematic innovations of Rubén Darío (which Machado had saluted in their day). Machado feels perfectly free to return to the Renaissance tradition of French poetry in his fondness for Ronsard.

25    Machado has chosen rhymed couplets of fourteen-syllable lines (Spanish alexandrines), a metrical and strophic pattern made popular by his *modernista* predecessors. The long dragging lines, with their internal pauses frequently displaced from the midpoint and their sense frequently overrunning the two-line unit, "telling" as well as "singing" of the physical strain of the climb, signify the difficulty of reaching and sustaining a genuine vision of the Castilian past and present, whose harshness other details of the scene underscore: the pungency of the crushed herbs, the merciless sun.

2. The mountain Machado is climbing is the barren Cerro de Santana located on the left bank of the Duero opposite the town. Compare No. 45, I, ending.

31/32. The bridge leading across to Soria, whose main section rises on the steep right bank of the Duero.

33-34/37-38. *El Duero cruza el corazón de roble / de Iberia y de Castilla* (literally, the Duero crosses the oaken heart of Iberia and of Castile): The image carries a suggestion of piercing by an arrow, that is, of vitality drained away, which is lost in my English.

54/58. Valencia was taken by the Cid for Alfonso VI of Castile in 1094. The feat is related in the second *Cantar* of the *Poema de mio Cid*.

61/65. *sopa de convento* (literally, convent soup) refers to leftovers from convent meals served to beggars and paupers.

64/67. The Spanish refers specifically to trade on the east coast of Spain, that is, to the more active commerce of the Catalans and Valencians.

66/70. *la guerra* (war): The reference is to the internal riots and unrest provoked by a punitive Spanish campaign of 1909 against rebellious Moroccan tribesmen.

67/71. *Castilla miserable* (Wretched Castile): Although the earlier harsh judgment of Castile is repeated in almost the same words, the speaker's indignation is finally spent, though his spirit is not restored. The immediate scene once more impinges on his consciousness, its harshness softened by the coming-on of evening. The inquisitiveness of the "two pretty weasels" sets off the earlier indifference of the "boors" and benumbed "philosophers."

26    Machado saw blasphemy as a necessary escape valve for a peasantry who viewed the Lord as one more arbitrary and oppressive overlord. An observation made by Juan de Mairena twenty years after this poem (1934) provides the best commentary on it: "Blasphemy belongs to the religion of the people. Beware of a nation where there is no blasphemy: atheism will be popular there. To forbid blasphemy with more or less severe punitive laws is to poison

the common people's heart, forcing them to be insincere in their dialogue with the divinity. Will God, who sees into hearts, allow himself to be deceived? You may be sure that he will sooner pardon blasphemy given utterance than that hypocritically shut up deep inside the soul or still more hypocritically turned into a prayer" (*JM*, 43; Belitt, 2-3).

1-2. In an admonitory *cantiga* of the thirteenth-century king of Castile, Alphonse the Learned (No. CIV in the edition of the Royal Spanish Academy, ed. Marqués de Valmar, Madrid [1889]), a gambler lets fly at God with a *saeta* (literally, an arrow, but in this case, by extension, a blasphemous threat), only to find his gaming table pierced the next moment by a bloody arrow. Compare, however, the following *saeta* of Abel Martín: "Hay blasfemia que se calla / o se trueca en oración; / hay otra que escupe al cielo / y es la que perdona Dios." (There's a blasphemy that is silent / or turns into a prayer; / there's another that spits at heaven / and it's this that God forgives.) (*JM*, 133).

47-50. These lines further attest Machado's regard for the sixteenth-century mystics.

61-62. "So neither is the future yet written anywhere nor the past," Machado-Mairena will still write in 1938 (*OPP*, 567), no doubt with the Civil War in mind but also as a corollary to a restatement of his abiding conviction that future-present-past form a single agglomerate that is in constant flux.

27    49/48. *viejo romancero:* The rich store of traditional balladry dating from the later Middle Ages.

51-52/50-51. The ending is ambiguous, suggesting at once Castile's historical spirit of maritime enterprise and a draining away of the vitality of the Spanish heartland. Compare No. 25, note to lines 33-34/37-38.

28    The Bergsonian conception of memory referred to later (note to lines 29-30 of No. 30) underlies this poem. Glendinning ("Philosophy of Henri Bergson"; see above, Introduction, Note 24) pertinently quotes Bergson to the effect that memory is "une survivance des images passées [qui] se mêleront constamment à notre perception du présent et pourront même s'y substituer" (*Matière et mémoire* [Paris: Presses Universitaires de France, 1946], 68). Machado may sometimes create an effect, as here, of encasing a given experience in surrounding layers of others which resemble it (for example, the "chorus of evenings and of dawns" of the last of the "Songs for Guiomar," No. 54, III). Sometimes, on the contrary, he seems to be peeling away these outer layers in order to regain one seemingly pristine experience inside, as in Poem 3 and Poem 47, IV. Sometimes the "peeling" may occur involuntarily (No. 42). Other poems are built, in a way peculiar to Machado, on an oscillation or a hesitation between "peeling away" and enveloping, between focusing and unfocusing. This pattern is embryonic in No. 19 and fully formed in

No. 5, both examined in the Introduction. It is clear in the first of the "Songs for Guiomar" (No. 54, I); see notes to this poem.

29     For a perceptive examination of this poem, see Geoffrey Ribbans, "The Unity of Antonio Machado's 'Campos de Soria,'" *Hispanic Review*, 41 (1973), 285-296.

9. Moncayo: A prominent peak to the east of Soria, in Aragon. Rising to 7,600 feet, it separates the basin of the Duero, which flows into the Atlantic, from that of the Ebro, which flows into the Mediterranean.

79/78. *Soria pura / cabeza de Extremadura* (literally, pure Soria, / chief town of Extremadura): Machado is quoting the words on the town's escutcheon. The "pure" originally denoted absence of any non-Christian blood in the town's population after it was taken from the Moors and resettled in the thirteenth century. Extremadura preserves its medieval sense, referring not to the region so called today, but to an advanced zone of recaptured Christian territory.

81/80. *castillo* (castle): A hotel now occupies the eminence above the river where the castle stood. Little of it can be seen today.

115/111. *San Polo y San Saturio:* Sanctuaries on the left bank of the Duero connected by a poplar-lined road, one of Machado's favorite walks. San Polo was until the fourteenth century a convent of the Knights Templar. A garden through which Machado used to walk now surrounds its ruins. The Hermitage (*Ermita*) of San Saturio is the Romanesque shrine of the patron saint of Soria. Remnants of "the old town walls" rise across the river from these sanctuaries.

141/136. *alto llano numantino* (high Numantian plain): The ruins of Numantia, an Iberian town famous for its nineteen-year resistance to the Romans, which ended with its capture by P. Cornelius Scipio in 133 B.C., are located three and a half miles northeast of Soria. The siege is the subject of Cervantes' early play *La Numancia*.

30     7. *Castilla la gentil* (Castile the noble): The epithet is found in *Poema de mio Cid*.

29-30. In this figure of the missing thread, Glendinning has plausibly seen an assimilation of the Bergsonian conception of memory in terms of *attaches, liens, fils* which bind the "survivals" of earlier perceptions to similar experiences of the moment ("Philosophy of Henri Bergson," 69). It is precisely the absence of such affective ties that Machado, using similar figures, will later deplore (*OPP*, 711) in discussing the free-floating imagery of the avant-garde poetic movements of the 1920s.

31     Title: José María Palacio, a close friend of Machado's in Soria, was owner and editor of the newspaper *El porvenir castellano*, in which this poem first appeared in 1916. A searching analysis of the poem by Claudio Guillén is found in the seventh essay, "Stylistics of Silence," of his *Literature as System* (Princeton: Princeton University Press, 1971).

32    Critics agree that Machado is moving beyond Bergson here. Glendinning (66–67), in agreement with A. Sánchez Barbudo in his *Estudios sobre Unamuno y Machado* (Madrid: Guadarrama, 1959), 264, concludes that, although allusions to Bergson's work or thought find their way into the poem because the passage of time is its subject, they do not in any way "predetermine" the view here taken of time. A passage of *Juan de Mairena*, though written in 1936, is remarkably apposite to the poem: "But let's forget clocks, sophistry's instruments, which seek to mix up time with mathematics. As poets, lovers of poetry, apprentice nightingales, just what do we know of mathematics? Very little. And that little superfluous . . . And as metaphysicians—this is what we'd like to be—we have no use for mathematics, since nothing *of what is* can be counted or measured. Our clocks have nothing to do with our time, an ultimate reality, psychic in nature, which likewise is not counted or measured. Of course our clocks may reduce it to nonsensicality . . . to the extreme of making us harbor a sort of trivial impatience to hear the *tock* when the *tick* has sounded. But that is actually an illusion" (*JM*, 236).

3. *gay saber:* The complex craft of love verse and song practiced by the fourteenth-century Provençal troubadors and their Catalan and Castilian followers. More commonly called *gaya ciencia*, it connotes a skilled art at the opposite pole from folk poetry. Machado is being slightly ironical at the expense of his earlier literary pretensions. He is more so at the expense of the latter-day *modernistas* in No. 24, line 16, where he changes *saber* (craft) to *trinar* (trill).

98–99. *Abro uno / de Unamuno* (I open one / by Unamuno): As Glendinning notes (67), the new book on Machado's table is presumably Unamuno's fundamental *Del sentimiento trágico de la vida* (The Tragic Sense of Life; 1913), in which the questions Machado proceeds to mull over—doubt and belief, meaning and meaninglessness, free will—figure as prominently as in Bergson, whose *Essai sur les données immédiates de la conscience* (Essay on the Immediate Data of Consciousness), though not a new book (1889), is evidently current reading for Machado, as the two subsequent references in the poem show.

104–105/107. From his position as Chancellor of the University of Salamanca (1901–1914) Unamuno launched books that wrestled from an essentially antirationalist standpoint with basic problems of nation and faith, and issued calls to moral action which made him for a decade the dominant ethical force in Spain. As early as his *Vida de Don Quijote y Sancho* (Life of Don Quijote and Sancho) in 1905, Unamuno had defiantly proclaimed madness that acted upon the higher dictates of conscience to be a truer, wiser, and more courageous form of reason. These vigorously asserted paradoxes lend force to Machado's allusions (line 84) to the alternatives involved.

112–113. Compare the *manantial sereno* which Machado, in the

"Retrato" (Portrait) that opens *Campos de Castilla* (No. 24, line 10/9), calls the source of his verse.

125-136/124-135. Machado's flippancy at this point toward Bergson, the adverse comparison with Kant, are significant indications of the direction of his thinking.

130/129. *el volatín inmortal* (the immortal handspring on the tightrope): "The allusion to Immanuel Kant is perhaps somewhat ambiguous. We understand by his 'handspring' not the 'Copernican overturn' in knowledge, but the superiority of the 'categorical imperative' to every other consideration" (J. M. Valverde, *Antonio Machado* [Madrid: Siglo Veinte, 1975], 125).

155/153. *Se platica* (People talking): There follows a striking sketch of the characteristically Spanish institution of the *tertulia*, the group bound together by the assumption that to converse for the sake of conversing, on one or many subjects, is a high form of human sociability. On this particular *tertulia*, see Rafael Láinez Alcalá, "La botica de Almazán," G-P, 90-91.

197. "The description of the 'yo fundamental' at the end of the poem . . . is clearly an allusion to Bergson's two 'mois' in the *Essai*" (Glendinning, "Philosophy of Henri Bergson," 66). Again Machado is not unwilling to entertain second thoughts.

**33**    The journey described in II is the first leg of Machado's trip with a companion eastward from Baeza in June 1915 to the sources of the Guadalquivir in the Cazorla Mountains.

63-64/66. *La Torre de Pero Gil*, more commonly Torreperogil—so Machado calls it elsewhere (*Poesie*, 886)—lies east of Ubeda, through which the coach has already passed.

88/90. Peal (pronounced as two syllables) is Peal de Becerro, a town at the edge of the Cazorla Range.

103-104/104-105. The bitter allusion to the destructive cannons of General Alexander Von Kluck, German general at the Battle of the Marne, 1914, sweeps away the earlier personal pain, the pessimism regarding Spanish society, and the mounting existential "nausea" in a final surge of Machado's "Jacobin blood," which sees only total destruction and rebuilding as a remedy for the ills of Spanish society.

**34**    The dates of first publication are given except when this is 1912.

I (1909). Fundamentally ironical since the parallel is only apparent between the immortal Christ, who miraculously walks on the Sea of Galilee, and mortal man, who, for all his symbolic walking on the trackless sea of existence, actually sinks into the sea of death.

II (1909), 2. In the original, the untranslatable shift in the gender of *mar* (sea) from masculine to feminine only increases the immensity of the unknowability.

III. See Introduction at Notes 124 and 125.

III, 3-4. Sarcasm toward a cult of institutionalized Catholicism. Compare "Continúa Unamuno a los místicos españoles, almas de fuego. ¡Pobres corazoncitos de Jesús, no os asustéis!" (Unamuno is the successor of the Spanish mystics, souls afire. Poor little hearts of Jesus, don't be alarmed!); *OPP,* 765 (1905).

IV. The lines anticipate the skepticism of No. 15 (1917) and undermine the hopefulness of the "Retrato" of 1908 (No. 24, line 26).

V (1916). The implications of I, III, and IV attain a pithy formulation.

VI. The irony of I is missing in this pure song-verse.

VII. This enigmatic *copla* may signify that procreation, rather than cerebration, is the way to self-perpetuation.

IX (1913).

X (1913). The usual "two Spains," the forward-looking and the reactionary, have here become in effect one. On this profoundly pessimistic note Machado chooses to end the series in the definitive version of the *Poesías completas* of 1917.

35    The dates of composition (when known) or of first publication of the parables are: I–III, 1915; IV–V, 1912; VI–VIII, 1917.

II. Written at San Lúcar de Barrameda, at the mouth of the Guadalquivir, the ancient land of Tarshish or Tartessos.

III. The point of this enigmatic parable turns on an untranslatable play of meaning in the last line between a colloquialism vaguely expressive of the vastness of the sea, and the symbolic force (death, mortality, the unknown beyond life) so often attaching to the sea in Machado (viz. No. 32, line 142/140, and No. 34, II and V).

IV. Assuming a tone of unconcern, Machado rings changes on *Vita brevis, ars longa,* the Hippocratic and Senecan saying long since become proverbial.

V, 1. The Spanish means both *in* and *on* the sea, a significant fusion of senses. The sea functions polysemically here to symbolize both pure consciousness and everlastingness, though it does not really lose the symbolic overtones alluded to apropos of III.

12. *caridad* (loving-kindness): This unselfconscious emphasis, like that on *filantropía* (love of humankind) in No. 24 strikes a distinctively Machadian note in its unpretentious and unhesitating assertion of the ethical, so much a part both of his nature and his *Institución* training. Perhaps "the pure stream / of loving-kindness that flows forever" comes as close as Machado ever did to defining God. One has only to look at Poem 33 for a case of what he understood by "unloving faith."

37    I, 4, 5. Rafael Láinez Alcalá ("Los paseos del poeta," G-P, 91-92) recalls seeing Machado on his promenades in Baeza gazing on the panorama of these mountains off to the east and south.

8/7. North of Baeza lie the "cub hills" of Sierra Morena, the main range crossing southern Spain and separating Andalusia from New Castile.

II, 15. According to Láinez Alcalá, Machado often used to walk the nine kilometers from Baeza to Ubeda; this black oak tree was a landmark on the way.

III, 21. *San Cristobalón* (Big old St. Chris): The augmentative expresses familiarity and affection, as well as the great stature of the brawny popular saint. *Cristóbal* is the Spanish form of *Christophoros*, the bearer of the Christ-child.

23-25/22-25. See Introduction at Note 76.

VIII, 54-55. The epithet *la llana* (literally, low-lying) accompanies the name of Cordova in old ballads; Macrì cites examples in *Poesie*, 1224.

**38**    II. Various details in this section suggest early spring as opposed to the inert landscape of winter in I. An ascending phase of the Heraclitean cycle is implied.

III. We are back at the bottom point of the cycle, with water contending with fire. Compare Fragment 76 in the Diels arrangement of Heraclitus (see Introduction, Note 91): "Fire is nourished by the death of water, water by the death of fire."

IV. Numerous details suggest a world reborn, a new mounting phase of the cycle.

25. The taps of the departing shower are exactly seven to accord with the "seven strings of the sun's lyre," the seven notes of the scale of Pythagorean world harmony.

V. These lines represent a lull between the high exultation of the ending of IV and its recurrence at the end of VI. On different interpretations of them, see my article cited in Introduction, Note 89.

VII, 55. *las cenizas* (the ash): Frequently in Machado "ash" carries a connotation of devitalized conceptuality, hollow abstraction.

58. *alalo* (voiceless; properly, unspeaking): Machado hispanicizes the Greek.

**39**    8. *Urbión:* Name of a prominent peak and range northwest of Soria, in which the Duero rises.

17. The same town square, surely that of Soria, appears in No. 40, VIII.

51. The plain is that of the delta of the Guadalquivir.

60. The allusion, as in VIII and in No. 31, is to the grave of Leonor in the cemetery on the hill in Soria called *El Espino*.

78. *Agua que brilla y no suena* (Water glistening but mute): Behind the laconism and almost disdainful tone, one senses an implicit contrast with the river of VIII, and perhaps a subconscious one between baroque and neobaroque poetry, brilliant in visual effect, and a plainer poetry of pulsation and marked temporality. One may perhaps read the same contrast into No. 41, LXXXII.

**40**    II, IV. The influence of the Japanese haiku, in vogue in the early 1920s, has been seen in these sections. (Compare IX.) Instead of the usual octosyllabic regularity of the three-line Spanish *solear*, they exhibit a distinct metrical pattern, though the strict 5-7-5 syllabic pattern of the haiku is not followed. They further conform to the haiku in their concentration on natural or seasonal imagery. For details of Machado's passing interest in this form, see Macrí, *Poesie,* 1228-1229.

IV, 11. *Aleluyas* (cries of hallelujah): The Spanish word has the additional meaning of a small Easter picture imprinted with this word that is tossed among the crowds on Easter eve.

VIII. Compare No. 39, III.

IX. Compare No. 54, note to lines 77-78.

X, 46. The famous, excellently preserved Roman aqueduct of Segovia.

XII, 53/54. *Santo Domingo:* A church in Soria near which Machado lived with Leonor.

XIII, 75. For the "little earthen jug," see No. 41, XIX.

XIV. In this lighter context (as against No. 25, lines 38-40/42-44), emigration can be seen as a temporary expedient, not a cause of depopulation.

**41**     Title: The translation of *cantares* as "song-verse" is intended to emphasize the imitation in such verse of oral poetry sung rather than spoken.

I. On the "neo-Leibnitzian" character of Machado's "new objectivity" here, see Valverde's remarks in *NCCA* (introduction), 63-64. In *Juan de Mairena,* 157, Machado admits that the otherness of "the eye you see" may be disquieting and the solitary unseeing countryside, consequently, a relief.

II. There is perhaps an allusion here to Heraclitus' "people who know neither how to speak nor how to listen" (ed. Diels, Fragment 15).

V. The answer seems not to be waking up, which, as LIII and LXXXI show, comes after living and dreaming, but either forgetting or remembering (the second necessarily contingent on the first), which prepare the way for the transformation that leads to the artistically productive apocryphal past. This is fully expounded in *JM,* 77 (1935): "My master thought . . . that love begins with remembering and that one could hardly remember anything that hadn't been previously forgotten." Similarly: "Two important things the poet must know: first, that the past is not only incomplete . . . but is capable of being completed at will; second, that forgetting is an active capability, without which there is no creation, properly speaking" (*OPP,* 538).

XI, 3-4. For the full implications of these two lines, see the remarks of Juan de Mairena quoted in the Introduction at Note 100.

XIII. The Spanish plays untranslatably on the suggestion in *toronjil* (rose-balm) of *toronja* (grapefruit).

XV, 1. *tu complementario* (your counterpart): The exact sense is "one who completes you." This may either be by complementing you or by offering an alternative usually not wholly opposed to you. (Abel

Martín and Juan de Mairena assume gradations of both relationships to Antonio Machado.) *Los complementarios* is significantly the title Machado chose for the notebook-journal he began in Baeza in 1912. The cover is reproduced in J. L. Cano, *Antonio Machado. Biografía ilustrada* (Barcelona: Destino, 1975), 83.

XVI. As Note 74 to the Introduction attests, Machado was fond of quoting this *solear* as the gist of his case against both what he saw as the revived baroque tendencies of his own day and the original poetry of the baroque. In Juan de Mairena's diatribe against the latter he writes: "The bee that sips from the honey and not from the flowers is further removed from any creative activity than the modest compiler of factual documents" (*NCCA*, 222-223).

XVIII, 4. Compare *la miel del sueño* (dream-honey), No. 38, line 43/42.

XXII. Compare *JM*, 263; Belitt, 115: "Naturalness in poetry is generally the thing well said . . . *Quod elixum est ne assato*, says a Pythagorean proverb . . . Anything roundabout usually means an avid search for the shortcut, the direct utterance."

XXIII. Valverde cites remarks dated 12 Feb. 1916 in Machado's notebook (*Comp.*, II, 45): "Everyone will think that my epigrams are written against someone . . . No one will realize that these epigrams are written against myself. And why not? I am Tartarin [compare LXXVII], I am the cricket . . . and the snail [compare XXV] and all the rest. Why shouldn't a man be taken aback by the sad figure he makes? Ought we to write to puff ourselves up and applaud ourselves? Or the contrary [?]"

XXIV. The application is to artists and craftsmen. See *JM*, 89, where the town in which Mairena lived is said to contain a lower class superior to the others: "an intelligent, refined, and sensitive working class of artisans who know their craft and for whom, as for the artist, doing things well is much more important than merely doing them."

XXV, 1. *Sin embargo* (Just the same): Acknowledging the irresistibility of second thoughts, Machado writes: "The *just the same* of Mairena was the note forever being sounded by the bass string on the guitar of his reflections" (*JM*, 140; Belitt, 52). Compare XXXIII, LXXXIX.

XXVI, 1. *hombres activos* (active men): Anti-Nietzschean, like XXXV.

XXVII. Valverde cites an eighteenth-century epigram: "Dr. Pandolofo was looking at the skull of an ass. Touched, he said, 'Heaven help me, to think what we are!' " (*NCCA*, 140).

XXIX. In this context which opposes literary leaders to literary epigones, the issue of voices and echoes can be met unequivocally, for once.

XXXI-XXXIII, XXXV. Directed against Nietzsche; see note of Valverde, *NCCA*, 141.

XXXIV. Both Italian sayings—"Either renew yourself or die" and

"Sailing is necessary (but living is not)"— are from D'Annunzio (see Macrì's note in *Poesie*, 1232), though neither is original with him: the first is taken from Nietzsche; the second originates with Plutarch, who ascribes it to Pompey. Of D'Annunzio, Machado would write during the Spanish Civil War: "A misreading of Nietzsche led to the imperialism of D'Annunzio; a misreading of D'Annunzio has made possible the Italy of Mussolini, that porter turned into a god" (*OPP*, 604).

XXXIX. The emphasis is on a fundamental complementarity as against an unnatural and superficial imitation. As in IV and XV, the borderline between self and other here becomes thin.

XLI. Introductory to XLII and XLIII.

XLII. An implicit rejection of narcissism, self-love. Compare a statement occasioned by Unamuno's *Abel Sánchez* in a 1918 letter to him: "Your Cain is certainly envy: hatred of our fellow-man through love of ourselves" (*OPP*, 923).

XLIV, 2. In the letter just cited, Machado writes: "I am beginning to understand the value of letters. In them one says what one feels, away from a social setting where a man can hear neither himself nor his fellow man." The "words" of line 1 are evidently written words.

XLVI. In 1937, when Machado has had considerable success as a playwright, in collaboration with his brother Manuel, he will have Juan de Mairena quote these lines and add: "These lines—by a ditty-maker of Seville who is ranging the steppes of Soria at present—should be taken to heart by our actors, who cannot achieve the slightest note of truth when they play characters like Hamlet, Segismundo, Don Juan, characters who can't be copied but must of necessity be imagined. Clipping from *The Lighthouse of Chipiona*, 1907" (*OPP*, 538-539). (The clipping and its source are obviously made up on the spur of the moment.)

LII, 2. Compare No. 40, VIII.

LIV. As Valverde notes (*NCCA*, Introduction, 34), Machado is speaking of himself here.

LV. For Valverde (*NCCA*, 145), Machado is here synthesizing the history of philosophy, from Cartesianism to the idealism "which casts doubt on existence, particularly that of the individual."

LXI. "Don Santos de Carrión [Sem Tob, the fourteenth-century rabbi of Carrión], an old poet who dyed his white hair, not to simulate youth, which he had lost, but to dissemble the certainty of his old age and justify the immaturity of his mind" (Juan de Mairena in 1938, *OPP*, 631). Agustín García Calvo, in his edition of Sem Tob's *Glosas de sabiduría o Proverbios morales y otras rimas* (Glosses of Wisdom or Moral Proverbs and Other Rhymes; Madrid: Alianza, 1974), includes the relevant lines with the "other rhymes" (147). Sem Tob took the *chria*, ultimately Greek in origin, from the ninth-century Syrian doctor and scholar Honain ben Isaac (223).

LXII. Valverde (*NCCA*, 147) sees here a possible self-caricature for an attempt to retain mentally what age is taking away. Compare the later Juan de Mairena: "Never stick the dead leaves of trees on with sealing wax. Because the wind grows angry, not tired, and carries off the dead leaves and the green ones" (*OPP*, 525).

LXIV. See Introduction at Notes 40 and 54, and compare the following remarks: "It is difficult to interpret the dreams which pull the bundle of our purposes apart in order to mix memories and fears in with them . . . With bad dreams that burden the heart of the sleeper, it is not hard to interpret rightly. These dreams are memories of what is past, woven and mussed up by the clumsy, shaky hand of an invisible character: fear" (*OPP*, 772-773).

LXIV, 7. *copo dorado* (gold ball): *Copo* is, properly speaking, the mass of unspun wool or flax on the spindle.

LXV, 1-3. As Valverde notes (*NCCA*, 147), this Pythagorean precept is usually construed to indicate generosity and respect for fertility.

LXVIII. In an amplified version in *JM*, 132, two new opening lines clinch the point with an example: "¡Quién fuera diamante puro!— dijo un pepino maduro" ("Oh, to be a pure diamond!" said a ripe cucumber).

LXXIV. One might paraphrase: "Hate thy neighbor as thyself."

LXXVII. Machado sardonically sees himself as Daudet's Tartarin de Tarascon, who brags eloquently of sallies he has never made, in contrast to Kant, who works out his whole *Critique of Pure Reason* without leaving his native Königsberg. (So Valverde observes, *NCCA*, 150.)

LXXXIII, 1. *Hesperia* (literally, the Western land): Greek term used for Spain (or Italy).

3-4. *rabo . . . por desollar* (literally, tail still to be flayed): Playing on the expressionn *Aún queda el rabo por desollar* (literally, The tail still remains to be flayed), used, among others, by Sancho Panza to indicate "You haven't heard the half of it yet," Machado enjoyed speaking somewhat equivocally of Spain as "the still-to-be-flayed tail of Europe." Compare *JM*, 255.

XCI, 3. The *cucaña* is a greased pole set up at public diversions with a challenge to all comers to shinny to its top. In XCVII it becomes simply the "dry" or desiccated pole. Its symbolism is made clear in the following remark of the later Juan de Mairena, which offers a key not only to XCI, but to XCII, XCVI, and XCVIII: " 'Revolution from above.' As if one were to say, noted Mairena, renewal of the tree at the crown. But the tree, he added, is renewed everywhere, and in particular, by the roots. Revolution from below sounds better to me. Of course 'revolution from above' is a misleading and misguided euphemism. Because the point is not renewal of the tree from the crown but—through the bark! Note that this revolution from above has always been entrusted to the old, on the one hand, and *youths* on the other (conservative, liberal, Catholic, monarchic, traditionalist, etc.)—in short, to the old. And it will end up one day in a counterrevolution from below . . . accompanied by an inevitable mass rebellion" (*OPP*, 528).

XCIII, 3-4. Compare the remark of Juan de Mairena quoted in the Introduction at Note 119: "Logical forms are never pontoons anchored in the river of Heraclitus but actual waves of its current" (*JM*, 210).

XCVIII, 3. Compare Luke 19:40: "And he answered and said unto them, I tell you that if these should hold their peace, the stones would immediately cry out." Valverde (*NCCA*, 154) cites, apropos of *corazones* (hearts), a reference in the *Apocryphal Songbook* to the "tone deafness of the heart which afflicts the masses, enslaved by mechanical work" (*NCCA*, 230).

XCIX, 1. *puro juego* (simply play): Despite these words, Machado's sympathy for the purely ludic element in the art of the 1920s is strictly limited, as the rest of this short poem shows.

**44**     15-19. Machado's concluding lines lead one to wonder if he did not know the famous quatrain by Michelangelo in which the latter's figure of Night from the Medici tombs speaks: "Caro m'è il sonno, e più l'esser di sasso, / mentre che 'l danno e la vergogna dura. / Non veder, non sentir m'è gran ventura; / però non mi destar, deh! parla basso." (Sleep is precious to me; more so, being of stone, / so long as wrongs and shameful acts persist. / Not to see, not to feel is greatest bliss, / so do not wake me, speak only in hushed tones.)

**47**     II. The lighted balcony window recalls that of the first of the "Dreams in Dialogue" (No. 45, I, line 8), suggesting a fusion of reminiscences.

III. One should compare the somewhat facile conclusion of this sonnet with the handling of similar imagery in the "Other Songs for Guiomar" (No. 55, VII).

IV. L. F. Vivanco, in "Retrato en el tiempo," *Papeles de Son Armadans*, Year 1, II, no. 5 (Sept. 1956), 249-268, has studied the development of this sonnet from a longer earlier poem (*Poesie*, 1026-1028). A facsimile of the autograph of the sonnet is found in *Comp.*, I, fol. 176r.

14. *piadosamente* (pityingly): The adverb makes clear the grounds of the father's apprehensiveness in a wave of retrospective fellow-feeling flowing back from this experienced present.

**48**     I, 7. There is an untranslatable play in the Spanish on the expression *¿Quién pondrá puertas al campo?* (literally, Who can set doors to the countryside?, that is, Who can set limits on the illimitable?).

II. The speaker, having assumed a bandit identity, fears exposure by the full moon, an eventuality more likely in feather grass (*esparto*) than among olive trees.

4/3. *Alicún*: Alicún de Ortega, a town southeast of Baeza in the province of Granada.

7. *Guadiana menor* (Lesser Guadiana): One of the most important tributaries of the upper Guadalquivir, unconnected with the Guadiana River proper.

III, 1. *Ubeda la grande* (the great town of Ubeda): There is humorous irony here, Ubeda being a small and provincial place.

2. Ubeda is not conspicuous for hills, and the idiomatic phrase *por los cerros de Ubeda* (over the hills of Ubeda) has come to connote anything out of the way or irrelevant.

IV, 1. *Sierra de Quesada* (Quesada Mountains): A range adjoining the Cazorla Mountains near the source of the Guadalquivir.

**49**   Abel Martín's explanation that love starts as a "sudden upsurge of the flow of life" which envelops but does not stop with the lovers, and his remark that "chastity is par excellence the virtue of the young and lewdness always a thing of the old" (*JM*, 192-193) provide the best comment on this sonnet.

5. *vuestra mutua primavera* (the spring you share—literally, your reciprocated spring): Compare *el mutuo jardín* (literally, the reciprocated garden) of the second of the "Songs for Guiomar" (No. 54, II). The reciprocation, the total complementarity, an unrealizable fantasy with Guiomar, here is taken for granted.

7. *la lúbrica pantera* (the wanton panther): As Valverde notes (*JM*, 194), Machado's panther harks back to the first canto of the *Divine Comedy*. But Dante, rather than fearing the animal when it blocks his path in the early spring morning, sees its beauty as a good omen.

**50**   For Abel Martín, the "Great Nought," God's gift to man, is "the nought made up of all the negations of everything that is" (All quotations in the notes to No. 50 are from *NCCA*, 212).

1. "In Abel Martín's theology, God is defined as absolute being and consequently nothing that *is* can be his work."

10, 11. Abstract thinking, as Juan de Mairena's exposition of his master's thought expressly states, is naturally the province of the "rational biped," not of the beast.

13. *canto de frontera* (borderline song): "Thus, the human mind possesses a concept of totality, that sum of all that is not, which loggically serves as a limit and borderline [*límite y frontera*] for the totality of everything that is."

**51**   6-8. The contrast between the *luz de acuario* (water-slanted light) and the *luz de osario* (light on a bone-heap) places in an existential context the familiar aesthetic dilemma between live temporality and dead abstraction. Compare note to No. 52, line 1, and the Introduction at Note 13. There is a recurrence here, not retained in the translations, of *acuario* (aquarium, standing for ocean) found in No. 34, VIII.

10-11. Images familiar from poems such as No. 17 reappear, more than ever now the symbols of the lost paradise of unrealized hopes. As occurs with the imagery of Poem 17, the *galería* (passageway) is both the tenor and the vehicle of the dream.

35. The obduracy of the existential barriers that mock human purposes is once more forcefully symbolized by the mountain imagery.

37-40. The same aspiration may be read back into the wonder at the superb assurance of the eagle in No. 48, I.

**52**    1. *el pez de fuego* (the goldfish): Swimming in its stream, the fish symbolizes the vital temporality with which the poet will seek to imbue his poem. (Compare Introduction at Note 13.) A limitation of this symbolism is evident here: the fish is confined to a basin and apparently to swimming in circles. The stage is thus set for the abstractions and delimitations to come.

3. Love, too, seems conceptualized and devitalized.

4-5. *la copla de marfil de la verde cigarra* (the ivory jingle of the green cicada): Traditionally the cicada symbolizes enduring vitality and art. (See Alan S. Trueblood, "Rubén Darío: the Sea and the Jungle," *Comparative Literature Studies*, 4 [1967], especially 429-432.) Machado evidently prefers to hedge the symbolism about with suggestions of exact instrumental effects, at times almost capricious ones. A characteristic example in Poem XIII (1907) speaks of "the sempiternal scissors of the singing cicada, the jovial monorhythm, half metal, half wood, which is the summer song" (*Poesie*, 246). The *copla de marfil* (ivory jingle) of the present instance is more fully called elsewhere *esta bolita de marfil sonora* (this little resonant ball of ivory [*OPP*, 729]), evoking something like the sound of the pea in a whistle. Here there is a suggestion of curbing what is live and natural by a mechanical sort of repetitiveness.

10. Inevitably the inversion (as in line 8) of the ordinary coordinates of the perceptual world in the perspective from the far side of our usual conceptions leads close to paradox. The anchor which has been sought so insistently (compare No. 30, lines 29-30 and note), but as a link to the shore rather than a line in the sea, is here jettisoned in an act of sheer speculative abstraction.

16. Valverde (*NCCA*, 237, note 57) points to the inversion here of the "famous Kantian idea of establishing the limits of reason in order to leave room for faith" (that is, faith in a transcendent moral order).

**53**    In the Spanish the artistic control fundamental to the poem finds external corroboration in the strict regularity of meter and in vowel rhyme or full rhyme. I have made no systematic attempt to carry these over into English. The poem has been treated at length as surrealistic by Luis Rosales, "Muerte y resurrección de Antonio Machado," *Cuadernos hispanoamericanos*, nos. 11-12 (1949), 435-479 (reproduced in G-P, 391-431). See also the commentary by Bernardo Gicovate, "El testimonio poético de Antonio Machado," *PMLA*, 71 (1956), 42-50.

I, 5. ¡*Masón, masón!*: Machado was a member of the Madrid lodge of the Masonic order. (See Joaquín Casalduero, quoting Emilio González López, in "Machado, poeta institucionalista y masón," *La Torre*, nos. 45–46 [Jan.–June 1964], 101.) The charge, which evidently reflects real gossip at Segovia (see No. 40, XII), ironically foreshadows later anticlerical overtones.

18. The making of lamps, now in decline, has traditionally been the main industry of Lucena, a town in the province of Cordova.

21-22. For Rosales ("Muerte y resurrección," 411, 420), the oak and the lemon tree are autobiographical symbols linking the "impurity" of age with the purity of youth.

25-26. Oblique anticipations of the execution by firing squad at dawn that appears in IV.

II, 30. Poem XXIII of *Soledades. Galerías. Otros poemas* (1907) begins: "En la desnuda tierra del camino / la hora florida brota" (From the bare earth of the road / flowering-time breaks forth [*Poesie*, 264]).

31. The reminiscence evoked by the previous line comes to nothing, but leads, with a radical shift of mood and setting, into a new reminiscence: the first of the "Highland Songs" (No. 39).

III, 34-36. The brooding and phantasmagoric ambiguities of these lines bring together reminiscences of earlier ones: No. 30, line 5; No. 45, II, lines 7-8. The play in Spanish on the nuances of *sombra*—applicable to things both live and dead—is a little attenuated in English because the two equivalents of *sombra*, "shade" and "shadow," although similarly charged semantically, have their own distinct overtones.

40. *la* (she): Presumably Leonor.

IV, 47-48. *hidalgos*: Gentry or lesser nobility, distinguished from inferiors by the possession of the right to beheading instead of hanging. This, as Valverde points out (*NCCA*, 242), is an issue in Calderón's *El Alcalde de Zalamea* (The Mayor of Zalamea), to which he sees an allusion here.

70. An allusion to garroting.

VI. This "sapling," though evidently not an olive, has affinities with roadside olive trees found in other verse of this period not included in this book (*Poesie*, especially 640, 1044). The underlying similarity is the providing of pleasure (beauty, shade) by what, in the case of the olive at least, is normally seen as a utilitarian tree. Compare the thoughts and afterthoughts on utilitarianism and art cited in the Introduction at Note 71.

VIII, 115-118. The implicit allusion to a child's top wound up and released adds to these lines the sinister overtones of the garroting of lines 70-72. Perhaps there are associations with "The Great Nought" as well.

121. Compare No. 41, XLIV.

IX, 126-136. Charon: In Lucian's "Voyage to the Underworld,"

Charon pushes his shades about in businesslike fashion with sarcastic comments, bickering over the price of the crossing and the scant space in the skiff. Lucian's Charon is joined in this by Clotho, presumably alluded to in "The Old Woman Spinning" for whom the square near the end of the poem (line 186) is named. The shades, for their part, quarrel among themselves with threats and counterthreats of being "strung up." See Lucian, *Selected Satires*, tr. Leonard Casson (New York: Norton, 1968), especially 186, 188.

130. *lago irrebogable* (lake of no return): As Macrì notes (*Poesie*, 1249), *irrebogable* (literally, not subject to rowing back) is a nonce word built on *irrevocable* and *bogar* (to row).

135.—*Sí, claro . . . y no tan claro* (Of course . . . ! What do you mean "of course"?): Self-parody involving a favorite dialectical-pedagogical trick of Juan de Mairena. Compare *JM*, 42 and 152.

x, 138-139. *un poeta con nombre de lucero* (a poet with a light-bearing name): *Lucero* (morning-star, day-star) refers to Lucifer, presumably also the "fairest angel" of No. 18. The allusion would evoke for the Spanish-speaking reader the root *luz* (light) in *Luzbel* (Lucifer).

140. The implication may be that Lucifer wears the pastoral amethyst ring of a bishop of the Church.

143-155. The confusing "twists and turns / and endless S-curves" through labyrinthine streets have their analogues in compositions of Abel Martín and Juan de Mairena roughly contemporaneous with the present passage. In this case, the seeming aimlessness heightens the nightmarish quality. For Abel Martín (*NCCA*, 202-203) the search arises from an erotic impulse; Juan de Mairena also attributes an alcoholic one to his master (*NCCA*, 215). In *JM*, 71-72, Machado writes: "There [in hell] one gives up hope in the theological sense, but not time and the expectation of an infinite series of misfortunes. Hell is the hair-raising dwelling-place of time."

xi, 156. —*Es ella . . .* ("It's she . . . "): Although Valverde (*NCCA*, 246) sees a possible reference to Leonor in xi, this figure in the Square of the Greatest Disillusion seems closer to Death. This remains the case in xii, where she is also half-identified with Love.

171-177. Compare Abel Martín's brief lines (*NCCA*, 202): "Por la calle de mis celos / en veinte rejas con otro / hablando siempre te veo." (Down my Jealousy Street / at twenty window grilles, always / I see you talking with others.)

186. As noted, "the Old Woman Spinning" may be identified with Clotho, first of the three Fates, holder of the distaff.

195. The implication of the "Dreary Cruet" escapes me.

198-199. *Pero duerme sola* (But she sleeps alone): As a figure of popular tradition and song, *Manola* [Lola] *no duerme sola* (doesn't sleep alone). "La Lola" figures in the popular play by Manuel and Antonio Machado, *La Lola se va a los puertos* (1929). Machado talks of this figure to Guiomar in a letter quoted in *OPP*, 932.

201. The play on *claro* (both "of course" and "bright") comes over into English with some difficulty.

**54**  I, 5. *dorado ovillo* (gold ball): The image expresses at the same time a sense of hope fulfilled (compare No. 41, LXIV) and of time acquiring meaning as an accumulation of experience, somewhat as in No. 43.

16-17/15. *la alborada / verdadera* (the one true dawning): The absolute breakthrough to the other, in love; this, as the final lines show, would peel away all prior disillusioning reversions to solitude.

II, 21/20. Valverde (*NCCA*, 249n.) suggests that the garden of the Alcázar of Segovia is the basis for the garden dreamed of here.

26/25. *almez* (lotus tree): I adopt the translation of Gerald Brenan in *South from Granada* (New York: Octagon, 1976), 73. The tree is of the elm family.

27/26. *agua santa* (sacred water): Compare No. 55, VII, line 55/54.

32-33/30-31. *se funden y complementan / nuestras horas* (where each fulfills the other / where our hours run together): Systematically in *Juan de Mairena* (221-222) Machado disproves what is here in any case only "contrived" (and in I, only a query): the existence of complementarity or union in love. Of course he recognizes the same inevitability of otherness further along in this poem as well (lines 40-43/39-42).

44-48/43-47. Less an appendage than they seem, these lines revert ludically to the illusion of fulfillment, reinserting love in the flow of time from which lines 23-24/22-23 had removed it, anticipating the rainbow of III, and harking back to the *alborada*—the "dawning"— of I.

III, 48-76/48-77. Insofar as a basis in experience is to be assumed for the first part of III, it would be the poet's weekly train trips back to Segovia from Madrid. After taking leave of Guiomar, he indulges the illusion that she is still with him and belongs to him.

50. Even this touch of lemon color retains overtones of inaccessibility, unattainability.

77/78. *celda de viajero* (traveler's cubicle): Machado thought in these terms of his lodgings in Segovia, which he left every weekend for Madrid. The same thought probably underlies No. 40, IX.

79/80. *el iris* (the rainbow): A conjunction of nostalgic mood and given circumstance (the rainbow and the departing shower) lifts the present moment out of onflowing time, the Heraclitean *panta rhei* of lines 83/84, creating (as in No. 17 and No. 38, IV) an effect of a timeless present which embraces the past.

80/81. The rainbow, with its Pythagorean association of cosmic harmony, overcomes the "planetary sadness" of the mountains, so often in Machado symbols of blockage and frustration, here a projection as well of the solitary melancholy of the poet's maturity.

82-84/83-85. In the original, the single afternoon invoked is successively of the present in the exclamation of line 82, of a particular remote past (preterit of line 83), and of a past of unlimited recurrence (imperfect of line 84).

85-88/86-89. The poet imaginatively recreates the adolescent fantasies of Guiomar.

**55**    I. Behind the fragmentary, sometimes evidently sensual images recalled there may be a particular episode, an occurrence on the beach at San Sebastián where Guiomar sometimes summered and Machado went to visit her. (See Justina Ruiz de Conde, *Antonio Machado y Guiomar* [Madrid: Insula, 1964], 144-145.) Nevertheless, the almost complete absence of finite verbs produces a sense of temporal rootlessness, making notions of past, present, and future irrelevant.

9. *cárcel y aposento* (my dungeon and lodging): compare Poem No. 40, IX, and No. 54, line 77/78.

10. Solitude is here projected upon the future as a desolate landscape.

VII, 51-55. The imagery recalls that of the sextet of the third of the sonnets of No. 47, but Machado seems to be specifically denying what was asserted there—and in the process displaying a gain of his verse in intensity, clarity, and breadth.

55/54. The *agua santa*, that is, water sacred in its purity, is perhaps a clue to that of the "Songs for Guiomar," No. 54, II, line 27/26.

59-61. *el diamante sin memoria* (the unremembering diamond): Compare "The diamond is cold but it is a product of fire and a great deal might be said about its story" (*Comp.*, I, fol. 15r [1914]). The remark is made apropos of the "eternal present" of Greek verse and confirms the classical character of the aesthetic expressed here.

VIII, 70. See No. 54, III, note to line 80/81, for the symbolism of these mountains, and No. 45, III, for an earlier occurrence of the same symbol.

73. *abanico de milagros* (fan of wonderments): The fan's opening carries a suggestion of the rainbow which elsewhere evokes resolution of conflict in harmony.

**56**    I, 6-7. A vivid expression of the familiar prolongation of a past, here enduring disturbingly, into a present.

10. *raíces* (roots): An emblem of the early stages of life, rapidly being lost as life ebbs.

11. *frontera* (border): Compare No. 50, line 13 and note.

12. In the existential world, which in this poem, in contrast to others, impinges on the realm of pure abstraction, retrospection will inevitably resurrect pain.

21. *cero* (cipher): The "Great Nought" of No. 50.

24. Compare Poem No. 52, line 7.

24-26. Juan de Mairena's comments shed different lights on these enigmatic lines. In November 1935 he speaks of his master's expressing in them "a fear, in no way a desire or a hope: the fear of dying and being damned, of being definitively erased from the light by the hand of God" (*JM*, 175–176). But in another comment of April of the same year, Mairena had seen in the lines a problem of a more philosophical kind, that of the "divine consciousness or divinization of human consciousness after death": "We must rethink consciousness as a light which advances in the dark lighting up the other, always the other. But this so very luminous conception of consciousness . . . is also the most obscure, so long as it isn't proven that there's a light capable of seeing what it itself illuminates" (*JM*, 138). The God-given shade cast by the mighty hand (line 24) raises problems of its own: "Because nothingness rather throws us into amazement than into shadows, said my master . . . since it is given to us rather to enjoy the shadow of the hand of God and meditate in its fresh breezes, than to be lulled to sleep in it" (*JM*, 175). On the other hand, Martín's fear, as just seen, is that of "being definitively erased from the light by the hand of God."

27-28. Compare and contrast with No. 52, line 8.

30. Martín's secret must be precisely the quandary he is in with regard to the possibility of a divinization of the human consciousness at death. About the death of his master, Mairena writes: "My poor master had a difficult agony, one full of struggle and uncertainty, with doubts as to his own poetics . . . and possibly more inclined toward the Buddhist nirvana than hopeful of the paradise of the just . . . Still, he must have been saved at the last moment, to judge by the final gesture of his agony, which was that of a person who literally swallows his own death without much fuss" (*JM*, 176).

II, 34. *soledad* (loneliness): Here an anguishing existential aloneness, a far cry from the *soledad* of the early work.

III, 37/38. *la musa esquiva* (the elusive muse): This is the "wonderworking muse" of the fourth of the "Dreams in Dialogue" (No. 45, IV, line 2).

45. *no eres tú quien yo creía* (you are not the muse I thought): that is, not *soledad*, mentioned in the opening line of the sonnet in question, but death.

IV, 50-53. Valverde comments (*NCCA*, 259): "Poetry and philosophy, for Martín-Machado, are, above all, inventing a man to do the poem or think the theory—in this case, a man 'to keep watch on sleep' in the guise of someone thinking about his own dreaming, a poet with a philosopher—although an ironical one—as complement."

54-58. These lines culminate in the inevitable nihilistic conclusion which had much earlier been brushed aside in "One Day's Poem" (No. 32, lines 140-141).

60. 'Thus Mairena, following Martín, symbolizes divine creation by a negative act of the divinity, by a voluntary blinding of the

'great eye which sees everything in seeing itself' " (*NCCA*, 228: Machado's résumé of Mairena's metaphysics).

v, 77-80. Abel Martín's death may be viewed in one sense as the reabsorption of his consciousness by the nothingness that is the original creation of God. Or it may be seen as his extinction through dazzlement, blinding, by the symbolic new light (line 72), once the protective shade of God's hand is removed.

57    10-11. *la marina panza* (literally, the maritime paunch): The diction is as dissonant in Spanish as in English, the most striking example of a possibly self-immunizing verbal whimsicality that will recur in the Stradivarius and the bleeding ear of lines 20 and 21.

12/11. The *nueva nave* (new ship) is perhaps a reminiscence of the *altera Argo* of Vergil's Messianic eclogue (IV.34) with its prophecy of a new unfolding of the order which the world has lived through once already.

14-17. The negative implications regarding original sin make the whole associative cluster reminiscent of the pristine "ancient world . . . untouched by Adam's sin" of the "Further Lines" of 1920 (No. 59).

21. *sangrábale el oído* (his ear was bleeding): The vertiginous pace of temporal flow has become too much for mortal ears, whose normal humming Juan de Mairena speaks of, as earlier seen, as "the most elemental sonic materialization of temporal flux" (*JM*, 72).

23. Valverde (*NCCA*, 261) finds a plausible key to the "shadows of giants bearing shields" in a passage of the undelivered draft of the speech of acceptance into the Royal Spanish Academy (1931) in which Machado refers to forces of reaction: "For the old phantoms are not fleeing without putting up resistance; many bear shields on their arms and are defending themselves boldly and heroically. But they all seem to be falling back" (*OPP*, 855).

25. Valverde notes that these slaves "probably symbolize work and the proletariat," that is, a new order destined to come into its own.

26-29. The *nihil* recalls the metaphysical nothingness of the previous Abel Martín poems. Its ambiguity, as Valverde observes (*NCCA*, 261), is occasioned by possible references to revolutionary nihilism and to annihilation of the world. The last meaning suits the Heraclitean context of the "zigzag of a road on the mountainside," since this combines the *hodos ano*— the way up—with the originating fire of lightning, the herald of a new cycle. Compare Poem No. 38.

59    4. Nausicaa: Virgin daughter of Alcinous, King of the Phaeacians, who discovers Odysseus on the Scherian shore where he has been cast up. Athena had directed her in a dream to go to the shore with her maidens to wash clothes. (*Odyssey*, Book VI).

5-11. Compare the *Homeric Hymn to Demeter*: "Her heart overflowing with sorrow, she sat by the path / near the Well of the Maiden,

where housewives came to draw water . . . / The daughters of
Celeos, son of Eleusis, espied her / as they came to the well to draw
water to fill their brass pitchers / to carry them back to the house of
their father— / four girls like goddesses, flowers of youthful grace"
(Thelma Sargent, *The Homeric Hymns. A Verse Translation* [New York:
Norton, 1973] 4). Machado makes the ensuing episode of the *Hymn*,
in particular Demeter's attempted immortalization of King Celeos'
child, Demophon, by immersion in renewing fire, the basis of the
initial poem, "Olivo del camino" (Roadside Olive), of *Nuevas canciones* (*NCCA*, No. CLIII, 107-111). Valverde (114) notes the express
application which Machado makes of the myth to social renewal in
the Preface to the second edition of *Soledades. Galerías. Otros Poemas*
(1919). The full text from which he quotes is in *OPP*, 48-49.

9. *pozos partenios* (virgin wells): Machado has adapted the Greek
*parthenios* (maidenly, virginal), which is also applied to pure, unde-
filed water.

63    In Rocafort, the late Don Tomás Navarro informed me, Machado
made his home with the large family of his younger brother, José,
and found little tranquillity for composing poetry except at night.

10. The famous fertile truck garden and orchard area around Valencia is irrigated at night with water from the Guadalaviar (Turia)
River, which runs through the city.

20. It is difficult not to read personal premonition into this line,
over and above its Machadian formulaic quality; compare, for example, No. 37, IV.

21-22. These lines, suggestive of the silted port of Old Valencia
and the receding coastline, also evoke a barren future. The ambiguity of the syntax—the *donde* (where) of line 21 fits with verbs in
either of the two preceding lines—heightens the effect of uncertainty attaching to the future.

64    Lorca was killed on 19 August 1936. The late Don Tomás Navarro told me of the powerful impression made by Machado's reading of his elegy at a Republican rally in the town square of Valencia. In an undated letter of 1936 or 1937, Machado wrote: "The
death of García Lorca has greatly saddened me . . . A stupid crime
has silenced his voice forever . . . Rereading, something I rarely do,
the lines I dedicated to García Lorca, I find in them the expression
of a genuine grief, not very highly elaborated aesthetically, and in
addition, through a subconscious effect, a sine qua non of all poetry, a feeling of bitter reproach, which implies an accusation
against Granada. For the fact is that Granada . . . is . . . one of the
stupidest cities in Spain, one of the most self-satisfied in its isola-
tion and through the influence of a degraded and idle aristocracy
and hopelessly provincial middle class. Could Granada have de-
fended its poet? I think so. It would have been easy for it to prove
to the Fascist assassins that Lorca was politically innocuous and that
the common people whom Federico loved and whose songs he col-

lected were not precisely those who sing 'the Internationale' " (*OPP*, 671-672). Machado evidently saw Lorca's death as politically motivated. Today the most authoritative account sees it as a personal vendetta (Ian Gibson, *The Death of Lorca* [Chicago: J. P. O'Hara, 1973]). On the interaction of political protest and traditional elegy in this poem, see B. W. Wardropper, "The Modern Spanish Elegy: Antonio Machado's Lament for Federico García Lorca," *Symposium*, 19 (1965), 162-170.

2. *una calle larga* (a long street). Uncannily reminiscent of that of No. 53, line 171.

# Key to Poem Numbers

*Selected poems*                                              *Standard numbering*

1   En el entierro de un amigo                                IV
2   Fue una clara tarde, triste y soñolienta                  VI
3   El limonero lánguido suspende                             VII
4   Yo escucho los cantos                                     VIII
5   Yo voy soñando caminos                                    XI
6   Horizonte                                                 XVII
7   Sobre la tierra amarga                                    XXII
8   Crece en la plaza en sombra                               XXXI
9   Al borde del sendero un día nos sen-
    tamos                                                     XXXV
10  Oh, dime, noche amiga, amada vieja                        XXXVII
11  La noria                                                  XLVI
12  El cadalso                                                XLVII
13  Las moscas                                                XLVIII
14  Glosa                                                     LVIII
15  Anoche cuando dormía                                      LIX
16  ¿Mi corazón se ha dormido?                                LX
17  Desgarrada la nube; el arco iris                          LXII
18  Y era el demonio de mi sueño, el
    ángel                                                     LXIII
19  ¡Oh tarde luminosa!                                       LXXVI
20  Es una tarde cenicienta y mustia                          LXXVII
21  Y ha de morir contigo el mundo mago                       LXXVIII
22  Tal vez la mano, en sueños                                LXXXVIII
23  Y podrás conocerte, recordando                            LXXXIX
24  Retrato                                                   XCVII
25  A orillas del Duero                                       XCVIII
26  El Dios ibero                                             CI
27  Orillas del Duero                                         CII
28  Eres tú, Guadarrama, viejo amigo                          CIV
29  Campos de Soria                                           CXIII
30  En estos campos de la tierra mía                          CXXV

| | | |
|---|---|---|
| 31 | *A José María Palacio* | CXXVI |
| 32 | *Poema de un día.* Meditaciones rurales | CXXVIII |
| 33 | *Los olivos* | CXXXII |
| 34 | *Proverbios y cantares* | CXXXVI |
| | I | II |
| | II | XV |
| | III | XX |
| | IV | XXI |
| | V | XXVIII |
| | VI | XXIX |
| | VII | XXXII |
| | VIII | XXXV |
| | IX | XLIV |
| | X | LIII |
| 35 | *Parábolas* | CXXXVII |
| 36 | *A don Francisco Giner de los Ríos* | CXXXIX |
| 37 | *Apuntes* | CLIV |
| 38 | *Galerías* | CLVI |
| 39 | *Canciones de tierras altas* | CLVIII |
| 40 | *Canciones* | CLIX |
| 41 | *Proverbios y cantares* | CLXI |
| 42 | *Los ojos* | CLXII |
| 43 | *Esto soñé* | CLXIV |
| 44 | *Al escultor Emiliano Barral* | CLXIV |
| 45 | *Los sueños dialogados* | CLXIV |
| 46 | *De mi cartera* | CLXIV |
| 47 | *Sonetos* (I-IV) | CLXV |
| 48 | *Viejas canciones* | CLXVI |
| 49 | *Rosa de fuego* | CLXVII |
| 50 | *Al gran Cero* | CLXVII |
| 51 | *Ultimas lamentaciones de Abel Martín* | CLXIX |
| 52 | *Siesta.* En memoria de Abel Martín | CLXX |
| 53 | *Recuerdos de sueño, fiebre y duermivela* | CLXXII |
| 54 | *Canciones a Guiomar* | CLXXIII |
| 55 | *Otras canciones a Guiomar* | CLXXIV |
| 56 | *Muerte de Abel Martín* | CLXXV |
| 57 | *Otro clima* | CLXXVI |
| 58 | *En dónde, sobre piedra aborrascada* | [XXVI, II]* |
| 59 | *Otras coplas* | [XL] |
| 60 | *Apunte de sierra* | [XLV] |
| 61 | *Recuerdo infantil (de Juan de Mairena)* | [XLVIII, I] |
| 62 | *El poeta recuerda las tierras de Soria* | [LI, II] |
| 63 | *Meditación* | [LII] |
| 64 | *El crimen fue en Granada* | [LIII] |

* Brackets indicate poems not included by Machado in any edition of the *Obras completas*.

# Index of Titles and First Lines

*Compositions of less than six lines are not included unless they are independently numbered (1–64) or the first in a series*

## Spanish

*A don Francisco Giner de los Ríos*   152
A dos leguas de Ubeda, la Torre   138
*A José María Palacio*   122
A la hora del rocío   216
*A orillas del Duero*   102
Abre el rosal de la carroña horrible   248
Abrió la ventana   258
Al borde del sendero un día nos sentamos   82
*Al escultor Emiliano Barral*   206
*Al gran Cero*   222
Anoche cuando dormía   90
*Apunte de sierra*   258
*Apuntes*   154

¡Bajar a los infiernos como el Dante!   234

Cabeza meditadora   150
Caminante, son tus huellas   142
*Campos de Soria*   112
*Canciones*   168
*Canciones a Guiomar*   240
*Canciones de tierras altas*   162
Canta, canta en claro rimo   170
Cantad conmigo en coro: Saber, nada sabemos   140
Cerca de Ubeda la grande   218
Colinas plateadas   118
Cómo en el alto llano tu figura   208
Como se fue el maestro   152
Con esta bendita fiebre   232

Conoces los invisibles   *192*
Contigo en Valonsadero   *174*
Crece en la plaza en sombra   *80*
¿Cuál es la verdad?   El río   *202*
Cuando el *Ser que se es* hizo la nada   *222*
Cuando murió su amada   *204*
Cuántas veces me borraste   *164*

*De mi cartera*   *212*
Del romance castellano   *196*
Desde mi ventana   *154*
Desgarrada la nube; el arco iris   *92*
Dice la razón: Busquemos   *150*
Dios no es el mar, está en el mar; riela   *148*
Dondequiera vaya   *156*

*El cadalso*   *86*
*El crimen fue en Granada.* A Federico García Lorca   *262*
*El Dios ibero*   *106*
El Dios que todos llevamos   *150*
El iris y el balcón   *158*
El limonero lánguido suspende   *74*
El monte azul, el río, las erectas   *158*
El ojo que ves no es   *176*
*El poeta recuerda las tierras de Soria*   *260*
El río despierta   *166*
¿Empañé tu memoria? ¡Cuántas veces!   *216*
En Córdoba, la serrana   *164*
En dónde, sobre piedra aborrascada   *256*
En el azul la banda   *158*
*En el entierro de un amigo*   *70*
En el silencio sigue   *160*
En estos campos de la tierra mía   *120*
En la sierra de Quesada   *220*
En medio del campo   *166*
En Santo Domingo   *172*
En un jardín te he soñado   *240*
En una tarde clara y amplia como el hastío   *80*
Entre montes de almagre y peñas grises   *160*
Era la tierra desnuda   *228*
Era un niño que soñaba   *144*
Erase de un marinero   *148*
Eres tú, Guadarrama, viejo amigo   *112*
Es el campo undulado, y los caminos   *114*
Es ella. . . Triste y severa   *236*
Es la parda encina   *162*

Es la tierra de Soria árida y fría   *112*
Es una tarde cenicienta y mustia   *96*
Esta luz de Sevilla. . . Es el palacio   *216*
Esta maldita fiebre   *226*
*Esto soñé*   206

Fue una clara tarde, triste y soñolienta   *70*

*Galerías*   *158*
*Glosa*   *88*

Hacia Madrid, una noche   *166*
Hasta borrarse en el cielo   *218*
Hay dos modos de conciencia   *142*
Hay fiesta en el prado verde   *172*
He vuelto a ver los álamos dorados   *118*
Heme aquí ya, profesor   *124*
*Horizonte*   *80*
Hoy, con la primavera   *222*

Igual que el ballestero   *106*
*Iris de la noche*   *166*

Junto a la sierra florida   *168*
Junto al agua fría   *232*

La aurora asomaba   *86*
La fuente y las cuatro   *170*
La nieve. En el mesón al campo abierto   *116*
*La noria*   *84*
La rima verbal y pobre   *212*
La tarde caía   *84*
Las ascuas de un crepúsculo, señora   *210*
¡Las figuras del campo sobre el cielo!   *114*
*Las moscas*   *86*
Las tierras labrantías   *112*
*Los ojos*   *204*
*Los olivos*   *134*
Los olivos grises   *156*
*Los sueños dialogados*   *208*
Los últimos vencejos revolean   *250*

Mediaba el mes de julio. Era un hermoso día   *102*
*Meditación*   *262*
¿Mi corazón se ha dormido?   *92*
Mi infancia son recuerdos de un patio de Sevilla   *100*
Mientras danzáis en corro   *174*
Mientras no suena un paso leve   *260*

Mientras traza su curva el pez de fuego   226
Muerte de Abel Martín   250

Ni mármol duro y eterno   212
No sabía   240
Nuestras vidas son los ríos   88

Oh cámaras del tiempo y galerías   254
¡Oh, claro, claro, claro! (53, iv)   228
¡Oh, claro, claro, claro! (53, xii)   236
Oh, dime, noche, amiga, amada vieja   82
¡Oh Guadalquivir!   200
¡Oh!, sí, conmigo vais, campos de Soria   120
Oh soledad, mi sola compañía   210
¡Oh tarde luminosa!   94
Orillas del Duero   108
Otra vez el mundo antiguo   258
Otras canciones a Guiomar   244
Otras coplas   258
Otro clima   254

Palacio, buen amigo   122
Para qué llamar caminos   140
Parábolas   144
Pero caer de cabeza   234
Poema de un día. Meditaciones rurales   124
Por la sierra blanca. . .   162
Por qué, decísme, hacia los altos llanos   208
Por un ventanal   154
Primavera soriana, primavera   108
Proverbios y cantares (34)   140
Proverbios y cantares (41)   176

Que apenas si de amor el ascua humea   248
Que el caminante es suma del camino   206
¡Qué gracia! En la Hesperia triste   198
Quién puso, entre las rocas de ceniza   160

Recuerdo infantil (de Juan de Mairena)   260
Recuerdos de sueño, fiebre y duermivela   226
Retrato   100
Rosa de fuego   220

Sabe esperar, aguarda que la marea fluya   148
Se abrió la puerta que tiene   162
Se le vio, caminando entre fusiles   262
Siembra la malva   192

*Siesta.* En memoria de Abel Martín    226
Sobre el olivar (37, ii)    154
Sobre el olivar (37, iv)    154
Sobre la limpia arena, en el tartesio llano    146
Sobre la tierra amarga    80
Sólo tu figura    244
*Sonetos*    214
Soria de montes azules    164
Soria fría, *Soria pura*    116

Tal vez la mano, en sueños    98
Te pintaré solitaria    248
Tejidos sois de primavera, amantes    220
Tierra le dieron una tarde horrible    70
Todo amor es fantasía    246
Tu poeta piensa en ti    242
Tuvo mi corazón, encrucijada    214

*Ultimas lamentaciones de Abel Martín*    222
Una centella blanca    158

Verás la maravilla del camino    214
*Viejas canciones*    216
Viejos olivos sedientos    134
¡Volar sin alas donde todo es cielo!    232
Vosotras, las familiares    86

Y era el demonio de mi sueño, el ángel    94
Y ha de morir contigo el mundo mago    98
Y podrás conocerte, recordando    98
...Y tu cincel me esculpía    206
Ya había un albor de luna    218
Ya hay un español que quiere    144
Ya su perfil zancudo en el regato    260
Ya va subiendo la luna    262
Yo escucho los cantos    76
Yo voy soñando caminos    78

## English

A fiesta is on in the meadow   *173*
A rent in the clouds   *93*
A white flash   *159*
A white moon showed   *219*
Above the orange grove   *263*
Against the blue, black string   *159*
*Along the Duero* (25)   *103*
*Along the Duero* (27)   *109*
And is the magic world to die with you   *99*
And the devil in my dream   *95*
And you can know yourself if you'll recall   *99*
. . .And your chisel picked me out   *207*
*Another Climate*   *255*
As the master had gone away   *153*
At high mass   *173*
*At the Burial of a Friend*   *71*

Back in the landscape of my native soil   *121*
Be content to wait, watch for the turning tide   *149*
Blue mountain, river, upward sweep   *159*
Blue mountains of Soria   *165*
But to plunge headfirst   *235*
By flowering hills   *169*

*Childhood Memory* (*of Juan de Mairena*)   *261*

Dawn was breaking   *87*
Do you know the invisible   *193*
*Dreams in Dialogue*   *209*

Evening was falling   *85*

*Flies*   *87*
For if the live coal of love so much as smoulder   *249*
*From My Portfolio*   *213*
*Further Lines*   *259*

*Gloss*   *89*
God is not the sea. He is of the sea   *149*
Guadarrama, is it you, old friend   *113*

Has my heart gone to sleep?   *93*
Have I soiled your memory? Countless times   *217*
He opened the window   *259*

He was seen, surrounded by rifles    263
Head lost in thought    151
Highland Songs    163
Horizon    81
How often, ashy land    165
Humble spring of Soria settling in    109

I could not tell    241
I dream my way    79
I dreamed you into a garden    241
I follow the songs    77
Idling once in a dream    99
I'll paint you all alone    249
In the Quesada mountains    221
In the silence    161
In the white hills    163
It was mid-July and a splendid day    103
It's she... grim and sad    237
Its unremembering of awful carrion    249
I've seen again the poplars showing gold    119

Jottings    155
Just like the gambling    107

Lady, the drab storm cloud comes apart    211
Last Lamentations of Abel Martín    223
Last night I had a dream    91
Late swifts in wheeling flight    251
Listless the lemon tree suspends    75
Love is imagining, always    247
Lovers, the stuff you're woven of is spring    221

Meditation    263
Memories of Dreaming, Fever, and Dozing    227
Moss grows in the shadows of the square    81
Mountain Note    259
My childhood is memories of a patio in Seville    101
My heart was where a hundred roads    215

Near the great town of Ubeda    219
Neither hard and timeless marble    213

Oh Guadalquivir!    201
Oh light-struck evening    95
Oh recesses of time and passageways    255
Oh solitude, sole sharer of my life    211

Oh tell me, friendly night, so long beloved   *83*
Oh, yes, yes, of course! (53, iv)   *229*
Oh, yes, yes, of course! (53, xii)   *237*
Old familiar flies   *87*
*Old Songs*   *217*
Olive trees gray   *157*
On a bright evening, vast as tedium   *81*
On the plain of Tarshish, the clean white sand   *147*
Once there was a sailor   *149*
*One Day's Poem. Rural Reflections*   *125*
One night in the Guadarrama   *167*
Only your figure   *245*
*Other Songs for Guiomar*   *245*
Our lives are rivers   *89*
Out on the land   *167*
Outside my window   *155*
Over the olive grove (37, ii)   *155*
Over the olive grove (37, iv)   *155*


Palacio, good friend   *123*
*Parables*   *145*
Parched old olive trees   *135*
*Passageways*   *159*
Past gray crags and red chalk mountains   *161*
Pilgrim, a wonder awaits you on the road   *215*
*Portrait*   *101*
*Proverbs and Song-Verse* (34)   *141*
*Proverbs and Song-Verse* (41)   *177*


Rainbow and balcony   *159*
*Rainbow at Night*   *167*
Reason says   *151*
Round Soria the land is dry and cold   *113*


*Siesta.* In Memory of Abel Martín   *227*
Silver hills, gray heights   *119*
Sing along with me: what we know is nothing   *141*
Sing, maidens   *175*
Sing, sing, in a clear rhythm   *171*
Snow. The inn looks out across the fields   *117*
So here I am   *125*
*Songs*   *169*
*Songs for Guiomar*   *241*
*Sonnets*   *215*
Soria, cold *pure town*   *117*
Sow mallow   *193*

Taking its spindly stance in a watercourse    261
That sapling no one sees    233
The ancient world again    259
The clear afternoon was drowsy and sad    71
*The Crime Was in Granada.* To Federico García Lorca    263
*The Death of Abel Martín*    251
The earth was bare    229
The eye you see is an eye    177
*The Eyes*    205
*The Flaming Rose*    221
The fountain with the four    171
*The Gallows*    87
The God we all carry within    151
The gray of oaks    163
The hinged door in my heart    163
*The Iberian God*    107
The larks climb so far    219
*The Olive Trees*    135
*The Poet Remembers the Soria Country*    261
The river awakens    167
*The Soria Country*    113
The traveler is the aggregate of the road    207
*The Waterwheel*    85
There was a child who dreamed    145
They put him in the ground one brutal afternoon    71
Think of it: a Spaniard    145
This is rolling country. The roads dip    115
This light of Seville. . . The great house once again    217
*This Was My Dream*    207
This withered, ashen afternoon    97
This wretched fever    227
Those figures on the land against the sky!    115
Though old ballads give you    197
Through a tall window    155
To be flying wingless where everything is sky!    233
*To Don Francisco Giner de los Ríos*    153
To go down to hell as Dante did!    235
*To José María Palacio*    123
*To the Great Nought*    223
*To the Sculptor Emiliano Barral*    207
Today with spring in the air    223
Two forms consciousness takes    143
Two leagues from Ubeda    139

Until he hears soft footsteps sound    261
Upcountry in Cordova    165
Upon the bitter land    81

Wayfarer, the only way    *143*
We settle down one day beside the path    *83*
What a joke! In gloomy Hesperia    *199*
When his beloved died    *205*
When the *Being that is* made nothingness    *223*
Where have I seen you, heaped    *257*
Wherever he goes    *157*  ·
Which is the truth?    *203*
While the goldfish traces flashing coils    *227*
Who set that golden broom    *161*
Why give the name of roads    *141*
With the morning dew    *217*
With this delightful fever    *233*
With you in Valonsadero    *175*
Worked fields    *113*

Yes, I have brought you along, landscapes of Soria    *121*
You wonder why my heart rejects this coast    *209*
Your figure in the highlands rises up    *209*
Your poet's thoughts    *243*